## Praise for ⌐ Seven-Book Series on Spiritual Psychology,

### Praise for *Everything Is Energy:*
### *New Ways to Heal Your Body, Mind and Spirit*

"This book affords a fascinating look at a wealth of information about important truths in a readable manner. I recommend it for seekers of truth of all persuasions."

—RANVILLE CLARK, M.D.,
psychiatrist, president of Psychiatric Center Chartered, Washington, D.C.

"Dr. Barrick blends Jungian dream work, Kabbalah, EMDR, and prayer into a tapestry of beautiful and practical approaches to healing of the imbalances and splits in psyche and soma.... Those of us who are also students of science know well that all things are energy, light, motion, all in an evolutionary dance. We are such things. And only through those means... energy, light, motion, and change can we be brought to our potential."

—ANNE DE VORE, Ph.D.,
Jungian analyst

"Dr. Barrick describes complex psychological processes in a style and language that is easily understood by the psychologically unsophisticated layman. Readers will appreciate both the depth and tenderness that pours through her writing. I think this is a brilliantly written book and many, many people will draw inspiration and timely illumination from it."

—KENNETH FRAZIER, L.P.C., D.A.P.A., A.C.P.E.

"Dr. Barrick has done an excellent job of interweaving the theories of experts with her clinical experience. I particularly appreciate the concepts about the labyrinth, which are key for people to understand during these trying times. I believe the book will be a great tool to help people achieve their personal victories."

—REV. TANI KINGSTON

"My overall reaction to the book is that it is vital, engaging and literally full of light. I felt the light coming through the pages to my physical body. There is a vitality that's very real. The examples are vibrant; they reveal the manifestation of miracles in everyday life through the willingness and courage to choose the Higher Self. And it's written with simplicity, humor and modesty, which make it compelling."

—PERLE RINE,
clinical psychologist, Israel

"In my opinion the book Everything Is Energy has the potential to become a classic. There is a profound spiritual depth and deep psychological understanding for every seeker of truth and enlightenment."

—REV. E. GENE VOSSELER,
public speaker, writer and spiritual counselor

"This book is a seminal work and required reading for all true seekers of truth, especially truth about self and one's life mission. It folds together the worldly understanding of one's personal psychology with the deeper spiritual understanding of our true self as it is hidden in the labyrinth of the soul. Dr. Barrick weaves an enthralling tale of the personal lives of her clients throughout."

—PATRICK WOLBERD, M.S.W., BCD,
licensed clinical social worker

### Praise for *A Spiritual Approach to Parenting: Secrets of Raising the 21st Century Child*

"Filled with remarkable insights into the psychology of the child's soul, this book goes way beyond current parenting approaches. By exploring children's deep spiritual needs through their developmental stages and ways to raise up the inner genius, A Spiritual Approach to Parenting offers real healing and hope to the many sensitive, bright children that have been mislabeled as 'learning disabled' or 'problem' children."

—DR. JOYE B. BENNETT,
child psychologist and co-editor of
Nurturing Your Baby's Soul: A Spiritual Guide for Expectant Parents

"As we welcome the Indigo and Crystal children who are our future leaders, Dr. Barrick has written a valuable and timely book. Drawing on ancient wisdom and personal experience, she offers sound advice to help parents support the growth and creativity of these wonderful, young people."

—CHRISTINE PAGE, M.D.,
media presenter and author of
Spiritual Alchemy: How to Transform Your Life

"Drawing from a rich background in psychology and religion, as a former professor at a major university, a practicing clinical therapist and a minister of many years' standing, Dr. Barrick has written with great clarity a profound book that couples wise insights with practical applications for everyday life.

"This is a must book for the Aquarian age families who are raising the advanced souls coming in as children today. Dr. Barrick's explanation of the developmental stages of life is priceless and unique in its depth of spiritual and psychological understanding. I love the book and highly recommend it."

—REV. E. GENE VOSSELER,
writer, spiritual counselor and former director of
social service programs for disadvantaged youth

**Praise for *Soul Reflections: Many Lives, Many Journeys***
"Soul Reflections takes you on a journey into your own inner dimensions of being, to a place of healing and light. Dr. Barrick has outlined a clear path for your soul's homeward journey, illumined by her many years of experience in guiding souls through life's difficult moments.

"A handbook for those whose hearts yearn for soul liberation. The reader will greatly benefit from the spiritual exercises and case histories in the book."

"Marilyn Barrick fervently believes in the power of lifting up deep, inner compassion as a potent tool for healing human sorrow and suffering. She offers us the possibility—nay, the promise—of spiritual companionship and support the moment we honor our brief time on earth as a gift to be opened, rather than as a problem to be solved.

"Dr. Barrick offers kindness, healing and hope to anyone who reads this book. She helps us heal the past while creating a luminous future for ourselves and for the family of the earth."

"In *Soul Reflections: Many Lives, Many Journeys*, Dr. Barrick blends profound wisdom and keen psychological insights with practical tools and exercises for personal application of the truths revealed.

"This book is a must-read for any serious seeker who hungers for knowledge of the path that can lead to enlightenment, God-realization and the ascension in the light."

**Praise for *Emotions: Transforming Anger, Fear and Pain***

"Marilyn Barrick is on the mark. While we search for the understanding of our physical, mental and spiritual selves, we often forget the source of the balance between all of them—our emotional self. This book addresses the issue magnificently. Read it and grow."

—DANNION BRINKLEY,

N.Y. Times best-selling author of *Saved by the Light* and *At Peace in the Light*

"Written in an easily understandable style, Emotions: Transforming Anger, Fear and Pain *offers a wealth of information. Dr. Barrick provides excellent methods for freeing ourselves from some of our most destructive emotions—thus opening the door to improved health at all levels. This book is deserving of wide reading and rereading."*

—RANVILLE S. CLARK, M.D.,

psychiatrist, Washington, D.C.

"Emotions *is a wise, heartfelt and deeply spiritual path that can lead you from fear to courage, anger to joy, and helplessness to effectiveness—whatever challenges you may be facing. I have found it tremendously helpful."*

—MARTIN L. ROSSMAN, M.D.,

author of *Guided Imagery for Self-Healing*

### Praise for *Dreams: Exploring the Secrets of Your Soul*

"This unique book on dreams integrates the soul's development on the spiritual path with personal dream work. . . . It invites us to consider a greater potential of the self beyond life's ordinary conflicts and helps us open up to a greater understanding of the purpose of life."

—RALPH YANEY, M.D.,

psychiatrist/psychoanalyst and author of *10,001*

### Praise for *Sacred Psychology of Change: Life as a Voyage of Transformation*

"This book asks us to 'focus our attention on the higher intelligence of our heart' and then describes in loving detail ways of doing just that. Those interested in the heart's ability to heal will find encouragement in these pages."

—RUTH BLY,
licensed psychologist, Jungian analyst, author

"A profound treasure of spiritual truths and their practical application based on the author's many successful years of personal and professional experience. Written in the language of the heart and with remarkable clarity and sensitivity, this book will lead you, chapter by chapter and step by step, to a profoundly healing dialogue with yourself—and through an exciting spiritual and psychological journey of change."

—KENNETH FRAZIER, L.P.C., D.A.P.A., A.C.P.E.

## Praise for *Sacred Psychology of Love:*
## *The Quest for Relationships That Unite Heart and Soul*

"In our search for the Beloved, whether inner or outer, we seek that mysterious blend of beauty and practicality which Dr. Marilyn Barrick masterfully conveys on every page. Synthesizing her knowledge of sacred text, her clinical expertise and her life's wisdom, she has written a book for anyone seeking to love or to be loved. With compassion and humor, she gives us an important tool for enriching relationships."

—ANNE DE VORE,
Jungian analyst

"A wonderful marriage of the mystical and practical, this soul-nourishing book is beautiful, healing and thought-provoking."

—SUE PATTON THOELE,
author of *Heart Centered Marriage*

# EVERYTHING IS
# ENERGY

*New Ways to Heal Your Body, Mind and Spirit*

Other Books in the Sacred Psychology Series
by Marilyn C. Barrick, Ph.D.

*Sacred Psychology of Love:*
*The Quest for Relationships That Unite Heart and Soul*

*Sacred Psychology of Change:*
*Life as a Voyage of Transformation*

*Dreams:*
*Exploring the Secrets of Your Soul*

*Emotions:*
*Transforming Anger, Fear and Pain*

*Soul Reflections:*
*Many Lives, Many Journeys*

*A Spiritual Approach to Parenting:*
*Secrets of Raising the 21st Century Child*

# EVERYTHING IS
# ENERGY

*New Ways to Heal Your Body, Mind and Spirit*

*Marilyn C. Barrick, Ph.D.*

SUMMIT UNIVERSITY PRESS

EVERYTHING IS ENERGY:
*New Ways to Heal Your Body, Mind and Spirit*
by Marilyn C. Barrick, Ph.D.

Library of Congress Control Number: 2005926093
ISBN: 1-932890-07-6

SUMMIT UNIVERSITY 🔥 PRESS®

09  08  07  06  05      5  4  3  2  1

I dedicate this book
To all who seek to understand
The power of energy for good or ill,
In self and sky and sea and land.
May each of us be ever blessed
With courage, zest and strength,
As we make our way along
Life's unfolding length.

As we walk the labyrinth of life,
Mindful of lessons to be learned,
May our journey be ever fruitful
With many victories earned.

May the angels and nature spirits
Guide us onward and ever higher,
Until we reach the heaven-world,
To which our soul and spirit aspire.

Let us be our brother's keeper,
In all ways great and small,
And choose to lend a helping hand
Along life's way—to all.

# Contents

# Acknowledgments

*Many special people have inspired and assisted me in writing this book on the healing of body, mind and spirit, particularly those individuals whose case studies have contributed to this seventh and last book in my* Spiritual Psychology *series. I am forever indebted to all who have delved deeply into the psychology of their soul and shared their reflections with me. Many appear in this or another book in the series disguised in identity but clearly represented in the spiritual and psychological truths their journey has revealed.*

*I am grateful to my family and friends who have supported my efforts and encouraged me to put my thoughts and reflections into print through the* Sacred Psychology *series. And I acknowledge with gratitude those who have helped to bring this book to fruition: my editors, formatters and those who contributed to the cover design. The suggestions of the reviewers are also much appreciated. Thank you for enriching the final product.*

*My love and gratitude to my spiritual teacher Elizabeth Clare Prophet who introduced me to the sacredness of the journey of life and to the ascended master[1] Kuthumi who inspired me to write down what I have learned during the journey.*

# Preface

*Energy is God. How gloriously we find him in all life.*

–MAITREYA

The majestic Rocky Mountains where I conduct my clinical practice and write my books are an inspiration to soul and spirit, and the purity of the atmosphere in the mountains is energizing.

This pure natural energy contributes to my work as a clinical psychologist, minister and writer by providing daily evidence of the remarkable influence that our surroundings have on the body, mind and spirit. It is a constant reminder that shifts and changes in energy—much like the noticeable freshness in the air after a rain—are key to healing hurtful memories, changing negative mind-sets and restoring equilibrium.

This is my mission statement: To inspire, illumine, nurture and empower those who come to me for assistance in fulfilling their special mission. It is the major purpose of my clinical practice, ministerial service, books, workshops and lectures and the self-help material I post on my web site.*

All of us lose track of our mission at times. We are distracted by the challenges of daily life or blindsided by situations

_____
*www.spiritualpsychology.com

that take us off course. Yet, difficult experiences can actually help us align with our inner compass, the Higher Self, because they trigger an assessment of what we value in life. Once we know our priorities, we can achieve them by setting specific goals and strategies. Soon we are back on track with our mission.

My practice as a spiritual psychologist reinforces my view that energy, both atmospheric and the energy comprising our physical being, is key to resolving trauma and moving through life with a positive stance. In this book, *Everything Is Energy: New Ways to Heal Your Body, Mind and Spirit,* I focus on the impact of difficult life experiences and how they influence our attitudes, mind-sets, emotions and body sensations. And I offer practical ways to heal the residue of trauma.

Using case history examples,[*] I describe how trauma leaves a residue, not only in the conscious mind but also at subconscious and unconscious levels and in the physical body. I place a major emphasis on how energy techniques can help us resolve the residue of trauma and bring about insight, resolution and healing. This shift in consciousness can occur not only in the body, mind and spirit but also in the depths of the soul.

It is my hope that the concepts in this book will awaken in the reader an awareness of our origin as souls of light, composed of divine energy, molded by the Creator and born on earth to fulfill a unique purpose. I believe that no matter what sorrows we encounter in our earthly life, when we put our hand in God's hand all of heaven will mobilize to help us. May your life journey be victorious!

---

[*]In the case examples in this book, names, places and details have been changed to protect the anonymity of the individuals whose stories are included.

# Introduction

*Write down what thou hast received.*

—KUTHUMI

In the privacy of mind, heart and soul, each of us harbors a sense of personal destiny. To fulfill that calling we journey through the ups and downs of life. Inwardly we travel through multilayers of consciousness: a superconscious that ignites our hopes and dreams,[2] a conscious mind that is our every-day companion, a subconscious that acts as a subliminal influence and an unconscious that can erupt unexpectedly and propel or deter the fulfillment of our destiny.

The superconscious is the source of our intuition, higher values and communion with God while the conscious mind is busy contemplating how to plan the day and address the daily doings. The subconscious is an inner reservoir that we tap when we try to remember something and say, "Wait a minute, it's just on the tip of my tongue." And in the depths of the unconscious, we store troublesome experiences that remain hidden until consciously addressed.

Many people revolve traumatic events for weeks or months after they occur. As a result, they may experience sleep disturbance, emotional upheaval and a habitual second-guessing of their actions. The resulting stress can ignite aches and pains even when there is not a physical injury. This is because the residual energy cycles through the memory, thoughts and emotions and lands in the physical body.

My role as a clinical psychologist is to help people resolve traumatic experiences and heal the residue of upsetting memories, self-limiting thoughts, distracting emotions, self-defeating behavior and related physical distress. Through a combination of spiritual psychology and the techniques of energy therapy, many people have experienced a complete turnaround in consciousness. As one of my clients put it, "I have a new lease on life!"

My interest in psychology and spirituality goes back to childhood. As a child, I used to imagine becoming a nurse, a doctor or a missionary. My father put his foot down on the missionary idea even though I had two girl cousins who ended up doing exactly that in Africa and South America.

When I entered high school, my dad suggested that if I was seriously interested in either nursing or medicine I should take pre-med courses. I decided to do that and the course work was a challenge—I would never have made it through physics without a great lab partner! I pursued a bachelor of nursing degree in college but ended up marrying and starting a family after a year in the program.

Once my children were in school I decided to finish college but realized nursing was no longer a practical goal. Since I was interested in the psychological impact of illness and trauma, I shifted my major to psychology.

After completing my undergraduate work and a Master of Science degree, I worked as a school psychologist for several years. Upon completion of my Ph.D. degree, I taught graduate courses for the psychology department and worked as a clinical psychologist in the University of Colorado counseling center. I also started a private practice. My childhood daydreams of being a doctor or nurse had come to fruition very differently than I had anticipated.

The ministry aspect of my life is rooted in my childhood faith, my interest in missionary work and my walk with Jesus as a teenager. Whenever I didn't know what to do I would ask Jesus to help me, and I always received an answer to my prayers. Our Baptist youth group was also a major influence. All of us took turns leading our Sunday evening youth service, including giving sermons. Afterwards we would play volleyball or go square dancing, and we often went swimming or hiking on Saturdays. Discussing our faith was a natural part of our time together.

In the 1960s and early '70s, when I was teaching at the university, students were exploring a smorgasbord of spiritual doctrines including Christianity, Eastern teachings and New Age concepts. I began to investigate faiths that were different from my upbringing in order to relate to the students' understanding of spirituality.

I had a client who was pursuing spirituality in a variety of ways including the practice of kriya yoga. One day in 1973, she told me about her experiences at a spiritual conference in Colorado Springs, Colorado, where she camped out in the wilderness and learned about the teachings of a New Age group, The Summit Lighthouse, founded by Mark L. Prophet and his wife, Elizabeth Clare Prophet. I lit up inside as she began telling me about these teachings, and I intuitively realized that I was meant to explore them. When I prayed for confirmation, I received a rush of light and energy.

In the months that followed, I frequently visited La Tourelle, the headquarters of The Summit Lighthouse in

Colorado Springs, to learn more about the spiritual teachings. I worked a summer at the University of Colorado to earn time off to attend a three-month spiritual retreat sponsored by The Summit Lighthouse in the spring of 1975. During those three months, we studied the dimensions of the soul, which is actually the root meaning of the word psychology.* I realized that my profession as a psychologist had been a perfect introduction to my adult spiritual path.

After the retreat, I returned to the counseling center and the psychology department at the University of Colorado as well as my private practice. And I continued to study the teachings of The Summit Lighthouse. Less than a year later, Mrs. Prophet asked me to come to La Tourelle to be the director of a small staff there; she and the rest of the staff were moving to Pasadena, California.

As my children were young adults and pretty much on their own, I resigned from the counseling center and psychology department at the University of Colorado and began my service with The Summit Lighthouse. I also continued my profession as a clinical psychologist in private practice several days a week.

Before moving to California, Mrs. Prophet gave me the spiritual blessing of lay minister. And I had a transforming energy experience. As she touched the crown of my head with an amethyst jewel, a major tingling of spiritual fire went through me. She asked if I had felt that. I said, "Yes!" And she responded, "It's a real flame, you know." I've never forgotten that sensation of feeling aglow from head to foot.

Thus began my spiritual profession as a lay minister, and I was on track for my mission as a spiritual psychologist. In the late 1970s, the headquarters of The Summit Lighthouse

---

* psyche (soul); ology (study of)

moved to Malibu, California, and later became known as Church Universal and Triumphant. In 1984, I became an ordained minister in the Church.

Over the years, I had the privilege of teaching, participating in lecture tours and serving as personnel director for The Summit Lighthouse and Church Universal and Triumphant, while continuing my private practice as a clinical psychologist. These activities continued when the organization moved its headquarters to Paradise Valley, Montana.

In 1997, when the organization went through a downsizing, I awoke in the middle of the night and talked to God about it. I asked the ascended master Kuthumi, who is known as the master psychologist, "What do I do now?" The answer was immediate and clear. A vision appeared before my closed eyes, words written in brilliant, shimmering fire: *Write Down What Thou Hast Received.* I realized this was divine direction and immediately began to write what became the seven-book *Spiritual Psychology* series.

Through my books, I hope to leave a legacy of inspiration and information to encourage my clients as well as people I may never see in person. I also desire to reach those who may not seek therapy or spiritual counseling but have concerns similar to my clients.

*Sacred Psychology of Love: The Quest for Relationships That Unite Heart and Soul* is about how to master the lessons of love and create enduring love relationships. The book is a synthesis of my understanding of sacred texts, my clinical expertise and what I have learned from life about the hidden dramas inherent in friendships, love relationships and marriage. The reader has the opportunity to learn how all of this relates to the union of heart and soul.

*Sacred Psychology of Change: Life as a Voyage of Transformation* focuses on how cycles of change and chaos can become a transformational opportunity. This book stresses the importance of an open heart, a creative mind-set and the maturing of the soul in order to navigate the waves of change. By way of storytelling and self-help exercises, the reader learns a variety of practical approaches to the challenging scenarios of our fast-moving world.

*Dreams: Exploring the Secrets of Your Soul* validates the concept that everyone and everything in a dream represents an aspect of the dreamer. This book makes clear to the reader that dreams not only connect with events in life but also express a dimension of the soul. In short, everything in your dream is you! Through learning how to remember our dreams and interpret their symbolism, we can decode the metaphorical messages of the soul and spirit. By so doing, we can shift our lives onto an upward track.

In *Emotions: Transforming Anger, Fear and Pain,* the book explains in depth how we can transform painful emotions and achieve a balance in body, mind and soul. The reader learns how to release anger, fear and grief in a healthy way and replace them with inner strength, courage and peace of mind. This book is an invaluable guidebook for everyone whose life is impacted by the turmoil and violence rampant in the world today.

*Soul Reflections: Many Lives, Many Journeys* speaks to the many people who are seeking spiritual awakening or are on a quest for enlightenment. While we may look to therapists, coaches and ministers for answers, ultimately the healing of soul and spirit is an inner journey. The book includes the study of factual and legendary heroes along with inspiring meditations and practical exercises that can help us transform painful experiences of the past.

*A Spiritual Approach to Parenting: Secrets of Raising the 21st Century Child* is about the families, teachers and mentors who are running full speed ahead to keep up with an ever-changing world. Included is a discussion of the Aquarian family, New Age children and young geniuses who have a special mission to fulfill. The book offers insights about these extraordinary children plus teachings on the cycles of life and their corresponding life lessons, an analysis of how karma and past-life records can impact marriage and family life—and what to do about it.

In *Everything Is Energy: New Ways to Heal Your Body, Mind and Spirit,* the reader learns the details of how our energy levels affect our attitudes, thoughts, emotions and physical well-being. The book includes examples and case histories that demonstrate how we can resolve old trauma by changing the associated energy patterns. The reader also gains knowledge about intuition, intention and spirituality and how they relate to energy work and the achievement of higher consciousness.

What is offered in this book is what my heart has confirmed. As you turn the pages, I suggest that you reflect upon your inspiring life experiences as well as traumas that may have left an uncomfortable residue—and how you might heal them. I also suggest that you define your purpose in life and how you plan to fulfill your special mission. I wish you well in your life journey. May God bless and keep you every step of the way until you return, victorious, to the heaven-world.

# 1
# *Walking the Labyrinth of Life*

*Round and round we go,*
*Where we stop nobody knows*

—AUTHOR UNKNOWN

*H*ave you ever thought of life as a labyrinth of intricate choices that require you to mobilize a strong will and sharp mind in order to be successful? It's an apt analogy because life is often like a labyrinth, with its circles and spirals, hills and valleys, all of which we may encounter along the way.

The labyrinth is an ancient symbol that represents the journey to one's center and a return to the world. This can help us understand and appreciate our journey in life. A labyrinth looks like a circle and within the circle is a spiral that weaves in and out returning ultimately to its origin.

As we silently wend our way through a labyrinth, we can focus upon it as a sacred space, a sacred walk with God. By walking the labyrinth in a meditative posture, we set ourselves to experience the return current of light and energy from our Maker.

A labyrinth in the mystical understanding of the word has only one path and no blind alleys. The path leads us in a gentle spiral to the center and out again. Walking a labyrinth is a right-brain activity, an experience where imagery, intuition and spirituality can be strengthened.

Some experts differentiate between a labyrinth and a maze. They speak of a maze as a path where many choices must be made and an analytical mind is necessary to find the center. In contrast, in a labyrinth we make only one choice, to enter or not to enter. The path leading to the center corresponds to the spiritual path, a spiraling upward to union with God.

When we walk through a labyrinth we first pause, affirm our intention and proceed at our own pace. As we pause again at the center of the labyrinth to meditate, we may experience a gift of light or a sacred understanding, a deeper connection with our Maker or perhaps simply a sense of inner peace. Walking a labyrinth as a sacred space becomes a meditation on the journey of the soul.

## The Labyrinth as Sacred Geometry

The Reverend Dr. Lauren Artress, an Episcopalian priest, psychotherapist and founder of a worldwide labyrinth project, describes the labyrinth as "sacred geometry."

In an interview with moderator Kathy Carmean,* Dr. Artress elaborated on this concept, saying:

> Geometry is sacred when it is mirrored from nature. The labyrinth is based on not only the circle—which is a universal symbol in all cultures around the world—but it's also based on the double spiral. If you think of ocean waves coming in and out, that's all spiral.... If you look at seashells you can see spirals. Spirals are in nature. So when geometry is reflecting that, it's called sacred....
>
> Another way of describing sacred geometry is frozen music, and I love that image, because, in a way, when we come to the labyrinth and begin to walk it, we're the frozen music... You move through this wonderfully gracious pattern, and it unfreezes you. It opens your heart. It opens your mind. It quiets yourself so you can find your basic flow and be in rhythm with yourself....
>
> It uses the metaphoric part of the brain. When you're walking the path, it is symbolic of your path in life. You realize that we're not only human beings on a spiritual path; we're spiritual beings on a human path.[3]

## Greek Mythology: The Labyrinth That Is a Maze

There is also a labyrinth-like path that is a maze, with confusing twists and turns, a jigsaw puzzle that has to be figured out. We get lost in a maze because it has blind alleys, cul-de-sacs, circling paths that go nowhere. Like life! Unless

---

*Kathy Carmean is a moderator for "One on One" interviews exploring the many sides of religion, faith formation and spirituality.

we think to mark the trail as we go along, we wander help-lessly around and around.

The ancient Greeks understood the difference between a labyrinth and a maze and likely used the terms not only liter-ally but also metaphorically. According to Greek mythology, Daedalus, the Athenian craftsman and architect, designed a maze-like labyrinth on the island of Crete for King Minos of the Minoans. In the maze was imprisoned the Minotaur, a man-eating monster that was half man and half bull.

This intricate network of passages was so skillfully designed that no one could escape from the deadly Minotaur. And Daedalus revealed the secret of the maze to only one person, Ariadne, the daughter of King Minos.

As the legend goes, the king demanded tribute from King Aegeus of Greece. That tribute included seven young men and seven young maidens. The Grecian young men and maidens were to be put into the maze, where they would get hopelessly lost and end up being devoured by the Minotaur.

Theseus, King Aegeus' son, volunteered to be one of the fourteen young people so that he could try to kill the Mino-taur and stop the sacrificial killings. And, unknown to King Minos, Ariadne was Theseus' lover. She told Theseus to lay down a trail of twine as he entered the labyrinth and follow it out after he killed the monster. Which he did!

Minos was furious when he learned what had happened, and he imprisoned Daedalus and his son Icarus in the labyrinth. However, according to legend, Daedalus made wax wings so they could fly out of the maze. Icarus flew too close to the sun; his wings melted and he fell into the sea. But Daedalus flew on to Sicily where King Cacalus gave him safe haven. King Minos pursued Daedalus but the daughters of

Cacalus succeeded in killing Minos. Thus, Daedalus's life was spared.

## Is This Legend Fact or Fiction?

How much of this is fact and how much fiction? No one really knows. However, early in the nineteenth century the explorer C. R. Cockerell and his companions visited the winding caves on the south side of Crete.

The group unwound a ball of twine to lay a trail lest they lose their way and never emerge from the underground labyrinth. By their own admission, the journey was intriguing, frightening and bewildering once their compass broke. They were fascinated but horrified by the obvious intentional death trap for those lost in these caves. Had they not had the foresight to mark the trail they would likely never have lived to tell the tale.

Some experts have believed that the caves Cockerell explored did not fit the legend because they were not located at Knossos on the island of Crete. However, modern archaeologists have actually discovered a labyrinth at Knossos. The curious thing about this labyrinth is that it was not in a cave beneath the palace, it was the palace itself.

The palace was huge, containing hundreds of rooms at many levels grouped around a central courtyard. While it was not a labyrinth, per se, to a visitor the palace must have seemed like an intimidating maze of corridors, staircases and rooms.

Labyrinths and mazes were favored places of initiation among many ancient societies. Remains of these mystic mazes have been found among the American Indians, Hindus, Persians, Egyptians and Greeks. Some of the mazes are merely involved pathways lined with stones; others are literally miles of gloomy caverns under temples or hollowed from the sides of mountains. The famous labyrinth of Crete was very likely a place of initiation into the Cretan mysteries.

## Theosophy and the Cretan Mysteries

In his book *Ancient Mystic Rites*, Theosophist C. W. Leadbeater says:

> When Sir Arthur Evans began his excavations on the site of ancient Knossos he not only laid bare the palace of King Minos, but also a series of successive strata indicative of a continuous civilization of a very high character stretching over a period of several thousand years. It was shown that the old legends of the labyrinth of Crete and the terrible Minotaur, supposed to dwell in its innermost depths, were based on fact, not on fancy. . . .
>
> In the palace of Minos at Knossos, as also in the palace of Phaestos—another Cretan site—we find pillared crypts and chambers which were indubitably of a sacred and initiatory character.[4]

## The Great Egyptian Labyrinth

Since ancient times, people have been fascinated by stories of the great Egyptian labyrinth and the mystery that surrounded it. In *Isis Unveiled*, Russian Theosophist Madame Helena Petrovna Blavatsky described this labyrinth as "the wonder of the world."

She wrote:

> King after king, and dynasty after dynasty had passed in a glittering pageant before the eyes of succeeding generations and their renown had filled habitable globe. The same pall of forgetfulness had fallen upon

them and their monuments alike, before the first of our historical authorities, Herodotus, preserved for posterity the remembrance of that wonder of the world, the great Labyrinth....

In Rawlinson's translation, Herodotus is made to say: "The passages excited in me infinite admiration as I passed from the courts into the chambers, and from thence into colonnades, and from colonnades into other houses, and again into courts unseen before. The roof was throughout of stone like the walls, and both were exquisitely carved all over with figures. Every court was surrounded with a colonnade, which was built of white stones, sculptured most exquisitely. At the corner of the Labyrinth stands a pyramid forty fathoms high, with large figures engraved on it, and it is entered by a vast subterranean passage."[5]

## *Understanding the Ancient Mysteries*

Manly P. Hall, in his renowned book, *An Encyclopedic Outline of Masonic, Hermetic, Kabbalistic and Rosicrucian Symbolical Philosophy*, published by the Philosophical Research Society, mentions the labyrinth in his discussion of the mysteries of Asar-Hapi, the ancient name for Serapis Bey, known as the hierarch of the ascension temple at Luxor.

Hall writes:

Labyrinths were also a striking feature in connection with the Rite of Serapis.... Labyrinths were symbolic of the involvements and illusions of the lower world through which wanders the soul of man in its search for truth....

In A.D. 385, Theodosius, that would-be exterminator of pagan philosophy, issued his memorable edict *De Idolo*

*Serapidis Diruenco*\*.... When the Christian soldiers, in
obedience to this order, entered the Serapeum at Alexandria to destroy the image of Serapis which had stood
there for centuries, so great was their veneration for the
god that they dared not touch the image lest the ground
should open at their feet and engulf them. At length,
overcoming their fear, they demolished the statue, sacked
the building, and finally as a fitting climax to their
offense burned the magnificent library which was housed
within the lofty apartments of the Serapeum....
  Christian symbols were found in the ruined foundations of this pagan temple. [And] Socrates, a church
historian of the fifth century, declared that after the pious
Christians had razed the Serapeum at Alexandria and
scattered the demons who dwelt there under the guise of
gods, beneath the foundations was found the monogram
of Christ![6]

## Labyrinths in the Unconscious Mind

Not only are there labyrinths in the outer world, there are
labyrinths in the hidden depths of ourselves. The ascended
master Lanello gave his students instruction about navigating
the labyrinth of the unconscious mind.

He taught:

  All of us know what it means to have pain and to
  have had it over prolonged periods as we wrestled with
  fallen angels and our own dweller-on-the-threshold.[†]
  Shall we be pressed down because of it? Shall we lose our
  joy? Shall we lose our verve and forget that God will
  wipe away all tears from our eyes?[7] I say a resounding no!

---

\* This essentially meant the idol of Serapis must be destroyed.
† The dweller-on-the-threshold is a term used to designate the anti-self, the
not-self or the synthetic self of any individual.

Even so, it is necessary for you to contemplate the journeying of your soul again and again through the valley of the shadow of death. Indeed, you must return to the scenes of past lives where you have succumbed to death or received an unjust death. For only you can clear those records, and this you must do by violet-flame* transmutation through your Mighty I AM Presence.†

Yes, beloved, you must travel through the labyrinth of your unconscious mind and you must fill the passageways with a brilliant light that banishes centuries of despair—all the while refusing to allow your members to be divided. It is the boulders of your pride that must be split! Yes, cleave them by the lightning of the Mind of God![8]

## Splitting the Boulders of Pride

We have all known people who strut around like peacocks and feel they have a right to be prideful. However, subtle forms of pride are also a problem for people who are striving to be humble in heart and soul. I have met many souls of light who, as a result of trying to overcome painful situations and a sense of inferiority, comfort themselves by exalting their virtues—and go overboard. They are often shocked to realize that they have fallen prey to the vice of pride, subtly manipulated by their dweller-on-the-threshold.

Here is an enumeration of the major aspects of pride and how they manifest in our psychology:

- **The nature of pride and recognizing its subtleties:** We all recognize pride in someone who is pompous, arrogant, putting everyone else down in favor of their own agenda. But pride can also be a rather subtle energy. For example,

---

*See Glossary: Violet flame
† For a pictorial representation of your I AM Presence, Christ Self and soul, see the Chart of Your Divine Self, p. 260.

a person who refuses to wear a hearing aid, insisting that everyone else needs to speak up! Or a person with poor eyesight who rejects the indignity of eyeglasses. Or the person who always begs to differ and has to have the last word.

- **Prideful behavior:** All of us can benefit from exploring and transmuting prideful attitudes and behavior in ourselves. We can ask ourselves, "What kind of subtle prideful behavior do I indulge in? Do I consider people who do not have my point of view to be ignorant or unreasonable? Do I look down my nose at street people? Do I think people who make a mistake are stupid? Do I have to have my way or my family or friends or colleagues regret it?"

- **Pride has been said to be the beginning of all sin:** Pride was the reason behind the fall of Lucifer, who led the revolt of the fallen angels. He said, "I am an archangel. I was here first. And God's human creation should bow down to me!" Lucifer fell because of his refusal to bow to the light of God in God's sons and daughters. And this has been the archetypal fall for many lightbearers.* How many times have we wanted another person to give in to our ideas, our position, our intelligence, our years on the spiritual path? And what is the right solution? We can choose to be true to ourself and to our God, to respect the Christ in all, to extend mercy and forgiveness to the wayward soul—our own soul and the souls of the people we meet on the road of life.

- **Pride acts as a poison:** Pride poisons our consciousness; when we are prideful we do not see clearly. We view life and other people through a veil of pride and arrogance, a sense that other people do not know what they are doing

---

* Souls of light on earth for a heavenly purpose

or talking about—usually because they do not agree with us. Because we do not see clearly we make mistakes in judgment, in perspective, in determining our course of action. And prideful action creates karma.*

- **What do we do when we see pride in ourselves?** When we recognize that pride, we can get down on our knees and ask God to help us surrender the pride of the human ego and to be humble. We can pray for those who seemingly persecute us. We can pray for clarity of vision and purpose. We can ask for the grace of understanding other people's point of view. And we can ask ourselves, "On what spiritual principle is my stand based? On what spiritual principle might the other person's stand be based? What would Jesus do in this situation?" And we can make it a point to listen with an open heart and mind. When we do this, we are on our way to a fruitful discussion instead of an angry, prideful shouting match. And even if we think the other person's stand is incorrect, we can bow to that person's free will and right to his or her own opinion.

- **Pride attracts negative energies:** When we indulge in prideful thinking and declarations, we are at the mercy of the negative energies we attract because of the vibration of pride. We may be totally unaware that we are indulging in pride. We may simply be convinced we are right! Maybe we are right, maybe we are not right; maybe there is a different point of view. Maybe there is some "right" in everyone's point of view. But a prideful attitude will likely propel us into a fit of exasperation and anger at people who do not agree with us. Thus, we need to pray for the binding of pride and anger. And it's wise to remember the French saying, *"Vive la différence!"* Hooray for the difference!

---

* Karma is the law of cause and effect. See Glossary for full explanation.

Out of differences often comes a broader understanding of a situation and better solutions to a problem.

- **Quarrels and wars between people and nations have been ignited out of pride:** Quarrels nearly always have pride at the root. And typically, at some level both people or nations are taking a prideful stance. I remember two people who worked together who simply could not stand each other. And the funny thing was, that which they could not stand in each other—a streak of meanness— each of them had in themselves. So one person said the other person was mean and proceeded to be just as mean in reacting to the meanness—if you know what I mean! Both were taking pride in the fact that the other person was at fault, when in reality each one was contributing to the discord. And if we look at pride on a planetary level, the Luciferian consciousness of pride is at the root of planetary wars and mayhem. Lucifer is the archetypal figure of the prideful fallen angels who said, "We know better than God. We will be as God." And that pride and rebellion was the root cause of the sinking of the ancient continent of Lemuria.

- **The pride and rebellion of the fallen angels** was also behind the barbarous actions of Genghis Khan, the Mogul conqueror in the 1100 and 1200s, as well as Adolf Hitler's infamous Third Reich and Stalin's murderous regime in Russia in the twentieth century. And we see the fallen angels behind today's atrocities in the Middle East and parts of Asia, the murder and mayhem of suicide bombers all over the world and the endless warring between Israel and Palestine. All of the murder and mayhem throughout the ages and continuing today is rooted in the fallen angels' pride and rebellion against God.

- **The saints have demonstrated humility, the antidote to pride:** Think of the humility of Christ Jesus, of the ascended master Lanello, of Mother Teresa, of Padre Pio and the saints throughout the ages. They have shown us the way. True humility is serving the Christ. So we ask ourselves, "Is what I am doing now serving the Christ?" If not, we need to surrender it and start over. When we let go of our human pride, we are in the right state of consciousness to pray for the clearing of the pride of the fallen angels. And when we surrender the pride, we need to replace it with higher qualities: sweet humility, obedience to our Christ Self, service to the Christ in all, compassion for the holy child. You can add to the list. As we do our own personal work, we can also invoke angels to clear a portion of planetary pride.

- **Pride manifests in our psychology:** Many people are working on healing their personal psychology or they would not be reading this book. And psychology, as you know, is the study of the soul. The soul may have unknowingly identified with the prideful energy of the fallen angels— and our outer consciousness may very well have followed suit. When we look at how pride manifests in our psychology, we are looking at both our daily habits and the underlying dynamics of our soul.

- **The roots of human pride:** The roots of pride are fertilized when we react to the atrocities of the fallen angels or adopt an attitude of "They can't do this to me!" And yet, they have done this to us in past lives and perhaps in this life. What did Jesus teach? He taught by word and deed the virtue of humility, which is the antidote to pride. Jesus humbled himself before God, before his interrogators and before the people. And he said, "What is that to thee? Follow thou me."

- **Disciplines from the Guru:** I remember numerous times when Elizabeth Clare Prophet in her role as Guru gave a discipline to a chela. The soul lesson in these situations always contained the element: Be humble before your God. She would put her staff in positions of humble service to help quell the pride of the ego and embrace the sweet humility of the Christ. Those who joyfully accepted the challenge benefited both spiritually and physically. Those who kicked against the pricks had the opportunity to look at their pride or whatever other substance the Guru perceived. This was a proving ground for the soul: Would the individual be upset out of pride or humbly accept the opportunity to learn the lesson? Once the lesson was learned, the individual was given a new opportunity depending on what the soul needed to learn and to do for God.

- **So let us remember** to center in our heart, to bow before God in sweet humility, to surrender our desires to God and pray for the binding of the dweller-on-the-threshold of pride.*

Once we understand how pride manifests in the labyrinth of our psychology, we are ready to accept who we really are as lightbearers, sons and daughters of God. Now we can focus on fulfilling our mission on earth. And our soul will rejoice!

### *Walking the Labyrinth: A Metaphor for the Journey of the Soul*

Walking the labyrinth becomes a metaphor for the journey to the sacred center of being and back into the world in which we live. We can continue this spiral for the rest of our life on earth and beyond. Every time we choose to go within

---

* You may use the Alchemical Energy Formula on p. 255.

and commune with God, we can emerge with a deeper appreciation of the sacredness of life and the journey.

When we choose to make our walk through the labyrinth of life a sacred walk, the journey itself fosters an enlightened understanding of our true identity as a son or daughter of God. Every time we go within and commune with God, we emerge with a deeper appreciation of the sacredness of life and of the journey. And, as we walk hand and hand with our Higher Self, we synchronize our mind and body with our soul and spirit.

## Accessing the Higher Self

We uplift our consciousness by focusing on the super-conscious, the consciousness of the Higher Self, a reservoir of our highest hopes and dreams, which we tap into through prayer, meditation and spiritual reverie. We are thereby pro-pelled into an awareness of the spiritual realm and the sacred centers of being.

In this state of consciousness, we more frequently expe-rience inspirational visions, high dreams, emotional tran-quility and a sense of inner peace and quietude. And we find it much easier to relate to challenging situations without los-ing our cool.

In order to facilitate progress on the homeward journey we do well to pray for divine guidance and to meditate upon the mission of our soul and the steps we need to take to ful-fill it. And we benefit greatly by asking our guardian angels to guide us to the spiritual retreats* where we may study and learn the higher precepts while our body sleeps at night.

When we first wake up is the easiest time to remember a retreat experience or a high dream and to meditate upon the

---

* Spiritual retreats are etheric retreats presided over by the ascended masters.

lessons for the soul and the outer self. Many people like to keep a pad and pen at their bedside to make notes when they first awaken and are still in touch with the inner experience or dream.[9]

We do well to pay attention to the thoughts or reveries we have upon awakening. We can gain vital insights by asking ourselves, "What is the metaphor? What is the spiritual lesson?" Our waking reveries are often metaphorical messages to the ego, the outer self, from the Higher Self. And lucid dreams or out-of-body experiences frequently stir us to address the unresolved issues of soul and spirit.

Many people find it both inspiring and practical to reflect on the journey of their soul and to ask their Higher Self, "What is the most important task I need to complete in order to fulfill my mission?" And we can all agree that a road map for the journey will be useful to avoid pitfalls along the way.

## *A Road Map for the Journey*

How do we create the map? We start from where we are, we mark where we want to go, and we map a route and guideposts along the way. This means mapping not only where we are in our state of consciousness, but also where we are in physical reality, including family and neighborhood responsibilities, what is required on the job, how we will finance the journey and what we will consider to be a victory. Many people believe that a mission statement with specifics on how to fulfill it is vital. And everyone benefits from daily prayer and good works.

I personally believe that whatever we are called to do in this life is intimately related to our soul's original purpose for being on earth. I have abundant evidence in my practice that each victory over the challenges of daily life gives the soul a boost upward. Enough boosts and we're there!

We hearten our soul and spirit when we pursue the fulfillment of our mission until we are victorious. And we can do it not only for ourselves but also for friends and loved ones and those we meet along the road of life. A touch on the shoulder, a smile of encouragement and a heartfelt belief that another person's mission is important can make all the difference to that individual.

We can inspire ourselves to keep on keeping on by chalking our victories, learning from our defeats and remembering that as we conduct ourselves in synchrony with our Higher Self, Christ Self or Buddha Self, we are leaving footprints in the sands of time for others to follow.

Here is a set of affirmations that can remind us of our higher goals and help us to stay focused during the tough times. I suggest giving the affirmations daily, beginning with a personal prayer for God's guidance and voicing the affirmations aloud.

Some people like to put their affirmations to music because they experience a special uplift from the combination of affirmation and song. Others like to stand up and shout the affirmations as fiats. Whatever is your pleasure, your soul and spirit will appreciate the boost upward. Bon voyage!

### I AM COMING HOME

I AM one with my soul and spirit.
I AM one with my Higher Self.
I AM pursing my life mission.
I AM forging a victory over every obstacle.
I AM striving to achieve my ascension in the light.
I AM winning through my effort and God's grace.
I AM coming Home to my Father-Mother God.

# 2

# *Here I Am Again!*

*"It's so silly," [Teddy] said. "All you do is
get the heck out of your body when you die. My gosh,
everybody's done it thousands and thousands of times.
Just because they don't remember it doesn't mean
they haven't done it. It's so silly."*

—J. D. SALINGER

During their therapy, many of my clients want to address traumas that they believe trace back to early life or even past-life experiences. I share with you now my thoughts about karma and reincarnation that come from my own experiences, dreams and remembrances, those of my clients, and explanations of Mark and Elizabeth Prophet.

I remember a vivid dream I had years ago. I was seated alone on a hillside watching a distant city that was on fire. The flames were shooting high in the air, it looked almost volcanic, and it gave me the shudders to think of what was happening to the people in the city.

I looked around me and saw people in the distance—I could not tell whether they were coming or going from the city. But they were trudging along as though they had the weight of the world on their shoulders. They were dressed in robes of some kind, not modern-day clothing. And there were no children, only adults.

All of a sudden, I was walking with them away from the city, and I felt a tremendous sadness. And then I remembered being on the hillside and suddenly I was there again. The people had vanished and the city was a heap of glowing rubble. A huge rush of water began to cover everything. As the water began creeping up the hill where I was sitting, I woke up in a cold sweat.

I realized that the dream was a metaphor, but it also felt so very real. It seemed like a past life though I could not exactly place it in time. I associated the dream with what happened to the ancient continent of Lemuria, which was destroyed through a combination of volcanic eruptions and tidal waves.

I decided to analyze my experience as a dream and reflected on what the different images meant to me. Fire = destruction. Flood = drowning. The people = looked ancient. And I realized that the metaphor had to do with old parts of me dying. The "me" I was identified with was alive and well but threatened by the flood of water. So, I free associated to "flood of water" and asked myself what I might be drowning in. What flashed through my mind were scenes of a family tragedy many years ago. Tears filled my eyes as I recalled what had happened and as I prayed for resolution, I felt the love of Jesus enfolding me. After a few moments, I felt a sense of resolution and inner peace.

"Aha!" I thought. It is a good dream because it is reminding me that Jesus loves me and that I am a survivor. Whether it is a past life or the tragedy in this life, I can let it go because it is over. I do not need to dig in the rubble, and

I do not need to drown in old sorrows. And I got the dream message: "Move on!"

At that time in my life, I had been feeling sad and could not exactly account for it. I had been digging around in my unconscious to figure out the sadness. I realized that life was good and there was no need to carry the rubble of old trauma. I could simply let it go. And I did, with the help of prayers and the violet transmuting flame. The dream has not recurred, which I trust means that I moved on in consciousness. If it was a past life, I am no longer stuck there!

### Ancient Roots of the Belief in Reincarnation

Mrs. Prophet has described the ancient roots of the belief in reincarnation and added her own perspective:[10]

> We've all had the sense of being familiar with a person or place that we've never contacted before in this life. Kind of an instantaneous like or dislike. Even love at first sight signifies an inner soul knowing.
>
> We have little hints but there is a reason why we specifically don't remember our past. God in his mercy pulls the shade when we enter the birth canal. It's a "curtain of forgetfulness." This is an act of mercy because we have an assignment for this life and we can't really focus on more than one life at a time and make a go of it.
>
> But now and then God raises the shade and shows us a frame or two from a previous life episode. This is for the quickening of our souls as to our responsibilities in this life and the commitments we made before coming into embodiment this time around. God sends his angels to teach us from the record of our own karmic book of life so that we can make enlightened choices and pass our tests.

Because even now at inner levels God is teaching
your soul about your karma and your past incarnations,
I am going to tell you how I first learned about karma
and reincarnation in the hopes that my story will ring a
bell for you. What I'm about to tell you is the first time
I recall God raising the shade for me.

### "Mother, What Happened?"

One day when I was about four years old I was
playing in my sandbox in Red Bank, New Jersey, where
I was born. I was in my play yard that my father had
made for me. It had a playhouse, a swing and sandbox
enclosed by a white picket fence with an arch and gate.
It was situated next to a delightful garden created by my
parents.

It was a beautiful day. Big white clouds were moving
through a deep blue sky. And I was alone, enjoying
myself in the sun, watching the sand slip through my
little fingers, drawing designs in the fresh earth and
making mudpies with cookie cutters and tin molds.

Then all of a sudden, as though someone had turned
a dial, I was playing in the sand along the Nile River in
Egypt and I was experiencing the beauty of that scene. It
was just as real as my play yard in Red Bank and just as
familiar. I was idling away the hours, splashing in the
water and feeling the warm sand on my body. My Egyptian mother was nearby. Somehow this too was my
world. I had known that river forever.

After some time (I don't know how much time had
passed), it was as though the dial turned again and I was
back at home in that little play yard. I wasn't dizzy.
I wasn't dazed. I was back to the present, very much
aware that I had been somewhere else.

So I jumped up and ran to find my mother. I found

her at the kitchen stove and I blurted out my story. I said, "Mother, what happened?" She sat me down and looked at me and said, "You have remembered a past life." With those words she opened another dimension. And I have never been the same.

Instead of ridiculing or denying what I had experienced, she explained that the soul does not accomplish her mission in one life. She told me that my soul was eternal. She said that our body is like a coat we wear. It gets worn out before we finish what we have to do. So God gives us a new mommy and a new daddy and we are born again so we can finish the work God sent us to do and finally return to our home of light in heaven. Even though we get a new body, we are still the same soul. And the soul has a continuous recollection of the past but we do not.

She explained all of this to me in simple childlike terms I understood. It was as though I had always known it and my mother was reawakening my soul memory.

### Karma Is Why We Are Still Here

Over the years she was to point out to me children who were born maimed or blind, others who were gifted, some who were born into wealthy homes and some into poverty. She attributed their inequality to karma and to their past exercise of free will. She said that there could be no such thing as divine or human justice if we had only one life, that God's justice could only be known in the outplaying of many lives in which we see past actions coming full circle in present circumstances.

Accustomed to praying to Jesus, my thoughts turned to him. I saw the logic of reincarnation and I said to myself, "God must have shown me this past life for a reason." But God didn't tell me the reason till I was well into adulthood. Then I realized that that life in Egypt was the key to the work I had to do in this life. No doubt through that glimpse into the distant past, there was transferred to me some substance of myself—perhaps some heavy karma that I had to balance today, thirty-three centuries later, or a mission I had not fulfilled whose time had come.

Since then God has revealed to me other incarnations and taught me lessons concerning positive or negative momentums that I must build on or undo. Thus, I have seen the causes behind the effects of bad karma that I had to balance in this life, and I have seen how my good karma put the wind in my sails to achieve my goals and more. Karma, in fact, is why we are all here.

### Life Is a Challenge and an Opportunity

You, too, have brought with you the momentums of your good karma as well as those of your bad karma that you must balance. You most certainly have positive or negative karma with family members and people you know or people you will meet. Life is a challenge and an opportunity.

Since the concepts of karma and reincarnation are *the* key to understanding our soul's journey, I ask you to stay with me this evening because I have much to say on the subject. I will not leave a stone unturned in bringing to you this teaching.

Based on my findings, you, then, can do your own research. You can meditate and consider what you come to in your own heart on this subject. You should not believe something because I say it but because the Lord Jesus Christ is speaking directly to you in your own heart and confirming the truth that I speak by the Holy Spirit.

I have walked and talked with Jesus all my life and Jesus has answered my questions about the scriptures, about the sermons of the pastors and ministers, about the Mass, about the rabbis, and so many things my heart would ponder. I have read my Bible and asked Jesus for answers, and he has never failed me.

And so I give you what I have received directly from Jesus as well as the research I have put together on karma, reincarnation and Christianity.

### Spiritual Beliefs of Ancient People

The belief in reincarnation is ancient and widespread. In 1886 the Reverend W. R. Alger wrote *A Critical History of the Doctrine of a Future Life*. It became the standard Christian work on the subject of immortality.

In his book Alger wrote: "No other doctrine has exerted so extensive, controlling, and permanent an influence upon mankind as that of ... metempsychosis [another word for reincarnation]—the notion that when the soul leaves the body it is born anew in another body, its rank, character, circumstance, and experience in each successive existence depending on its qualities, deeds, and attainments in ... preceding lives."[11]

Before the advent of Christianity, reincarnation was a part of the spiritual beliefs of many of the peoples of Europe, including the early Teutonic tribes, the Finns, Icelanders, Lapps, Norwegians, Swedes, Danes, early Saxons and the Celts of Ireland, Scotland, England, Brittany, Gaul and Wales.

The Welsh have even claimed that it was the Celts who originally carried the belief in reincarnation to India.[12] Author Ignatius Donnelly suggests that the Celts' belief in reincarnation was derived from the inhabitants of the lost continent of Atlantis who migrated to Ireland.[13]

In ancient Greece both Pythagoras and Plato believed in reincarnation. In the sixth century B.C., Pythagoras taught that the soul had many incarnations, which were opportunities for the soul to purify and perfect herself. "The human soul is immortal," he said, "for it resembles the heavenly stars, and (like them) is involved in perpetual motion."[14] According to biographer Diogenes Laertius, Pythagoras claimed that he had been embodied in the past as Aethalides and Euphorbus, who died at the hands of Menelaus at Troy.[15]

### Reincarnation and the Soul

In the fourth century B.C., Plato taught that the soul is immortal and that its circumstances in its current life depend on its disposition formed in a previous life. In book 10 of *The Republic*, he tells the story of a group of souls about to embody who are advised by a prophet: "Virtue owns no master. He who honors her shall have more of her, and he who slights her less. The responsibility lies with the chooser. Heaven is guiltless."[16]

According to some scholars, statements made by the first-century Jewish historian Josephus indicate that the Pharisees and Essenes also believed in reincarnation. Others believe these are references to the resurrection of the dead in new bodies.

In *The Wars of the Jews*, Josephus writes, "[The Pharisees] say that all souls are incorruptible; but that the souls of good men are only removed into other bodies—but that the souls of bad men are subject to eternal punishment."[17]

And in *The Antiquities of the Jews*, he says, "[the Pharisees] also believe that souls have an immortal vigor in them, and that under the earth there will be rewards or punishments, according as they have lived virtuously or viciously in this life, and the latter are to be detained in an everlasting prison, but that the former shall have power to revive and live again."[18]

Reincarnation was also taught by students of the Kabbalah, a system of Jewish esoteric mysticism that flowered in the thirteenth century. Reincarnation is still a part of the religious beliefs of the Jewish Hasidic movement, founded in the eighteenth century.

Some tribes of American Indians as well as numerous tribes in Central and South America have believed in reincarnation. Today the belief in reincarnation also exists among over one hundred tribes in Africa as well as among Eskimo and Central Australian tribes and many peoples of the Pacific, including Hawaiians, Tahitians, Melanesians and Okinawans.

The most elaborately developed concepts of reincarnation are found in the religious traditions of India, especially Hinduism, Buddhism, Jainism and Sikhism. In these religions, reincarnation is linked with the law of karma.

## How Karma Impacts Our Life

*Karma* is a Sanskrit word meaning "act, action, work or deed." In Hinduism *karma* originally referred to sacred actions performed in Vedic rituals and later evolved to mean moral deeds. It then became associated with the concept of reincarnation in another body or form of life.

Some in the Eastern religious traditions believe that as a result of past misdeeds or cruelty, a human can reembody as an animal or can regress to an animal-like state. Others, like the Jains, do not see the animal state as a punishment but as a necessary experience in one's spiritual evolution.

Pythagoras may have subscribed to this theory. One of his contemporaries once told the following story: "They say that while walking past a dog that was being beaten, Pythagoras took pity and said, 'Stop! Strike no more! In his body abides the soul of a dear friend of mine, whose voice I recognized as he was crying.'"[19]

You see, every dog and dogma—has his day!

## The Law of Cause and Effect

According to the law of karma as it is taught in the East, your thoughts, words and deeds in past lives have determined the conditions of your present life; and your thoughts, words and deeds in this life will determine your destiny in future lives.

It's a bit difficult to accept that. People like to blame their parents or circumstances or heredity or what happened to them when they were children or the opportunities they've missed—everything but themselves.

I think that the Church's doctrine of the vicarious atonement (that Jesus Christ paid the debt for our sins) perpetuates our sense of wanting someone else to carry the burden of our karma, in other words, the burden of our sin.

If some calamity happens to us, we think, "Well, this is so-and-so's fault." Or "I was a victim of circumstances." Or "I was at the wrong place at the wrong time." Some people blame God and stay angry at him for the rest of their lives. These attitudes are wrong. We have to get into the driver's seat and take responsibility for our lives and our actions. And when we do we begin to see that there is justice in the universe.

I myself have certainly not had an easy life. I recall petitioning the Lords of Karma before I took embodiment to allow me to take on a major portion of my

karma at birth, and they did. And I accept that most of
the things that have happened to me, good or bad, have
come about by my own doings.

I say "most" because people initiate original acts of
negative karma every day. People willfully harm people,
just as nation inflicts harm upon nation where there is no
antecedent of a prior karma between them. Thus the
injured party is not the recipient of returning karma of
the past, but the victim of an initial act of wrongdoing.
That is why we can truthfully say that not everything
that happens to us is the result of our own doings.

### Initiations of the Soul

Then there is the situation of the initiation of our
souls. This comes from the Cosmic Christ. And there is
temptation. This comes from the Antichrist. Initiation
and temptation are the means God allows for the testing
of our souls. The story of Job is a classic example of
calamity which God allows so that our love for him can
be tested. These trials teach us lessons. When we pass
through them without compromising our honor, we are
ready for the next trial and the next until we graduate
from earth's schoolroom.

So our good karma brings untold blessings as the
harvest of our good works. Our bad karma brings the
harvest of what we have sown in error. And we do not
escape one jot or one tittle of it.[20] But it is true that we
may receive good or bad energy from others, neither of
which we deserve. Every day people exercise their free
will to be kind or unkind—regardless of past karma.
They are making new karma and they will receive blessing or bane accordingly, just as we do when we initiate
actions that are wise or unwise.

Initiations, including persecution and the crucifixion,

are sent by God to strengthen us and restore our souls back to him. Temptation is a testing of the mettle of the soul. Since we cannot always tell whether the good fortune that befalls us is due to our good karma or the sheer mercy and grace of God, and we do not know if adversity is our bad karma coming back to haunt us or temptation or trial or soul testing or the highest levels of initiation from God, we must therefore deal with every circumstance with a positive, grateful attitude. We must determine that we will deal justly with ourselves, our God and our fellowman so that there will be a victory, a blessing and a resolution for all concerned.

So you see there are circumstances in our lives that cannot be classified strictly as karma—except it be our karmic lot to endure all things because it is we who left off from the presence of God in the first place. And now we have the karma of finding our way back to him "by the sweat of the brow" until our original sin of turning away from God be balanced.

In my sense, then, of God and the universe, I have only gratitude for the lessons I have learned from my karma. For I understood the law of karma in my heart before it was ever taught to me. My motto is: There is no injustice anywhere in the universe. Amazing as it may seem, if we knew all the circumstances and ramifications of our past lives, our past "rights" and "wrongs," we would see clearly that this is true.

### Words and Deeds as Teachers

If we understood the continuity of being and all that we have said and done in past ages, we would see that our words and deeds return to us as teachers. And if they are not so nice, we should understand that not-so-nice things happen to us so that we can self-correct. They happen so that we can see how it feels to be on the receiving end of what we have sent forth in this or a previous lifetime.

I think it is the coming of age of a man, a woman or a child when the soul reaches that point of maturity where she can say, "Whatever comes to me, I will receive it with rejoicing. For I know that as I balance and resolve that situation I can look forward to my communion with God and ultimately to that day when I can attain permanent reunion with my Divine Father and my Divine Mother."

So Hinduism and Buddhism teach that the law of karma is a universal law of cause and effect that affects everyone. As Newton's third law of motion states: For every action there is an equal and opposite reaction.

The law of karma operates automatically and without prejudice. This is why there is no injustice. We think that some people get away with everything while we get away with nothing. That makes us chafe at the bit and wonder if there is a just God.

We simply have to be at peace and remember the teaching from Deuteronomy that Paul referred to: "Vengeance is mine. I will repay, saith the Lord."[21] Therefore it is ours to forgive. God will mete out his justice and we certainly do not wish harm upon anyone, even those who are our self-styled enemies.

We know that karma functions on an individual as well as a group level. As the twentieth-century yogi Paramahansa Yogananda wrote: "The cumulative actions of human beings within communities, nations, or the world as a whole constitute mass karma, which produces local or far-ranging effects according to the degree and preponderance of good or evil. The thoughts and actions of every man, therefore, contribute to the good or ill of this world and all peoples in it."[22]

There is, then, such a thing as personal karma, something very personal, for instance, between you and me alone; it functions one-on-one. And then there is group karma. Entire nations or towns or families have made karma because of their stand against life. They commit acts together as one body and therefore they must reembody together. The Mafia families, for instance, come back together again and again because of their karma.

## America: Atlantis Come Again

Mrs. Prophet went on to describe America as "Atlantis come again," an opportunity for souls who lived on Atlantis to fulfill a destiny that was aborted in those ancient times. She taught:

It has been said, and it is true, that America is Atlantis come again, that most of us lived on Atlantis and are here to make right those things that we didn't do right and to have our victory. Atlantis was a teeming continent with great advances in science and technology. Many of our scientists have brought back the same inventions that they patented on Atlantis.

If you read the book *A Dweller on Two Planets* by Phylos the Thibetan,[23] you may find yourself identifying with the sights and scenes of that lost continent. You may even find that God will open your memory and reveal to you a past life and tell you what you have to do today to complete a major chapter in your life story. You see, life is a tremendous opportunity.

I pray daily for the awakening of the people of America to their divine destiny—for them to know that they are Atlanteans come again and that they have a mission to bring America and the world into a golden age like the one we knew 25,000 years ago on Atlantis.

And I pray, as it is my calling, that I can help you find the answers to your questions so that you can make the most of every moment of the rest of your life and come Home to God with a good report—so that you can joyously stand before the Court of the Sacred Fire at the conclusion of this life and hear the divine approbation: "Well done, thou good and faithful servant. Thou hast been faithful over a few things of thy karma, I will make thee ruler over many things."[24]

## *The Lessons of the Suernis*

The leader of another ancient civilization, the ascended master Ernon, tells the story of karma repeated again and again by the people of Suern who had major lessons to learn, and of his efforts, as the Rai of Suern, to get them back on track.

He gave the following instruction to his students in a dictation to Mrs. Prophet:[25]

I come, then, to tell you of the lessons learned—lessons that I have learned, lessons that the Suernis have learned and lessons that you have learned.

Of the two million who came with the Lord Christ to the land of Suern, who were his adherents and had considerable development of the Christ embodied within them, the one million who [eventually] ascended were in a state of higher love and higher grace. It was by their love for the living Christ and the source whence he had come that they ascended from that land.

The one million who did not ascend, although they had Christ-attainment, did not have the sufficiency of love to sustain that level of devotion that would allow them to merit the ascension. And so the residue of their karma held them back and eventually did overtake them as they did multiply the negative momentums and did gradually let go of the positive momentums. Thus, increment by increment the sacred fire[26] fell, almost unnoticeably yet precipitously.

### Jesus' Call to Repentance

These individuals have come to be known as the lost sheep of the house of Israel.[27] Thus, when Jesus came two thousand years ago he declared, "I am not sent but unto the lost sheep of the house of Israel."*

He came to call to repentance and to call to the path of the Divine Mother these [remaining] one million souls. Most of them are still embodied upon earth today, often in positions of leadership. They retain as a shadow the vestige of the former self and former Christ light, yet even that shadow of their former days of glory does place them above their peers in many fields....

Many of these are self-satisfied in their accomplishments, in their attainments, and yet they do not return [to their former] devotion to the Lord Christ. Others [not of the one million] have come forward to take up the calling to be his disciples and in measures of devotion have outdistanced the original remnant. Yet in ancient times that remnant did have greater attainment than that to which the newer followers of Jesus have attained.

### A Quickening and a Knowledge

Thus, beloved, the teachings of the ascended masters, given freely, are a specific transfer, a quickening and a knowledge unto those who had them 35,000 years ago in the golden age of Atlantis and in many centuries prior to that; for those souls had been with Jesus long before the fullness of their time came in that golden age.

---

* Matt. 15:24.

Therefore understand that the traditions found in the Western Bible contain fragments of this ancient teaching. These fragments have been filled in by the ascended masters today, your beloved Saint Germain, your El Morya and, of course, the Lord Jesus Christ. Many others have joined them until the saints robed in white in numberless numbers have come forward to give this teaching not only to those who had it long ago but also to those who will take it up now as a new study, for they are newer souls and have not had this background [that the older souls have had].

The souls who have been on earth for tens of thousands of years and more are familiar with the teaching even if they were not a part of this remnant of the one million. And therefore, when those for whom this teaching is a reading of the law [written] in their inward parts* come to our meetings and receive the teaching, they instantly confirm it by the ancient record that is written in their own book of life.†...

Ascended Master Ernon went on to explain that free will and the option of self-mastery is available to reembodied individuals from ancient civilizations and the golden age of Atlantis, in particular to the rebellious Suernis. However, to overcome a momentum of rebellion that has lasted lifetimes would take tremendous effort and dedication to the cause of truth.

When you think about it, most of us resist being told what to do, even when it's in our best interest. We can appreciate how difficult it would be to overcome a momentum on rebellion that has been built over lifetimes. As we reflect

---

* Jer. 31:33; Heb. 8:10; 10:16.
† The book of the records of their comings and goings and their karma.

on that drama, we might ask ourselves, "Do I rebel against taking an action suggested by someone else, even if I know it's the right thing to do? If so, why? Do I want to change that habit? If so, what do I want to do instead?"

Once we answer these questions to our satisfaction, we can practice replacing our rebellious attitude with right action, which is for most of us a giant step forward toward self-mastery and spiritual maturity. And if perchance we were one of the ancient Suernis, we may be balancing karma from ancient times.

In his dictation, Rai Ernon also discussed the role that devotion to the Divine Mother plays in the attainment of self-mastery and adeptship.

He explained:

> Now understand, beloved, that I sought with all of my heart to bring the ancient Suernis into a love and a devotion of the Divine Mother. For it is the Divine Mother who gives the attainment and the mastery and the raising up of her light whereby the individual may have mastery over himself, his circumstances and the elements, may command the forces and the elementals. Beloved ones, this experiment was such a disaster that not since then has a high adept ever been empowered in a position of rulership to compel adherence to the moral code of the conserving of the sacred fire.

> To this day, then, the option for self-mastery [is left to the] freewill decision of everyone upon earth. The decision of how to spend the light of the crystal cord descending from the I AM Presence and the light of the Divine Mother rising upon the spinal altar remains the province of every individual in the privacy of his personal counsel with God.

That is not to say, however, that the individual who does choose to continue to squander that light in lasciviousness and all manner of lust is free of the karma of so doing, for the light belongs to God: it is the descending light of Alpha and the rising light of Omega.

Thus, the path of adeptship is open to all. As you have been counseled to seek power and empowerment for the healing of the nations and for the saving of these cycles [of opportunity] in the last days of the age of Pisces, so I counsel you that the raising up of this light by pure love and devotion to the Trinity and the Divine Mother will give you that power which you so desire.

The question is: Will you desire that power enough to allow yourself to be weaned from its misuses and the scattering and the diminishment of your forces?

So, beloved, this is the question that is upon you. Those who love much and are much loved, of them much is expected and they expect much of themselves. And because their love of Jesus is so great, they are able to wield the power of the sacred fire and through mantra and meditation to arrive at the place where their chakras are always filled, their lamps are trimmed, and they have the wherewithal to transfer a light to those in whom the fire has gone out.

With what light, then, shall the fire be rekindled in those who have let it go out?

May it be with your light but may [its transfer] be always by the permission and under the jurisdiction of Jesus Christ. The oil of your lamps is a sacred gift and it must be given [only] to those who are worthy and committed in its use, else you will find yourself running out of your own light by distributing it without discrimination.

Rai Ernon also shared an important lesson learned, how he offered too much love to the detriment of the Suernis, and how they became as spoiled children, wasting the light that was given to them in wanton sexual behavior. He explained that this ancient drama had now come full circle.

He taught his students:

> My desire then, was so very great, and I did learn the lessons of too much love and how too much love for the child, in giving so much, does spoil the child. And therefore this evolution of Suernis who were under me have remained in that state of being spoiled and self-indulgent and have, many of them, remained stubborn and stiff-necked [children] to the present.
>
> Though they were under the guru Moses, though they were under Abraham and the patriarchs, though they have had many opportunities—visited by the arch-angels and by servants of God who have dotted the centuries as the Sons of the Solitude* come again and again—yet, in this day, still in rebellion against those ancient days of my love, they insist upon the misuse of the sacred fire as a continued defiance of me *personally!*
>
> They have never forgotten or forgiven me in my attempt to convince them to restrain their uses of the sacred fire, whereby they might be empowered not only to command the energies for the conveniences of life but, of course, to enter into a path that would bring them ultimate reunion with God. . . .

### Wooing the Suernis to a Path of Love

> Now, therefore, I come to you to ask your assistance. For I desire, of course, once again to woo the reincarnated Suernis to a path of love, to an inner awakening; for

_____
* See Glossary.

many of them, though they yet carry their anger, suffer from depression.

It is a deep depression, for they know at unconscious levels of being that in my person and in the persons of other Sons of the Solitude they have lost the truest friend they ever had. They know that they do not have that tie to the living Christ and yet they do not desire to surrender their substance [their misqualified energy and misuse of the sacred fire][28] to bend the knee, to confess that they have espoused the golden-calf consciousness and civilization, and to leave all this behind them for the love of the mighty one of God, the Lord Christ.

Thus, it is an hour when you see a karma repeated again and again. The cycles of opportunity [to overcome the] repetition of this karma are coming to a close for the Suernis. When I speak of the Suernis, I am not speaking of the one million souls who yet have the option to take that ascension but of the rebellious ones who embodied through them as the Suernis who rebelled against me....

## The Opportunity of Adeptship

Adeptship today, then, is by free will. Alas, the Path is not prominent in the West. Many have never heard of such a path or, if they have, fear it as something that they would call occult. As you know, *occult* simply means "hidden," that which is the hidden wisdom that is unveiled to the initiate.

But there is a path, beloved, and it is under the ascended masters. And since my ascension I have been able to work with many who have lovingly received my ministration and who have desired the techniques of full God-mastery for one reason and one alone: the purest love of God and the desire to help his own. Thus I have graduated to the place of being able to work with those who are certainly suffused with the love of Christ and therefore can make rapid and light strides on this path of progress....

I, too, am grateful that the story of my involvement in the land of Suern has been recorded in the book by Phylos the Thibetan,[29] for with the understanding [of my experience] many will see that to force the issue of the path of spirituality [or celibacy, using the sacred fire only for procreation], is not wise. This includes not forcing [the spiritual path] upon children but rather acquainting them with their options and allowing them to choose when [or if] they desire to make a more than ordinary commitment to the Path.

## The Greatest Teacher Is the Best Example

Thus, beloved, the greatest teacher is the best example. I sought to be that example in the land of Suern and [the record shows that I did succeed].

[Nevertheless], the example unto those who want none of it is never sufficient; but the record that is left in akasha of your example will always be there. And you will rejoice to see from inner levels and other octaves as you move on in your journey to the Sun how souls will come along and suddenly find themselves locked in [the replica of] your Electronic Presence that you have left along the byways of life.

Locking in to the record of your being, they will suddenly rejoice in gladness and know that the day has come for their intimate and personal association with an unascended or ascended master who will take them all the way to the point of their God-realization.

# 3

# *Fulfilling the Destiny of the Soul*

*There is a point of endurance.*
*It is in the inner silence.*
*It is in the closing-out*
*Of all of the conditions of turmoil*
*Of the outer world.*
*It is in the finding of the point of light*
*In the heart.*

—GAUTAMA BUDDHA

*T*oday we live in times of tremendous change including major changes in the perspective of what our lives are all about. I believe it is time to heal the ancient records of leaving off from God. It is time for each of us to claim the victory of divine love in the Aquarian Age. This can be quite difficult if we are holding onto old baggage from previous embodiments.

For those who have been on the spiritual path for lifetimes, it is the time to complete our mission on earth. It is time to return to permanent, conscious union with God and to make our ascension at the conclusion of this lifetime or to remain as bodhisattvas to assist the rest of the lightbearers to make it home. Yet, we are unlikely to win our victory if we are still weighed down with old baggage!

In order to fulfill our soul's destiny, we need to have some idea of the personal mission our soul came to accomplish. Sometimes, the process of psychotherapy will reveal clues to our soul's original mission. We can also pray, meditate, set our goals and ask God to remind us of the mission we originally set out to fulfill—and what that means in this life. Sometimes we get a flash of inspiration or words or images that make it clear. Or God may answer us by encouraging us to look at our natural gifts and talents. Or by reminding us of certain mystical teachings or an inner prompting we have not yet acted on.

We may find it necessary to review our life choices in order to understand that the high road has always been there at a choice point—whether we understood it or not. Sometimes our mission was on the horizon when we were children, adolescents or young adults, but we did not necessarily recognize it as such.

I believe that I was trained before this lifetime to be a spiritual teacher, to help souls wake up to their true purpose. Yet, I had my karma to balance and lessons to learn, and I did not necessarily make the wisest choices until I matured emotionally. It was through time and hard knocks that I eventually learned to differentiate between sympathy and compassion. And that was a big key for me.

The proverbial story about the difference between sympathy and compassion is a man sinking in the quicksand, yelling for help. The sympathetic passerby jumps in and tries to pull him out—they both go down. The compassionate passerby grabs a nearby branch and extends it, keeping safely out of the quicksand—he succeeds in saving the man and himself! You can guess that if my challenge was to be compassionate, not sympathetic, which passerby I often was!

I have had many teachers and life experiences that have helped me to overcome the tendency toward sympathy, taught me how to outwit deception, sharpened my spiritual discernment and given me necessary advice to correct a habit that was not serving my soul.

Mrs. Prophet gave me a personal instruction that I would like to pass on to you. She said, "Don't fault yourself for the flaws in the diamond of your being. Remember, only synthetic gems have no flaws." Of course, she didn't mean that I shouldn't try to correct those flaws! Self-correction under God's direction is the name of the game for everyone who is pursing enlightenment.

When we are serious about our spiritual journey on earth, we take a good look at what we can offer to God and to the people in our life. We begin the process of dumping old baggage overboard—troublesome memories, wrong motivations or attitudes, negative thoughts, hurtful feelings and bad habits. This may be with the aid of therapy in addition to prayer and meditation. We align ourselves with the inner compass of our Higher Self (Christ Self, Buddha Self, Krishna, Tiferet). And we set our sail to fulfill our divine destiny. That means staying attuned to the great God Flame* within our heart and taking the high road no matter what!

The ascended master Afra gave his students this simple direction, "Be true to yourself and to God." That is great advice. This means being true to the best of ourselves in whatever we undertake: spiritual studies, education or professional

---

*The divine spark, the flame of God ensconced within the secret chamber of the heart; the soul's point of contact with the I AM Presence and Holy Christ Self.

training situations, the world of work and play, family life, serving our community. In everything we do on a daily basis to fulfill our mission, we are called to be true to our Higher Self and to God.

Each of us came into this life blessed by God and our guardian angel to fulfill a special mission, to offer a gift to the children of God on earth. In fulfilling our mission, we have the opportunity to redeem imperfect choices and to create good karma.

## A Look at Cosmic History

Let's look at ancient history, a time when the ascended masters tell us that cosmic councils had decreed that earth should be no more because no one was upholding the light. They also tell us that the first three root races* on earth made their ascension. It was during the evolution of the fourth root race that fallen angels entered the picture after Lucifer's rebellion and refusal to bend the knee to the sons of God. That proud one said, "I was here first. I refuse to bow down to the sons and daughters of God." Consequently, Lucifer and the angels who aligned themselves with him were cast out of heaven and the drama of Good and Evil began on earth.

The ascended masters teach that earth then became a dark star, eventually so dark that the decree for its dissolution went forth. Enter Sanat Kumara and the 144,000 who accompanied him to earth. Some of you may know the story. Sanat Kumara, also known as the Ancient of Days, stood before the Cosmic Council and vowed that he would come

---

*A root race is a group of souls who embody together and have a unique archetypal pattern, divine plan and mission to fulfill on earth.

to earth and hold the flame for earth's evolutions to be reawakened if the council would spare the earth.

Sanat Kumara told the story in a dictation he gave through Mrs. Prophet.

He told his devotees:

> ...I came to focus the light of threefold flame at Shamballa thousands of years ago, responding to the call not of mankind, not of cosmic councils but the call of my own heartbeat. For mankind were yet too dense to call. They knew not how to call nor that they were in need of the call. And therefore, in meditation upon the rhythm of my own heart flame and that pulse of God within me, I perceived its absence on Terra. I came and I meditated upon that flame until Gautama and Maitreya responded to the flame."[30]

Many lightbearers, perhaps ourselves, chose to come to earth with Sanat Kumara to help hold the spiritual balance and to assist the souls of the fourth root race to return to God. Or we may have come with other legions of light at a later point. Or we may have been part of the fourth root race. One way or another we embodied on earth, gradually lost our attunement to God and were led astray by the fallen angels as recorded in the Book of Enoch.[31]

Ultimately, we became entangled with the forces of darkness, compromised or forgot our mission, didn't see through the plots and ploys of the fallen angels, made the karma of leaving off from God and did not fulfill what we had agreed to do when we came to this planet. And here we are today, thousands of years and who knows how many lifetimes later, awakening to the realization that we are here to fulfill a spiritual mission.

### The Role of Psychotherapy

Psychotherapy is a way in which we can access, understand and release hurtful dramas of the past that are fueling negative habit patterns. When we reflect on the worst moments of our life we often discover they are connected in some way. At some level they track back to our soul's original mission, our leaving off from God and lifetimes of believing that the introjects unconsciously incorporated from traumatic experiences were our true identity. Those traumatic moments were frequently karmic in nature and related to lessons that our soul needed to learn.

Sometimes we unconsciously identify with the records of our original departure from God. And if we have not done the spiritual and psychological work to resolve the patterns that we have been holding onto since that time, we are likely to step right back into the record and repeat it.

When ancient patterns emerge, most of us tend to identify with them instead of understanding that they are the same attitudes, motivations, thought patterns, feelings and actions that may have taken us off track in the first place. This is a major reason that Jesus Christ, Gautama Buddha, Mohandas Gandhi and other great teachers have taught spiritual precepts and demonstrated them in their lives.

By being true to the spiritual precepts we honor, we can stay on track. Take the Golden Rule, for example. This spiritual teaching, "Do unto others as you would have them do unto you," appears in all the major religions in some form. This teaching reminds us of an important moral precept that we are called to relate to others with kindness, mercy and generosity—regardless of how other people happen to be behaving at the moment.

When people come to me for therapy, I explain that the first step in resolving painful experiences is to pray for guidance. And the second is to attune to the Higher Self through prayer, meditation or decrees.* The third is to do the psychological work it takes to let go of the hurtful experiences and to change the habit patterns that are sparking self-defeating behavior.

Of course, there are no magic solutions. The healing process involves effort and a willingness to let go of old habits, and one session is not likely to solve all our problems. However, I have found that psychotherapy combined with spirituality can take an individual a long way down the road to emotional and mental well-being. I include God in my sessions. And I tell my clients, "Pray as if it all depended on God and take action as if it all depends on you!"

We benefit by looking squarely at our negative motivations, thoughts, feelings and habits, calling a spade a spade and doing the spiritual and psychological work to let go of the patterns of the not-self, the part of us that is not serving the Higher Self.

We can ask ourselves, "Would I do this in the presence of my God?" and if the answer is "Not on your life!" we know that this is a motivation, thought, feeling or habit pattern that needs to go.

We do our prayers, get counseling as needed and simply refuse to tolerate the old habit the next time it comes up. We refuse the next time and the next time, and keep on refusing. And each time that habit rears its head, we replace it with a positive action. We have determined that we want that old habit gone, once and for all, and we absolutely refuse to pick

_____
*See Glossary: Decree

it up again even if it waves frantically at us. And we practice the positive action until it replaces the negative reaction. And we keep accenting the positive until the new habit is firmly in place.

We remind ourselves that our goal is to be who we really are, and that when we are in a state of higher consciousness we can be happy and fulfilled no matter what is going on around us. We develop spiritual practices that reinforce who we really are. And we pursue friendships and job opportunities that support our new thrust rather than holding onto people and situations that are not in keeping with who we are or desire to become. This is a process of enlightened self-interest.

### *Addictive Habits Track Back to Soul Pain*

I have had clients who suffer from addictions, which in my experience frequently track back to soul pain. Once the individual recognizes and goes through the process of healing that pain, the addiction loses much of its power. Of course, the person still needs help to overcome the habit that became an addiction.

If a recovering alcoholic goes to work in a bar or a restaurant where she has to serve drinks, she is asking for trouble. If a recovering rage-aholic continues to work in a very frustrating and anger-provoking job, he is asking for trouble. If recovering sex-aholics continue to flirt or keep company with the people they have been involved with sexually, they are asking for trouble. The remedy for addiction is abstinence, removing oneself from the contributing environment and getting the help of a support group.

A recovering alcoholic needs to attend AA meetings to foster recovery from alcoholism and a job where there is zero contact with liquor, wine or beer. The recovering sex-aholic needs an SA support group and to avoid associating with people or websites that fuel the addiction. The rage-aholic also needs a support group and a job where calm behavior is valued. Anyone beset with an addiction needs help to say "No!" to situations of enticement.

Many people set up situations that are seemingly innocent but contain the potential to set off or reinforce their negative patterns. We have to catch on to how we do that and ask God to help us stop it. I remember Mrs. Prophet giving an amusing and helpful instruction to a person who was overly focused on the opposite sex. She said, "When you see one coming, just turn around and run the other way. And I mean, run!" The point was to outwit the negative pattern controlling the soul.

The goal is to set up situations that are conducive to being who we are at the level of the Higher Self instead of reinforcing habits that do not serve us well. We can achieve the goal if we focus on being true to our Higher Self, examine situations ahead of time and focus on constructive behavior.

## *Case Study: Stuck in a Black Hole*

To make the point, here is a case study of a thirty-year-old man. We will call him Dave. His dilemma was that he mistrusted his own judgment and followed the lead of other people instead of being true to himself. Every time he realized he had been led down the primrose path, he would berate himself. But then he would do it again—and again. Embarrassment finally propelled him into therapy.

The drama began with Dave's father and older brother and expanded to teachers, colleagues and dominant men. After he gave me some background and we discussed the situation, I asked Dave to focus on his earliest memory of self-destructive behavior and to tell me his negative thought about himself.

Dave went back to when he was a six-year-old. His negative thought about himself was "I'm stupid," an echo of what his father and older brother often told him. He felt put down, abandoned and desolate. He did not remember a particular scene but he said it felt like being in a black hole. So, we focused on that image.

At first, the child part of him decided therapy wasn't going to work. We did some preparatory inner child work, and Dave went back and forth deciding whether he was going to take this seriously. Finally, he visualized himself in a deep, black hole that he could barely see out of. It became very real to him, and we began the process of bilateral brain stimulation using a headset with an alternating tone.

When Dave felt stuck, I suggested he try visualizing his Higher Self or favorite ascended master as the good father helping him. The good father told him he could come out of the hole anytime he really wanted to. But the child part wouldn't budge. Even though the hole was miserable, it was somewhat safe. He was afraid of what would happen if he did come out.

So we focused on the fear and resumed the bilateral brain stimulation. The child part gradually began to feel less fearful. He began to get curious about what was outside the hole. Dave, as the good father, told him he would show him all kinds of interesting things when he decided to come out.

I want to interject here that the black hole was symbolic of real experiences this man had as a child where he was often bullied, rejected and left alone. He was working with the residue of these experiences. His child part needed to be healed.

Dave kept visualizing the good father part of him coaxing the child to come out of the hole. Finally, young Dave did just that. He stuck his head out of the hole, looked around and held out his hand to his good father. He talked about how awful he had felt in the hole all by himself. Then he asked the good father to put a lid on the hole. The father did just that and gave him a hug. All this was spontaneous imagery and dialogue on Dave's part.

We were coming down the home stretch with the "black hole" drama when suddenly Dave began to look very serious and drawn. He was experiencing what he believed was a past life in which he had been injured and wanted to die because of the pain. He had essentially given up and wasted the remaining years of that life. Dave got in touch with feelings of guilt and disgust with himself. We processed that until the intense feelings began to diminish. Then I suggested that he ask God to forgive him and that he forgive himself. He said, "That's easier said than done, but I'll try." He prayed, and we kept on going.

All of a sudden, he said, "What's past is past." He visibly brightened up and said he had just realized it was his choice to be really alive or to keep ducking into his hole or giving up.

He had flashed back to the original concerns he had about dominant men controlling his life. He said he had given them that control by not standing up for himself. And now he understood his astrological reading, which indicated that he had come into embodiment to help others but had gotten mixed up with people who were playing out their dark side. He had failed to stand up for himself and ended up completely at their mercy. They had essentially wiped him out, and he had blamed God for not rescuing him.

All of a sudden in the middle of this realization, his six-year-old inner child popped back in and said, "That's it! It's not God's fault. I'm standing up for myself, and I'm never going back in that hole again. Come on. Help me fill it up with dirt." So, with imagery, they did just that. When Dave got through, he felt good.

We finished the session by having the good father and the inner child make a pact that they would make it together. Dave's final affirmation was, "I am standing up for myself with my hand in God's hand." He followed this session with prayer work and standing up for himself with God's help every time he had an opportunity. He began to build a momentum on mobilizing his inner strength to replace the habit of hiding out or giving up. He maintained contact with his soul. And, ultimately, he established a positive regime that took the place of the old habits.

We can see that a major key to moving on in life spiritually and psychologically is to learn the lessons the soul is meant to learn from life experiences. I view spiritual psychotherapy as an Aquarian tool that can help us understand and process hurtful experiences from this life and past lives, memories that have created deep soul pain and remain with us as energetic residue.

The ascended masters do not encourage their students to focus inordinately on past lives; thus, we do not actively pursue the memory of past-life experiences. However, if a memory emerges spontaneously, we view it as a prompter to master the lessons inherent in the experience—and apply what we learn to life today.

Once we step forward to process the old dramas and release the pent-up emotions we have been harboring, we begin to claim the reality of who we are as lightbearers, as sons and daughters of God. Then we are in a position to fulfill the mission of our soul in the age of Aquarius. As a wise teacher once said, "The journey of a thousand miles begins with a single step."

## *Developing Trust in God*

One of my clients, Jack, told me in his first session, "I know God is up there somewhere but it's hard for me to trust him. Why is it that when I prayed for a miracle, it didn't happen?"

I asked Jack to tell me what had happened. And he was quick to respond, "My best friend, Dan, had a bad accident so I prayed really hard for him. And then, instead of getting better, he died. That really shook me up. Why didn't God answer my prayers?"

I responded, "That's a tough one. And yet, I know that God does answer our prayers—but it's not always the answer we expect. Have you asked God why it might have been Dan's time to go?"

Jack replied, "No, I'm kind of mad at God. He took my best friend away."

"I understand how you feel, but let's look at it from Dan's point of view. How do you think he felt about dying?" I asked.

"Well, that's part of it," Jack said. "Dan kept telling me that he had a premonition that he wasn't going to live long. And I kept telling him not to be morbid, that he was too young and healthy to be having thoughts like that."

"How old was Dan?" I asked.

"He had just turned 24 and he had his whole life ahead of him," Jack replied. "Why did God take him?"

"Let's ask," I replied. "I'd like you to do a spiritual exercise with me and we'll ask God at a certain point in the exercise. Okay?"

"Okay," Jack mumbled.

"First, I want you to get in touch with your physical heartbeat. Put your hand over your heart, a little to the left of the center of your chest, and stay with it until you feel your heartbeat."

Jack did exactly what I asked, which was a good sign. After a few moments of quiet, he said, "Okay, I've got it."

"Great, stay with it for a little while," I responded.

After a few moments, I continued the instruction. "Now stay in touch with your physical heartbeat and also pay attention to your breathing. It's a double focus—on the heartbeat and your breathing. Let me know when you are in touch with both of them at once."

Jack took a few deep breaths and was quiet for a moment or two, and then he said, "Okay, I've got them."

"That's good," I replied. "Now stay in touch with your breath and heartbeat while you remember or imagine a beautiful scene in nature, like skiing on a sunny day where the snow is glistening or any other great experience you've had in your life. Take a moment to get in touch with that."

"Okay," Jack said. "I've got it."

I responded, "Now put all three together, the heartbeat, the breathing and the memory of that great experience. And stay with it until I give you another instruction."

Jack did exactly as instructed. Several minutes later I suggested that he ask God, "Why did you take my friend away?" I told Jack to be aware of the response, which could be in words or an image or a flash of insight.

Jack closed his eyes and communed with God. He was quiet for several moments and tears rolled down his cheeks. He brushed them away and a few minutes later opened his eyes and smiled.

"That was something!" he told me. "Do you want to know why Dan needed to leave when he did? It's because he has another mission to do for God. And you know what? God told me he loves me. And you know what else? I believe Him." Jack and I both burst into laughter—and it was laughter of pure joy.

Jack kept in touch with me and it was clear that God had turned around this young man's consciousness. He shifted his major to theology and is now a pastor in his denomination. He called several years later to say, "I thought you would like to know that I am at peace about Dan. He has his mission for God and I have mine. And remember that movie, 'It's a Wonderful Life'? I feel just like Jimmy Stewart. I've turned my life around 180 degrees. It's a great life, isn't it?"

We never know exactly why the dramas of life occur as they do, but when we trust God and our Higher Self we make it through. And so do our families, friends and loved ones. When we feel a bit down, we can cheer ourselves up by anticipating a grand reunion with friends of the ages when we arrive in the heaven-world!

## Meditation on Destiny

Here is a beautiful meditation that can help us reconnect with our sense of higher destiny. This meditation was given to Mrs. Prophet by the ascended lady master Venus, Sanat

Kumara's twin flame.* Lady Venus assists the lightbearers from the etheric realm, and she desires that every lightbearer win their victory.

I suggest that you center in your heart and meditate upon her words of love and their meaning to your soul:

> I am a Mother of love, and love, too, comes in many guises. And so, strength is the quotient of love anchored within your heart. And steadfastness and each quality of light as you surrender, as you sacrifice, as you obey the laws of God come what may, is a love greater than the self. And only the love that transcends the self can be victorious; only the love that goes beyond [the self] and is confident of victory because of its momentum of love, only that love can win.

Now then, weigh in the balance the decision of the hour, which may well become the decision of a lifetime. For you know, as decisions go, one decision leads to the next and you find yourself step by step farther and farther from the center or closer and closer to the heart of the [Divine] Mother.

So, then, count each decision as a mark on the path of attainment. Count each decision as an expenditure, not only of your own light but [also] of the light with which hierarchy has vested you. Count each decision as you pass the hours and decide what to do each day with your life, and count that a decision that involves all of cosmos.

---

*Each of us has a twin soul, or twin flame, who was created with us in the beginning. God created you and your twin flame out of a single "white-fire body." He separated this white-fire ovoid into two spheres of being—one with a masculine polarity and the other with a feminine polarity, but each with the same spiritual origin and unique pattern of identity. For further information on twin flames, I suggest my book *Sacred Psychology of Love: The Quest for Relationships That Unite Heart and Soul* (see bibliography).

Go out into the grass, into the fields in the evening. Lie on your back, look up at the stars and think in your heart, "Lady Venus is there. Sanat Kumara is there; millions of cosmic beings twinkle in the sky, and here am I. Here am I smelling the grasses and the fragrances of springtime. Here am I with a life and a potential. I can become a star. As Saint Germain has said, with a million, two million right decisions, I can win my ascension. I will begin right where I am. I will decide to be [one with] God."

If this is your decision and you will it through and through, then act upon the consequences of being God where you are. And you will know and you will see the meaning of the flame of responsibility. And perchance you will remember the hour when cosmic councils convened, when no one on Terra had enough light to sustain or magnetize a threefold flame large enough to keep the evolutions and a planet in rotation.

You will recall how cosmic councils decided there was no purpose, no further reason for being for Terra. And the Flaming One, Sanat Kumara, my own beloved, appeared before those councils, saying, "I have a flame. I AM a living flame. I will go to Terra to keep the flame of life until some respond—enough to keep that flame for the multitudes."

Will you remember that that holy offering was an offering of one who had a sense of cosmic responsibility, a sense of responsibility to each one of you and to all mankind?

There are evolutions in this world and in other worlds who are looking to you, each one of you, as you are seated in this hall this night. They look to you and they wonder, what is the mark of responsibility? What is the reach of responsibility? What is the vision of responsibility of these who call themselves Keepers of the Flame?

Will they remember? Will they remember that in
their heart is the fire that can start a world turning, an
evolution glowing? Will they remember that there are
souls who will win if they win and who will lose if they
lose, if they fail to choose to be God where they are?...

Terra is a key to victory in this entire solar system.
And this solar system itself is a key to victory in this sec-
tor of the galaxy, and on and on. How do you know
when and where the dominos will fall when you make a
decision to be or not to be?[32]

## *To Be or Not to Be*

Do you see how the drama comes full circle to the decision to be or not to be who we really are? That is why we do
our spiritual and psychological work. We want to rediscover
the inner gifts and graces that we came into embodiment
to express, to discover how we got off track, the archetypal
situation and figure who derailed us, and to understand how
we have repeated that pattern over many lifetimes.

It is important to understand the interchange of energy
with the fallen angels. Because of the transfer of energy over
the arc of attention, we took in their energy and consciousness. And particularly when the interaction was cruel or
sadistic, we were so vulnerable that we absorbed the energy
of our tormentors. Then we identified with it. That is the reason that many people think they are evil when they are really
children of the light.

It is similar to what psychologists teach about introjects
in inner child work. We introject (take in) the energy patterns, attitudes, styles of thinking, feeling and behaving of
our parents or parent figures. In the same way, we have
taken in, "introjected," the consciousness of the fallen angels

who caused our fall. As long as we harbor that energy, it gives us deep soul pain. We think we are the bad ones. We are deluded into thinking that we are evil.

I believe Carl Jung made a tremendous contribution in his concept of the "shadow," both the positive and negative aspects of the shadow. We can understand the positive shadow as the conglomerate of the unconscious parts of ourself that are aspects of who we are as a soul created by our Maker. And we can think of the negative shadow as made up primarily of patterns of evil that we have unwittingly taken in from forces of darkness. It is important to realize that the negative shadow is not reflective of our soul and spirit nor does it reflect our true identity as a son or daughter of God.

Most of us are familiar with the shadow as the dark side, "the devil made me do it" kind of attitude that collaborates with our negative thoughts, desires and behavior. Yet, we hesitate to acknowledge that we harbor a dark side within ourselves. We prefer to identify with our positive motives, ideas, emotions and actions.

Consequently, the dark side recedes into the subconscious or unconscious realms where it continues to torment us through nightmares or negative thinking. Another unfortunate aspect of this trick of human nature is that whatever we repress we unwittingly project onto others. This contaminates our view of other people and keeps us from seeing ourselves clearly and acknowledging our own shadowy motives and attitudes.

Several years ago, I saw a movie on TV about the battle of the "son of Lucifer" and an angel of light for the soul of a man who could not learn his lesson. This man's lesson was about ignoring God, being dishonest in his dealings and unfaithful to his loving, ever-praying wife. He went through traumatic dreams and experiences that finally forced him to confront his soul-weaknesses. Finally, through major calamities and his wife's fervent prayers, he bent the knee.

His lesson was threefold: first, to open his heart to God and ask for help; second, to surrender his habitual gambling and dishonesty games; third, to demonstrate his love for his wife by being faithful to her instead of just talking about it. After many mishaps, he finally did it. He learned his lesson. Instantly, the son of Lucifer disappeared in a great shower of sparks and smoke. It was a dynamic and instructive movie!

To me the moral of that story is twofold:

1. God is only a prayer away.
2. Evil has no power in the face of Good.

## *Reclaiming Our Real Self*

However, until we learn the lesson we create problematic experiences. The key to reclaiming who we really are, spiritually and psychologically, is to master the lessons in our daily encounters. As we do so, we increase in self-mastery and identify more and more with our Higher Self, our Real Self. We take charge of our motives, thoughts, feelings and actions instead of being ruled by them. And we begin to heal the issues of our soul.

When we contact the pain of the soul and recognize the influence of the dark side, we have taken the first step. We are on our way to healing our psyche from the wounds inflicted by the fallen angels, as well as the records of whatever mistakes we made that led to our fall from grace. And we begin to realize that the influence of evil has plagued our soul over many lifetimes.

Once we understand how we got off track in the first place and how introjects of fallen angel patterns are activated by similar circumstances in our lives today, we can determine to get back on track. To do so, we need to transmute the energy patterns that we took in from the fallen angels at the time of our original leaving off from God. And we need to reclaim the lost fragments of our soul.*

We can pray for the transmuting action of the violet flame to dissolve our negative patterns and replace them with divine matrices. And we can humbly ask God to restore to us the fragments of our soul.[33] We can practice the nonattachment of the Buddha in difficult situations. And we can choose to view our negative tendencies as the "not-self" instead of the "real me."

There is another important ingredient—courage! The spiritual meaning of the word "courage" is "coming of age of the heart." It is a wonderful feeling to mobilize the courage to face the old records and their outmoded patterns of behavior, to realize "that's not me!" and to do the work of letting go and claiming a new beginning. Once we get our head above water, so to speak, we are ready to set a new pattern for our victory in this life and our soul's ultimate return to oneness with God.

In order to do this we intensify our devotion to God. We study the scriptures of our faith, meditate on how to apply what we learn, offer our prayers, decrees, chants, fiats or affirmations—and choose to be obedient to moral precepts. We straighten out our life, and we do it with joy and excitement because we're back on track!

---

*Everything within us is energy, including the soul; when the soul is abused or traumatized, soul fragments (energy particles) may be transferred to the perpetrator.

# 4

# A Jump-Start to Healing

*What lies behind us and what lies before us are tiny matters compared to what lies within us.*

—RALPH WALDO EMERSON

ainful memories, a tormented mind, disturbing emotions and physical pain can often be relieved through energy therapy. This is a method of bilateral brain stimulation for the healing of stress and anxiety that is a residue of traumatic experiences. The method was discovered and developed by Dr. Francine Shapiro, a licensed psychologist and senior research fellow at the Mental Research Institute in Palo Alto, California.[34]

I think of energy work as giving a jump-start to the healing of disturbing experiences because it stimulates our own internal energy processing. It is a type of psychotherapy that integrates successful elements of traditional talk therapy with a gentle method of bilateral brain stimulation through eye movement, sound or touch, which in turn triggers the brain's information processing system.

The client focuses on a distressing experience and the accompanying thoughts, emotions and body sensations. During the session, other related experiences may surface because the unconscious holds everything together according to similar vibration, circumstances, thoughts, emotions and body sensations.

The bilateral brain stimulation triggers the individual's internal energy network. Often a person will remember other situations that have generated similar thoughts, feelings and body sensations. The focus shifts to those memories because everything the client becomes aware of during a session is related. Thus, although the major therapeutic focus is on neutralizing the trauma initially chosen by the client, the individual processes whatever comes up along the way.

Of course, what the client remembers is not physically happening in the present moment. It is an event re-created by the mind from the recent or distant past as a memory and may or may not be completely accurate. Yet, whatever we carry in memory at an unconscious or subconscious level triggers conscious thoughts, emotions and body sensations.

Most people revolve hurtful experiences subconsciously or unconsciously, and clients sometimes say, "It feels like my soul is in pain." They also describe upsetting experiences from the past (including emotions, beliefs, physical sensations and behaviors) as "stuck" in their nervous system. One client added, "I've been like a puppet on a string when a similar scenario occurs. I tend to react the same way I used to even though I tried to bury the past. I'm certainly glad to be getting rid of this stuff!"

I believe the internal processing quickened by bilateral brain stimulation is a God-given, built-in gift, a path to emotional freedom. And I have an intuitive sense that the method has been rediscovered because it is time for people to let go of old trauma in order to fulfill their soul's destiny in the twenty-first century.

## *Research and Development*

EMDR has been extensively researched since it was first discovered in 1987 and is viewed today by many mental health professionals as a highly effective method for treating trauma and post-traumatic stress disorder.[35] As one of the most extensively researched and supported methods for treating the aftermath of traumatic happenings, EMDR is practiced around the world, particularly in areas where people have gone through war, earthquakes, fires, floods, hurricanes, bombings, etc.

Practitioners have several choices for bilateral brain stimulation. They can use a computer-type screen that shows a light pattern for the client to track with the eyes (adjustable for speed), back and forth, back and forth. A second method uses a set of headphones and the client listens to a tone (adjustable for volume and pitch) alternating between the right and left ear. A third method uses a gentle left-right vibrating device held in the palms of the hands. When I work with young children, I may ask them to slap my hands back and forth, alternating their two hands—they think that's lots of fun.

Any kind of bilateral brain stimulation appears to work. If we think about it, we realize that walking, running, swimming, biking, dancing—physical activities of all kinds—are also forms of bilateral brain stimulation. Perhaps that is one reason that people who exercise regularly tend to handle their emotions better than those who lead a more sedentary lifestyle.

### *Similarities in EMDR Processing and REM Sleep*

The mental, emotional and physical processing that occurs during the EMDR treatment is similar to what happens during REM sleep.* As you may know, in REM sleep we process through dreams whatever is disturbing to us. A great deal of dream research has been done in sleep labs and results indicate that when REM sleep is interrupted over a period of time, a person becomes quite agitated. REM sleep seems to help us to process and therefore stay on top of problematic experiences.[36] Both REM sleep and the EMDR method enable the processing of emotions and experiential information, and a vast amount of learning and insight can occur during a very short time period.

When I learned about the EMDR technique in 1995, I realized that the bilateral-brain stimulation training would be an excellent addition to my therapeutic repertoire. I knew that when my clients were upset or fixated on a trauma and I had them shift their focus quickly from one object to another, the upset or fixation seemed to fade. At that time, I thought of it as a distraction technique, but now I realized there was more to it.

I arranged to take both levels of training from Dr. Shapiro. I have always believed in going to the "horse's mouth," so to speak, for training. I appreciated the fact that Shapiro trained only clinicians with professional credentials and background. That way there was much less chance of someone unqualified misusing the method.

For the past ten years, I have included this work in my practice and have kept current with innovations. Every session

---

* REM refers to the periodic rapid eye movement during the stages of sleep associated with dreaming.

is unique because it is based on the client's way of processing life experiences rather than a particular therapeutic persuasion. Each session taps into the vast ocean of energetic patterns that we call memories or records. What surfaces in the client's consciousness during the session relates to the immediate drama the person wants to resolve as well as to similar experiences from the past and apprehensions about the future.

EMDR clinicians have successfully treated over a million individuals suffering from the aftermath of assault, domestic violence, rape, "bad trip" drug experiences, combat, loss of loved ones, accidents, serious illness, childhood traumas, natural disasters, and recurrent nightmares.

## A Young Woman's Relief from Suffering

In 1995, a trained EMDR team was sent to the site of the Oklahoma City bombing that killed 167 people and left thousands emotionally devastated. The FBI requested the help of these clinicians to relieve the suffering of victims and rescue workers alike. One young woman's experience illustrates EMDR's effectiveness in relieving trauma.

Linda had been enjoying the morning air on the balcony of her seventeenth floor apartment. She had just gone inside, preparing to leave for her job, when the bomb exploded across the street. The force of the blast blew her off her feet into the kitchen and demolished her living room and kitchen walls. When she regained consciousness, jagged glass and debris were scattered all over the place. Horrified, she thought a nuclear warhead had struck.

Disoriented, Linda ran downstairs into the mayhem on the street. She was not physically injured, but she was an emotional wreck. When she reported for work, she could not concentrate and her mind would blank out. She had difficulty eating and sleeping. She simply could not cope.

After two months, Linda's employer insisted that she seek treatment and took her to a psychiatrist who decided Linda should be hospitalized and medicated. She was shocked and refused. The psychiatrist then referred her to the EMDR free clinic where a team of psychotherapists was helping victims of the bombing. Linda and her employer decided it was worth a try.

The therapist did the standard screening and preparation for EMDR and asked Linda to focus on a specific aspect of the tragedy while her eyes followed the therapist's back-and-forth hand movements. Linda began to cry as she remembered the details of the bombing. She said later that it was like reliving everything that had happened.

Another session two days later brought back more memories. However, instead of reliving the trauma, she found herself observing it. And she remembered details she had not remembered before. She said it was like watching a movie instead of falling into her emotions. As soon as she left the session she called her boss with the good news, "I'm ba-a-ack!"[37]

EMDR teams have been sent to San Francisco and Los Angeles after earthquakes, to New York City after 9/11 and to Bosnia to train psychiatrists and psychologists to work with the holocaust victims. Today EMDR therapy is known around the world for its success in disaster-relief work, and crisis-intervention teams go to disaster sites on a regular basis.

### EMDR versus Hypnosis

People sometimes ask if EMDR is hypnosis. The answer is "No, it is not." Brainwave research shows that people are either in an "awake" beta state or a light alpha state—the meditative state.

I would like to mention my personal reasons for not using hypnosis in my psychotherapy practice. In the first place, many spiritual teachers warn against using hypnosis, self-hypnosis or autosuggestion. Secondly, I have had my own internal stop sign. During my graduate school training, the experienced hypnotherapist who was training us could not hypnotize me although I was not consciously resisting. I remember thinking at the time, "I guess I'm not supposed to do this." Third, I know the reality of the spiritual teaching that a hypnotist's state of consciousness can be transferred to the client without any specific intention of the hypnotist. Here is a story that backs up that statement.

When I was in graduate school, one of my fellow students told me a story that shocked me and left a lasting impression. He had been a close friend of a medical doctor, a hypnotherapist, who used hypnosis to help people with addictions such as smoking, drugs and alcohol. He was having good results. However, this doctor had a shock that stopped him on a dime.

Doctor X began to have patients coming back to him saying things like, "Doctor, I'm so glad you helped me with my smoking habit. I'm not having trouble with that anymore. But a strange thing is happening to me. I've suddenly developed an addiction to porn magazines. I've never had that problem before in my life. Can you help me?"

After several of his patients came back to him with similar requests, the doctor stopped hypnosis entirely and moved his medical practice to another area of the country. Why? You guessed it. The doctor had his own secret vice—pornography.

He was brought face to face with the realization that through hypnosis he had transferred to these patients his own addiction, which he had no intention whatsoever of doing. It so scared him that he said he would never again have anything to do with hypnosis.

My explanation of what happened to the doctor is that energy travels over the arc of attention. It is like the way you can feel someone looking at you from across a room. Wherever our attention goes, the energy flows. This is particularly true when we are in a passive state of being totally receptive to someone else's suggestions, which is the case with hypnosis. The bottom line is that we need to be cautious because we do not know the contents of the subconscious and unconscious or even of the conscious mind of a practitioner, even as the patients of this doctor did not know about his secret vice.

I believe the reason to avoid hypnosis, self-hypnosis or subliminal tapes is that in such an open, receptive state of consciousness we can easily link into negative energies unless we have the spiritual mastery of an adept—in which case, we wouldn't be doing it anyway. We can be completely unaware of negative energies that could penetrate our energy field when we are off guard. So, the best solution is to remain awake and attentive when working with a health practitioner.

## *The Role of the Soul*

As a spiritually oriented psychologist, I can verify that prayer makes a big difference in the therapeutic outcome. And that makes perfect sense if we recall that psychology means the study of the soul.

In my practice, I have been brought face to face with the reality that the soul is active in the therapeutic process. What we often call "inner child" work is actually "soul work."* Through my clients' experiences, as well as spiritual study, I have learned that the soul has lived many lifetimes and that traumatic experiences in this life are often just the tip of the iceberg of past-life trauma.

Here is an example of this kind of trauma surfacing during the therapeutic process. Harry,† a 40-year-old construction worker, entered therapy because of a self-destructive pattern that was getting him into a lot of trouble. Harry always thought he knew best and he took pride in letting his friends know that. However, his friends were not particularly interested in being lorded over by Harry.

He decided to get therapy because friends were exiting his life and his wife kept saying, "I told you so." Harry could not understand it. From his point of view, "I just say what I think and they go ballistic. Why don't they appreciate good advice?"

I couldn't answer that one so I suggested we focus on helping him understand himself instead of other people's reactions. At that point, Harry was upset and announced, "Nobody ever listens to me!"

I noticed a change in his tone of voice and commented on it. He responded, "I don't know where that came from. It's like that happens to me sometimes. I sound off, and I don't

---

* Clients typically say "inner child" when referring to early life experiences and "soul" when referencing a past life. Dialogues include the adult and inner child, inner child and inner critic, masculine and feminine, the individual and the soul. I often ask the client to alternate between two chairs to clarify who is speaking.

† Names, places and certain details have been changed to protect the anonymity of the individuals whose case illustrations appear in this book.

know where it comes from."

I suggested that Harry ask the part of him that was sounding off, "What's going on?"

Harry looked a bit disgusted but tried it anyway. "Okay, what's going on, whoever you are?"

I was quiet and Harry looked puzzled. "It is something going on inside of me. But I don't understand it."

I responded, "Try talking to that inner part of you."

"What do you mean?" Harry asked.

"Just act as if it's a part of you that you don't recognize, and see what you can find out," I replied.

"Okay, who are you?" he grumbled.

To his shock, he heard himself say, "I'm your soul, and I'm fed up with you ignoring me."

"What do you mean?" Harry asked cautiously.

"I mean you never listen to me, and I've been around a lot longer than you have!" was the reply.

Harry looked at me questioningly.

I responded, "Just keep going. You're doing fine."

"Okay," Harry said. "What do you know that I don't know?"

And that was the beginning of a dialogue with his soul, who let Harry know in no uncertain terms that she was tired of being ignored. Furthermore, she had a lot to say. And if he didn't listen, she'd jolly well make her points while he was talking to other people.

At first Harry was somewhat amused and at a loss. But as he and his soul began to dialogue in earnest, he began to get interested. And he found out a lot about himself that he actually knew at a subconscious level but had not let himself focus on consciously.

In the course of the conversation with his soul, he learned that telling other people what to do was actually coming from his soul, who desperately wanted to be appreciated. She thought that giving advice to other people would get Harry to listen to her.

Once Harry understood this, he asked me, "What do I do now?"

I suggested that he tell his soul that he appreciates her for who she is as his inner partner—and assure her that he will listen to her, that he cares about her.

He did so and his soul began to calm down. Harry was amazed. "It's like having a friend inside me," he remarked.

I suggested that he ask his soul, "What can I do for you right now?"

Harry did that. And his soul responded, "Just love me."

At that point, I suggested that Harry put his arms around himself and let his soul know he loved her.

Surprisingly, he did just that. And as he did so, his bravado and tough guy act melted away.

After a few minutes, Harry told me he realized telling other people what to do was his soul's cry for help. He was excited to understand that when he and his soul were at peace he did not need to tell other people what to do.

This was the beginning of a major turnaround for Harry. Whenever he felt like sounding off, he would excuse himself and go talk to his soul. When she was at peace, he would come back and interact appropriately. He could scarcely believe that he was beginning to turn himself around. He began getting along better with his friends. And his wife was delighted with what she called Harry's "psychological makeover."

## Resolving Traumas of the Past

People who are intent on healing their traumas and fulfilling their life mission often discover, as Harry did, that it is the soul who is in pain, not just the outer self. So, they embark on a journey to heal the pain, inwardly and outwardly. Soul transformation is an amazing process, and I have discovered how powerful it can be from my work with people who seek to heal records of trauma. Most people are born with symptoms of anxiety, depression, sometimes a very morbid sense that life is all about pain and suffering. And yet they have a sense of hope or they would not come for a therapy session.

At some point, they begin to realize that their difficult experiences are laden with the hidden jewels of valuable insights, the potential of balancing karma and a renewed opportunity for the soul. In hindsight, through contemplative meditation, they come to realize that each challenging life experience is a mystery to be unraveled, a chapter in the book of life, often prompting a U-turn to dump old baggage or to seek clues to a new direction.

We often carry a residue of hurtful experiences at a subconscious or unconscious level. The subconscious refers to thoughts or memories that are, as we say, "just on the tip of my tongue." Unconscious memories are "hidden" in less accessible realms of consciousness. Such memories may come to the surface through dreams or free association or when we find ourselves in a situation that is similar in vibration, circumstance, thought, feeling or physical impact to the repressed memory.

Why do we continue to be troubled with old memories or hurtful experiences from this or past lives? I believe we continue to revolve key experiences until we understand our mistakes, learn the necessary lessons and balance the karma of our misdeeds. When we have difficulty letting go of a traumatic experience in this life, we may discover a past-life trauma that is fueling the pain.

Sometimes we notice there is a repetitive theme to distressing happenings. Once we are aware of a theme, we can ask ourselves, "What purpose does it serve? What do I need to learn?" At that point, other memories including past-life records may begin to surface.

At the level of soul and spirit, we are determined to master the lessons of life in order to heal our deepest soul-pain, the pain of separation from God and our Higher Self. We seek a clear vision of our mission on earth and of the path to oneness with our Creator. I believe that we draw to us experiences that confront us with our karmic lessons—until we learn those lessons.

### The Story of Karma on Planet Earth

In her book *Saint Germain's Prophecy for the New Millennium,* Elizabeth Clare Prophet explains the story of karma on planet Earth.

She writes:

> The story of earth is a complex one, one where the truth is sometimes stranger than fiction. Like an intricate novel woven with many plots and subplots, what we face today is the crisscrossing of many karmic patterns.
>
> Some chapters of our ancient history tell of vast golden-age civilizations on the lost continents of Lemuria and Atlantis. Many of us lived there in previous incarnations and may have a soul memory of these times when we were guided by masters and adepts of great

attainment. We knew the laws of the universe and applied them. We were spiritually developed. We enjoyed a quality of life far superior to what we have today.

We may also have an inner awareness of a time when, under the influence of fallen angels, we betrayed our spiritual mentors. This is where the plot thickens.

### Earth Is a Crossroads

Earth is a crossroads. It has been home to good, sweet and beautiful people. It has also hosted rebel angels and those influenced by them—those who did not use their talents and free will to do good and help others.[38]

The records and artifacts of ancient Sumer, Egypt, India and even the Incan civilization bear witness to these visitors. With their advanced knowledge of science and technology, they taught the arts of war. They bred deception, greed and allegiance to the ego. In the chronicles of earth's history, their dark threads of infamy are subtly interwoven with golden threads sown by the good people of earth.

Influenced by these cosmic rebels, the civilization of Lemuria experienced a decline. Her people, who once walked and talked with God's representatives, lost their native spiritual vision and abilities. This spiritual decline, coupled with misuses of power, the abuse of technology, and the unbridled pursuit of pleasure and the ego, resulted in the sinking of Lemuria many thousands of years ago. Today, all that remains of Lemuria is the Ring of Fire, the ring of volcanoes on the boundaries of the Pacific Ocean along the west coast of the Americas and the east coast of Asia.

After the downfall of Lemuria, another golden-age civilization arose on the ancient continent of Atlantis. In his dialogues, Plato recounts that on "the island of Atlantis there was a great and wonderful empire" that ruled Africa as far as Egypt, Europe as far as Italy, and "parts of the continent" (thought to be a reference to the Americas).

There came a time on Atlantis, too, when many people abandoned their first love and their allegiance to the divine light within. Their scientists even went so far as to create grotesque forms by interbreeding man and animals through genetic engineering. The half-man, half-goat forms we read about in mythology are a soul memory of these events. The once-great continents of Lemuria and Atlantis now lie beneath the oceans, their triumphs and their failures deep in the unconscious of the race.

### Nothing Happens By Chance

Since then the ages have rolled on like cars on a giant Ferris wheel. Civilizations have risen and flowered, then declined and disappeared. The people of Lemuria and Atlantis have reincarnated again and again throughout these civilizations, making good and bad karma along the way. Many have gravitated to the Americas. It is against this backdrop that you and I are about to take our place on the stage of cosmic history.

As we enter the new millennium, we the citizens of planet Earth face not only our own personal karmic equations, but also world karma born of the interplay of many forces. It is a complex tapestry. Once again we are faced with ultimate choices. Will we sustain the connection to our spiritual roots that in the past allowed us to create golden-age communities? Or will we fall prey to the brittle intellect and the hardened heart, to materialism and worldly sophistication?

Some believe that the new millennium will be a golden age no matter what. That thesis doesn't take into account our free will. The actions we take will determine the course of our lives and the lives of future generations. The new era will become a golden age only if we make that golden age a reality.

Nothing in the universe happens by chance or by wish. No one else can do it for us, not the saints or adepts, not those who have lived before, not those who will live in the future. We must play our parts—parts that we have been waiting lifetimes to play.[39]

## *Healing the Traumas of the Soul*

In the process of therapy, people who are delving deep into the issues of their soul sometimes experience a past-life recall. This can happen in the course of the session or in preparing for it and, at times, the awareness comes in the form of a dream. That makes sense because our dreams reflect the unresolved issues and concerns of the soul, which surface from the unconscious and subconscious during sleep and as we are awakening.

The residue of these ancient traumas can often be cleared in the process of energy therapy. What do I mean by "being cleared"? Clearing means that the associated memory dissipates, the negative emotions neutralize, negative thoughts shift to a positive perspective and the body is relieved of physical symptoms related to the trauma.

I have done this kind of therapy successfully with many different people and situations. These traumas vary from accidents, illness, violence or sexual abuse to setbacks on the job or tension between colleagues or family members to community, church and spiritual dilemmas. Some people remember traumas from past lifetimes, how they died or were abducted or became entangled with evil.

In my therapy sessions, I begin and end with a spiritual invocation, and my clients and I offer prayers throughout the session as needed. This establishes a safe space for our work and invokes the assistance of the angels and our spiritual overseers. And we conclude each session with the client connecting a positive affirmation with the neutralized traumatic memory, e.g., "I am at peace with my soul."

I suggest meditation or prayer work as a follow-through at home including prayers to Archangel Michael for protection, violet flame decrees for transmutation and prayers for the light of God to guide the soul.* And I remind my clients that they can ask the angels to bind the negative habits of the naughty self and to cut the soul free from whatever is deterring the fulfillment of their divine destiny.

I believe that the battle of good and evil is the major issue in today's world and that it is a primary reason that people are drawn to movies such as *Star Wars* or *Lord of the Rings*. In the privacy of their mind, heart and soul, many people are pondering the dilemma of good and evil and are praying for divine intercession.

I also believe there are many paths to understanding the infinite nature of God. This is one reason that we have all of the world's major religions. Each of them was developed from the perspective of people who lived in a particular culture at a certain time in history. Yet, at the level of mystical understanding all true religions merge into oneness with the Creator.

Whatever negative drama we face, we can pray for wisdom

* See pp. 249–59 for these prayers and decrees.

and discernment, clear vision, a compassionate heart and the transmutation of doubt and fear. And we can ask God to help us replace any negative attitudes, thoughts, feelings and habits with a sense of higher purpose, wisdom and compassion, the inner resolve to be true to our Higher Self and a solid plan to meet the challenge with courage and determination.

### Alice's Story: A Past-Life Drama Come Full Circle

In the process of psychotherapy, I have seen people process life and death scenes, afterlife experiences and the reentry of the soul into a new body and a new life.

I will never forget Alice, a woman in her thirties, who requested EMDR therapy to understand her anger toward a particular man in her life.

She said, "I don't know what it is about Glen, but I go into a rage whenever I think about him. It's a good thing I'm not seeing much of him anymore. But I would like to understand it, and I'd like to get rid of the anger. It doesn't seem reasonable to get so mad at him. I think it's from another lifetime."

That was the preamble to her inner processing. When Alice focused on her anger toward Glen, she suddenly found herself in the middle of a scene in which a man had beaten, raped and left her for dead. She focused on his face and realized it was Glen, whom she was so angry with in this life.

She became more agitated as the scenes flashed by. She survived the rape scene but was crippled from it and never got over her fury. In fact, to the end of her days in that lifetime, she swore to get even with him no matter what it took.

As she said to me, "No wonder I can't stand Glen! He's the guy who beat me, raped me and left me for dead in that lifetime. He deserves whatever awful thing happens to him in this life!"

Alice was not about to forgive the rapist or to let the whole matter go. She was stuck in her rage. It was as though she had forgotten that she had come for therapy to resolve her anger. Now she was adamantly demanding vengeance.

From her angry outburst, it was obvious that she had appointed herself judge, jury and executioner of the man in the past life that she believed to be Glen in this life. Her fury was rapidly escalating instead of abating.

I silently prayed to God for her illumination and clear vision. And as we continued the session, Alice flashed back to an earlier lifetime where in a fit of jealousy and rage she had knifed and killed Glen. He had sworn vengeance on her, which resulted in the rape she had gone through in the later lifetime.

Alice was horrified to realize that she might have started the whole thing. She cried out, "I can't believe it! I've been the pot calling the kettle black, haven't I? God help me!"

"Of course, God will help you. He loves you," I responded. "Remember, these are simply records of old trauma. Once you understand the past, you can make a new decision."

Alice was now ready to consider forgiveness and some kind of resolution, but she could not seem to let go. As she continued processing, scene after scene from other lifetimes came up, and in each one either she was getting even with him or he was getting even with her. They had been chasing and killing each other over lifetimes, and at this point she was not sure who had started it.

Alice finally sighed and said, "This simply has to stop. As the Bible says, 'Vengeance is mine, saith the Lord.'"

I suggested she pray to her guardian angel to help her to forgive Glen. After a time, she began to look more peaceful, and a few minutes later she relaxed, smiled and said, "Okay, let's talk."

Alice told me that in her imagery she and Glen had gone to an etheric retreat* and talked the whole thing over. They realized that their anger and vengeance had created the drama. And they agreed it was time to bury the past and to heal the anger with love and forgiveness. In Alice's meditation, they forgave each other and prayed for God's love to heal them. Alice said she felt peaceful and happy.

We checked it out one more time by having her focus on the original trauma. She stayed peaceful. She decided on an affirmation to connect with the neutralized drama: "I am God's love in action here."

Alice told me how relieved she was to have let go of the anger and to feel like the loving person she intuitively knows she is. In a follow-up session a few weeks later, she was still at peace. In fact, it was hard for her to imagine the drama had ever happened. Alice summed it up: "It's like I'm a new person, thank God."

Not all sessions are this dramatic, but I get confirmation on an ongoing basis of the power of love and forgiveness. I am happily reassured of the continuity of life and opportunity for the soul and of the validity of the teachings of Jesus, Gautama Buddha, Krishna and all the great adepts that the nature of God is *Love*.

I believe that God blesses us with opportunities to heal our hurts and to open our hearts to one another. When we meet the trials of life with a loving heart and a willingness to forgive, we win a victory within ourselves—and we feel the return current of God's love.

---

* A spiritual retreat in the etheric octave, the highest plane in the dimension of Matter; a plane that is as concrete and real as the physical plane but is experienced through the senses of the soul in a dimension and a consciousness beyond physical awareness.

## *A Meditation on the Heart*

I close this chapter with a meditation on the heart that I often suggest to my clients for the transformation of painful experiences as well as understanding the inherent lessons. Take a moment to identify an experience that makes you cringe when you remember it. Once you are in touch with the emotional impact, follow these instructions:

Place your hand over your heart (a little to the left of the center of your chest). Move your hand around until you can feel your physical heartbeat. Notice the gentle thump, thump, thump of the heart. Close your eyes and stay focused on the heartbeat for a full minute or two.

Continue to be aware of the heartbeat as you also place your attention on your breath. Breathe in and out, in and out, in and out. Put your full attention on the combination of the heartbeat and the breathing. Stay with that for another minute or two.

Stay with the awareness of your heartbeat and breathing as you think of a beautiful, uplifting experience that arouses appreciation, exhilaration or inspiration. You might think of sunlight sparkling on the water in a beautiful lake, a rainbow in the sky or the snowy heights of a majestic mountain. Or it could be the thrill of sailing or surfing, ice-skating or swooping down a ski slope. Or simply a blissful moment of inspiration, a feeling of exultation or victory.

Focus on the combination of your heartbeat, the rhythm of your breathing and the beautiful experience for several minutes.

Now ask yourself, "What is my lesson? What is the lesson for my soul?" Accept whatever comes to mind. Write it down for further contemplation.[40]

# 5

# *The Dweller and the Y in the Path*

*The trek upward is worth the inconvenience.*

—EL MORYA

*T*here comes a time for every seeker on the spiritual path when we are faced with what is known as the Y in the path—this is the point of testing where we choose either to glorify God or to glorify the lesser ego. We either identify with our Higher Self, our Christ Self, or we identify with the self-serving human ego, which quickly propels us into the clutches of the dweller-on-the-threshold. We cannot have it both ways—good and evil do not reside together. One or the other ultimately wins out.

## *The Dweller as the Not-Self*

Mrs. Prophet gave a teaching about what happens when an individual does not transmute the dweller-on-the-threshold, which she aptly labeled the "not-self."

> Confusing the lower self for the Greater Self through his own self-created spiritual blindness, he enthrones the

dweller-on-the-threshold in the place of his Holy Christ Self. His personality, his psyche, his stream of consciousness all flow into the not-self.

Instead of saying, "I and my Father are One," he declares, "I and my ego are one," and it is so. . . . Behold Rudyard Kipling's 'man who would be king' who meets his fate in the abyss of the astral plane. Though he thinks he is in control, the nonentity [the egotistical not-self] eventuates in nonexistence. . . .

You see, the one who embodies that dweller—being self-willed, and inordinately imposing his will on others, having passed the point of the Y—is actually incarnating that momentum of evil, which is the equivalent of the light he had when he departed from the temple and fell from grace. In other words, he has inverted his original dispensation of light to generate evil. Moreover, he has deified that evil and himself as its progenitor.

Now, evil, in itself, is misqualified energy. . . . It is a veil of illusion—an energy veil, or *e-veil,* enshrouding the Deity and all his marvelous works. Illusion, or *maya,* as the Hindus call it, then appears more real than Reality itself. In fact, men's illusions become their gods, and evil is deified. . . .

This is why John the Baptist and Jesus Christ as well as the prophets and the avatars of all ages have come to the earth. . . . They come because they want to give a reprieve to the blessed children of God who are tormented by these fallen ones and yet have not the ability—the externalized Christ consciousness—to move against them.[41]

Each of us has the opportunity to make the right choice when we come to that point of the Y. If we follow the path of the saints and sages, we choose to surrender the will of the human self and align our will with the Higher Self. We pray for the binding of the carnal mind and dweller-on-the-threshold that would tell us to do otherwise. And we ask the angels to help us to be true to our ideals and to God's plan for our soul.

We pray for guidance from our favorite saints and ascended masters. We pursue our soul's union with our Higher Self. And we determine to choose the high road in each circumstance of life. In every decision we make, we ask ourselves, "Will this bring me and my soul closer to our union with the Higher Self?" And if we slip or fall along the way, we dust ourselves off, determine to do better and keep moving onward and upward! Ultimately, by effort and by grace, we can enter the bliss of reunion with the Divine.

### Walking the Maze of Human Creation

Why is it that we aren't already there? Perhaps because even though we desire to walk the high road, we find it isn't that easy. We can get lost in our human wishing or willing, fall prey to seductive temptation, succumb to expediency or ignore the prompting of conscience—and the dweller claps his hands with glee for we are but a step away from toppling into a pit of confusion and despair.

Mrs. Prophet talked to her students about the hazards of trying to penetrate the maze of human creation before committing to the will of God. She described the effort it takes to recognize and surrender the human will that so often leads us astray.

She said:

> Putting on the will of God is a wrestling, a groaning, a travailing until you are able to go through the very intense temptations and the labyrinth [maze] of human

creation and wrestle with it all and through it all be confident that when you get to the will of God, that is your first and foremost love and you will live by it.

And you go through this process and God will take you through it in the most dense areas of your own consciousness, the areas that need the training, that need the exposure. You don't know what your human will is until it's juxtaposed with God's will. So you bump into somebody who has a great virtue on a certain aspect of God's will like Kuthumi or like Djwal Kul and you get in their aura and all of a sudden you realize you have a human will because it's very much opposite to the master's will.

And then you say, "Hmm, you know, I wonder if I want to give this up.... I'm not so sure, I'll have to think about that." You don't really want to give it up but you're into this routine of surrendering so you go give your surrender decrees[42] and you say "I surrender it." But you didn't really surrender it in your desire body. You didn't really allow God to take his knife and carve it out of you. And so it stays there.

And you say all the right words and you say "I surrender," and you give calls and you sit and do Astreas,* but you're not engaged. And the first time you come up against a direct physical encounter, whether it's with the messenger or with a chela or some boss in the business in the world, it doesn't matter. But you come up with the encounter and there's the energy all over again. The surrender didn't happen, because God doesn't come in and take it from you....

You have to have an inner will that says, "I *will* do this, I won't do that, because I perceive God's will. I know

---

* Astrea is a cosmic being who wields an energy circle and sword of blue-white fire that cuts us free from unwanted energies when we recite her decree (see Alchemical Energy Formulas, p. 253).

it's best for me and I know it's the best way I'm going to
be able to help the rest of the world, and so I'll do it. I'll
shut my eyes and I'll clench my fists, and I'll go through
this dark night of the soul and I'll come out on the other
side, because I know it's right and I have the courage of
my conviction."[43]

## Outwitting the Labyrinth of Darkness and Despair

In a lecture on the major religions of the world, Mrs.
Prophet also talked about the labyrinth of darkness and
despair, and she gave her students keys for outwitting that
state of consciousness.

She explained:

> Seized by a suicide entity or an entity of anger or an
> entity of aggressive mental suggestion*—at the moment
> we're seized, this is reality. But there comes a point in our
> experience when we know that it is unreality. At the
> moment when we know it's unreality, we should write it
> down.... Let's write about what we really experience.
> Let's say, "I have experienced unreality and I know it's
> unreal," and then let's list what we know to be unreal.
>
> Then when our consciousness or our egos try to
> take us another round through that labyrinth of darkness
> and despair and illusion, we get out our notebooks and
> we say, "Hmm, I've been here before. It's the same old
> unreality. It should be shattered. It can be shattered;
> I know it can be shattered because I have lived at the
> heights of God-Reality."[44]

---

*An aggressive mental suggestion is a strong suggestion, projected either
from within or without the psyche, that comes into your head and will not
leave you alone. It does not originate in the mind of God nor is it native
to the soul but it can strongly influence the soul to make one wrong turn
after the other on the highway of life.

Once we differentiate between reality and unreality we can shatter unreality and choose reality. We can ask ourselves, "Okay, is this true reality or is this some kind of unreality?" We can ask our Higher Self to help us understand the soul lesson, we can give prayers and fiats for the binding of the dweller of unreality, for the binding of the entities, and we can invoke the violet transmuting flame to clean up the debris.*

Once we have a sense of clarity and higher vision we can ask ourselves, "What would Jesus or Saint Germain or the Blessed Mother have me do?" And act accordingly.

When we differentiate reality from unreality by our intuitive assessment and the vibration of a situation, we can shatter the unreality and choose reality. We can ask ourselves, "What would my Higher Self do? How would my favorite saint or an ascended master deal with this situation?" When we do this on an ongoing basis, we develop clarity and a sense of joyful anticipation in our decision-making.

If we apply the legend of the Minotaur to the labyrinth of consciousness, we can liken the Minotaur to the dweller-on-the-threshold. That dweller lurks at the threshold of self-awareness, where elements from the unconscious move through the subconscious into conscious awareness. The dweller, our inner opponent, often confuses us, prompting us to take a wrong turn, the wrong choice in the labyrinth of life.

We can think of the mythological sacrifice of seven maidens and seven young men to the Minotaur as analogous to our soul and spirit beset by the dweller-on-the-threshold. We can view the Minotaur within as the dweller-on-the-threshold attempting to consume the soul (feminine) and the spirit (masculine) in the seven chakras.

---

*See pp. 249–59 for these prayers and decrees.

This results in the plummeting downward of the energy and the hindering of the soul's mission. Why? Because the energy stays locked in the lower chakras instead of rising from the base-of-the-spine to the crown for the soul's enlightenment. Through spiritual resolve, mental sharpness, emotional balance and right action we can reverse that process and win the victory for our soul and spirit.

## Fixing the Seemingly Unfixable

In order to resolve the cause and core of problems that may seem unfixable or a constant stumbling block on our spiritual path, we benefit from seeking spiritual counsel and/or psychotherapy to help us navigate the labyrinth of human creation.

For example, when we have problems such as low self-esteem, fear and anxiety, anger or depression, they are typically unresolved at the subconscious or unconscious levels of being. We will carry the baggage of old traumas and reactions to people and situations until the soul understands and learns the necessary lesson.

Combining spiritual contemplation, prayer and decrees with psychotherapy is an excellent way to resolve these issues, both at the conscious level and at the level of the soul.

The ascended master Kuthumi, the master psychologist, has offered to assist us in resolving our psychology. In a dictation through Mrs. Prophet, Kuthumi said:

> Thus, I come, the joyful student, to announce to you the most precious dispensation, which comes from Maitreya, placed upon me by him with all diligence and the same concern for the step-up of your lives. This dispensation is my assignment to work with each one of

you individually for your physical health and for the
healing of your psychology that we might swiftly get to
the very cause and core of physical as well as spiritual
and emotional conditions that there be no more setbacks or indulgences and surely not two steps forward
and one step back.

Thus, from this hour, if you will call to me and make
a determination in your heart to transcend the former
self, I will tutor you both through your own heart and
any messenger I may send your way.[45]

## *The Labyrinth of Human Creation*

Mrs. Prophet has also spoken about getting beyond the
safe harbor of the intellect and trusting the ascended master
Lord Maitreya[46] to lead us through the psychological labyrinth of our human creation and our karma.

She said:

> What happens here can be cataclysmic in the world
> of the individual, where in order to now begin to draw
> forth and become the Christ, he has to leave the moor-
> ings of the safe harbor of the intellect and the psyche, or
> the psychic senses.
>
> He must be able to board the ship of Maitreya and
> trust the captain to know that that universal mind in
> him, in Maitreya, . . . will guide him through the laby-
> rinth he must pass through in order to fully internalize
> that mind himself. And the labyrinth is the electronic belt
> that you pass through from the seat-of-the-soul chakra
> on your journey to the heart chakra and the secret
> chamber of the heart.* And that includes all of the
> human creation that came out of wrong desire, the desire
> body that's attached to the solar plexus.

---

* See the Glossary, p. 286.

Now, all karma, negative karma, comes from wrong desire. So you see, it *is* a labyrinth. We go round and round and round the spirals of that electronic belt daily on our cosmic clock.[47] And we are carving tunnels out of granite every single time we are decreeing and doing Astreas and doing violet flame, and each day we're getting closer and closer to the place of union. But on the way, we have to slay all these beasts on those lines.[48]

## The Labyrinth of Problematic Situations

The ascended master Serapis Bey gave spiritual instruction to people who tend to revolve problematic situations:

There is a key in the disciplines to higher consciousness. The key is not to become entangled in the labyrinth of human questioning and the fears and the doubts and specters of the night that haunt that labyrinth. You do not have to trace the meanderings of the carnal mind and the human consciousness through all of the levels of the subconscious in order to come to the knowledge of truth, in order to come to reality or to overcome in love.

The key is not to be drawn by curiosity or a fascination with horror or a gluttony for the things of the senses, drawing you down into more and more astral experiences and psychic phenomena. The key—instead of taking a thousand steps through the astral plane—is to take one step into the arms of the I AM Presence, into the plane of the Christ mind where the oneness and the wholeness of the Great Pyramid, the oneness and the wholeness, is the dissolving action.

### Transcend the Cycles

Transcend your cycles! Do not follow those negative spirals round and round and round, down and down unto the death manifestation in the very crypt of the electronic belt. But with one invocation to the ascension fire, let that flame leap and arc from spiral to spiral, consuming on contact the debris. The flame is not linear; it need not travel over the lines of human creation. And so your soul, enveloped in the flame, also need not remain any longer in the consciousness that the only way out is through the labyrinth.

I say, transcend it! This means that in the moment when you would indulge your pettiness, your argumentation, your human nonsense, your dalliance in childishness, in that moment you instantly let go and you let God be the light that swallows you up in the victory of love. And the love that is your victory is your own love that is God made manifest within you.

And our God is the all-consuming fire of love.

### Meditate on the Love of God

Love God enough so that you do not need to satisfy human desire. You do not have to appease the carnal mind and give it what it wants so that you will have a moment's peace, an hour's peace. You do not have to engage your energies in imperfection. As much as you think that it is sometimes necessary, I tell you that by meditating within—within the heart and upon the three-fold flame of Life—by meditating upon the Presence and keeping that steady flow of energy of loving God arcing to him and his love returning, completing the whole of the two arcs as the two halves of the circle, *you can transcend the former cycles.*

### Become as a Little Child

If you can sustain your attention upon your I AM Presence and upon the light, you will receive the energy necessary to deal with all outer circumstances (karma) and that without traveling through them in your emotions, in your mental concepts, in your memory, and in physical labor. Think, then, upon this. The disciplines for higher consciousness demand that you prove how it is that you can be in the world and yet not of this world.

And how is it so? To the disciplined one, astute in the understanding of the Law and its counterfeit creation, the first step is to become as a little child. You must become the child of innocence before you can mature to the Christed man and the Christed woman. Do not, then, try to become the full Master of Galilee before you have traced the coils of God consciousness and of Christ consciousness, which are lawfully yours to trace—not the labyrinth of the carnal mind, but the blueprint of the etheric path of initiation. And therefore, become as the little child.[49]

## *The Maze of Human Creation*

In her lecture on the "Studies of the Human Aura," Mrs. Prophet taught about the labyrinth as the maze of human creation.

She said:

It is frightful because when you are that far on the exterior of identity, how are you going to get back to reality? By what course can we take the minds of those who are so enmeshed and so ensnared? How can we take them through the labyrinth that they have created— the labyrinth, the maze, of their human creation? How can we lead them through that whole canyon of mortality back to reality?

It's practically impossible. And therefore the only way that they're going to get back to the center of reality is

for us to so ignite the planet with the Christ consciousness that the Christ consciousness itself becomes the
towering inferno, the sacred fire, that consumes all these
canyons of the miasma and maya so that *it* goes up in
smoke, and they can instantly come into the center of
God-awareness.

## Walking the Labyrinth of Life

In her mini-book *Alchemy of the Heart: How to Give
and Receive More Love,* Mrs. Prophet talked about how as
we walk the labyrinth of life, the critical issues in our lives
revolve around our innate need to give love and receive love.
She said:

> When we feel compelled to take those torturous
> twists and turns, painful as they may be, it's because
> we're trying to recapture the experience of divine love
> that is native to our soul.
>
> The labyrinth takes us over the high peaks and into
> the deep chasms of our own inner terrain. The land-
> scape has been shaped by our karma—the consequences
> of the choices we have made in the past to love or not to
> love. Each time we come to a Y in the road, we again
> come face-to-face with the choice—to love or not to
> love, to open our heart and share our gifts or to shut
> down and pretend no one is home.[51]

## Navigating the Labyrinth of Karma

In the Eastern teachings, the ancient Gurus put their disciples through extremely difficult tests. The individual had to
see through all kinds of illusions, all kinds of obstacles where
he had to conquer his lesser self before ultimately arriving at
the abode of the Guru and being accepted as a chela.

This was the trek of Milarepa, the Great Yogi, under the tutelage of his Guru Marpa, which is explained in detail in my fifth book, *Soul Reflections: Many Lives, Many Journeys,* published in 2003. I recommend that you read the book if you have not already done so. It is about the journey of the soul under the tutelage of the adepts and masters. And Milarepa is such a lovable example because he has so many lessons to learn and gets himself in so much trouble along the way, yet his heart is right with God and ultimately he wins his victory.

Mrs. Prophet talked about how the individual who seeks discipleship to a Guru must make his way through the labyrinth of human karma where he faces frightening experiences and difficult obstacles in order to earn the right to receive the mysteries given by the Guru. The adept is called to overcome his fears and human frailties in order to achieve adeptship.

She said:

> It is simply a very long, winding course where one finally winds up on the other side face to face with the Great Initiator [Lord Maitreya], who says, "You have gone through all of this darkness, and I have known you have gone through it. I have been with you. And you had to make it on your own. You have achieved and you have attained, and you are now ready for the mysteries of the inner circle, which are given in the temples of the Brotherhood.[52]

The cosmic being Helios gave a dictation through Mrs. Prophet in which he encouraged the lightbearers to keep on moving through the labyrinth of life, no matter what outer circumstances might occur.

He said:

You are beloved of Alpha and Omega, each one of you. And you have a destiny that must proceed in an orderly fashion through the labyrinth of life until you are free once again.

You must not be discouraged by outer circumstances. You must not be discouraged by conditions that seem to surround you. You must not be discouraged when ill health at times has manifested. You must not be discouraged when tramp thoughts seek to manifest in your world. You must determine that you will definitely proceed in that fashion of keeping on keeping on, which is the divine God Presence within you acting in the world.

Whenever you are acting according to the Presence, you are then keeping on keeping on. When you are feeling sorry for yourself or you have permitted yourself to enter into a state of darkened consciousness, at that moment is the time when you must call as you have never called before; for your very life does depend upon your calls made to us so that we can come into your world and give you that buoyant feeling of God freedom which we are.

We are so willing, so completely willing, blessed ones, to establish in you a focus of our presence. We welcome each extension of ourselves upon earth and we are happy to pour into your world those golden drops of anointing unguent that will free you from a feeling of uncomfortability and make you to feel comfortable in the Presence, comfortable in the awareness of God, comfortable in that power that forgives sins and understands how that it will call the beloved son to His own heart.

You will be called, then, to my heart each time that

you invoke my name. Each time that you call forth my flame to surround you, I will come and I will assist you in finding your freedom. For there is no ascended being, no cosmic being, regardless how mighty they may be called...who will not answer the calls of the very least among the children of men and will also help them to find their freedom.[53]

The ascended master Jesus Christ gave these comforting words in a dictation:

Come home to my heart, ye who are bruised. Come home to my heart. I will not whip you. I will not beat you. I will not condemn you. I will show you the way out of the labyrinth that you have created for yourself.

I will show you that you need the living Christ, that you need the patterns that are in the heavens to be made manifest as the patterns in the earth. For surely you can all understand that in the process of attaining the ascension, you are perfecting those patterns in the earth and ultimately you are perfecting your way of bringing them back to their original mold of perfection.[54]

## The Goal of the Ascension

Mrs. Prophet has encouraged her students to remember that the ascension, the return to the heaven-world, waits at the end of the labyrinth.

She said:

Just remember, God wants you Home at the end of this life, and you have asked for it. And he is giving us the obstacle course or the labyrinth or whatever you want to call it. But he is taking us through those paths that we must walk to have our victory. Just remember this, God has a right to test us. That's his right. And it's our right to accept the testing graciously.[55]

Mrs. Prophet has lectured on the wisdom of striving for the ascension once we have 51 percent of our karma balanced. She said:

> So if you're smart, you take your ascension at fifty-one percent.... And when you reach this victory, you can easily feel, "Well, I've arrived at fifty-one percent. Nothing's going to stop me now." And really, you haven't come to the most difficult tests. These are the tests that are spoken about, in the West as well as the East, of the saints, of the terrific amount of challenges that they had to go through—the dark night of the soul, the dark night of the spirit, going through the labyrinth of human creation, meeting the dragon, slaying the dragons, all kinds of metaphors have been told in the stories of Greek mythology or in the books of the East.
>
> Beloved Jesus has instructed us to study and resolve our psychology as a means of navigating some of the labyrinth of the subconscious and finding the key to our Christhood. And he gave us these words of comfort and encouragement: "Know that my love is sufficient unto you to resolve every unresolved problem—a spiritual problem, a problem in the psyche or in your psychology, a problem of the mind or the heart or the desires."[56]

Thus, the soul moves through the spirals of being and many layers of karma before we come to the feet of the ascended masters. Once we learn about the masters, our Christ Self and our spiritual path, we can surrender the elements of our lower nature and strive for oneness with God. We are meant to walk the path of soul testing and initiation to fulfill our destiny on earth and make it all the way Home to God.

I suggest that you close your eyes and visualize your soul as a brilliant sphere of light moving up a golden crystal spiral to the secret chamber of your heart and journeying all the way up the crystal cord and through the crown chakra to the higher octaves of light. May this visualization be a meditation for you and your soul unto your victory!

# 6

# *Fables and Stories Reveal Human Nature*

*Incline your ear to wisdom,
and apply your heart to understanding.*

—PROVERBS 2:2

*M*ost of us have heard of fables written in ancient times, passed down through the centuries and now referenced in encyclopedias and books on cultural literacy. I believe that these stories are about human nature and that they apply to our lives today.

Historians attribute one compilation of fables to Aesop, a Greek storyteller, sixth century B.C. The main characters were animals and simple people and their stories taught rules of moral conduct. The fables included "The Boy Who Cried Wolf," "The Fox and the Grapes" and "The Tortoise and the Hare." I'd like to share these three fables with you because the morals of these stories are as apt today as they were in ancient times.

### *Aesop's Fables: What Can We Learn?*

In Aesop's fable "The Boy Who Cried Wolf," the story is about a young shepherd who had a habit of yelling for help to drive off wolves that were attacking his sheep. When the people from the village would rush out to help him, he would laugh and say it was a joke!

After several repetitions of his foolish trick, the villagers wearied of rushing to help only to be laughed at. The day arrived when wolves actually did attack the sheep herd. The startled shepherd cried out for help, but this time no one came. The villagers were fed up with his pranks so they ignored him. And the wolves killed and devoured his sheep.

In keeping with this fable, when people today sound a false alarm we say they are "crying wolf!" The results are similar to what happened in Aesop's fable. After the first time or two, the person sounding the false alarm is ignored. In some cases, an individual is arrested for a false alarm. And people say, "It serves him right!" The moral of the story is never to cry wolf and always to be truthful.

In another of Aesop's fables, "The Fox and the Grapes," a hungry fox tries to pluck grapes from a bunch dangling above his head, but no matter how many times he tries he can't quite reach them. As he trots off to forage elsewhere, he mutters in disgust, "Those grapes are probably sour anyway."

This fable led to a common expression, "sour grapes," meaning that when a person tries for something and cannot achieve it, he might announce to friends or colleagues, "That's okay. I didn't really want it anyway. So I didn't give it my best shot."

Most people admit privately that they have done this at one time or another to avoid public embarrassment—and they ended up feeling equally embarrassed about the lie. But they feel it would have been even more embarrassing to reverse their story. It would seem that a good moral for this story would be, "Tell the truth to yourself and you will be able to tell the truth to others."

In a third Aesop fable, "The Tortoise and the Hare," the tortoise and the hare agree to race each other. Of course, the hare is totally confident that he will win so he takes a nap along the way. The tortoise understands that he cannot slack off if he is to have any chance of winning. So, he plods along at a steady pace, quietly passes by the sleeping hare and ends up winning the race.

The moral of this fable applies equally well to people caught in the whirlwind of modern-day competition, including politics, business and industry, marketing and sales, TV and film production, sports events, arts and crafts shows, scientists and inventors, writers and musicians and neighborhood competitions for beautiful homes and gardens.

The lesson is clear: overconfidence leads to slacking off and losing ground, while determination and steady effort propels the victor across the finish line. Thus, ancient wisdom can help us solve today's problems if we apply the lessons recorded in history and fables. We realize anew the truth of the words in Ecclesiastes, that "there is no new thing under the sun."[57]

## *Soul Dialogue: Getting Back on Track*

Whether we look at ancient fables or modern-day life, we realize that human nature does not change that much. That is why understanding our soul is important. At the level of the soul, each of us has a special mission to fulfill. When we are fulfilling it, we feel balanced and joyful. When we are not, we feel out of balance and unfulfilled.

Consequently, we tend to get caught up in the merry-go-round of daily life instead of asking ourselves, "What is the mission of my soul? Am I pursuing it? If not, how can I get back on track?" This brings us to soul dialogue, which is an important way of getting back on track.

I remember Gloria, a lovely young woman who was not certain what she needed to be doing with her life. She had been downsized from her job and decided that this was an opportunity for a new beginning. That brought her to me as a client.

Gloria had this nagging feeling that her soul was not happy with her. When I asked her to tell me more about that, she said that she used to have contact with her soul. Now she could not seem to contact her soul; it was as if her soul did not trust her anymore.

I suggested that we use a two-chair technique, where Gloria would sit in one chair when she was talking for herself and shift to the other chair when she was talking for her soul. Gloria said she thought that would help because when she tried to dialogue by herself she always was mixed up as to who was who.

So began a soul dialogue in which Gloria pleaded with her soul to talk to her about what she was feeling. It did not take long for her soul to respond. Here is the dialogue they had with one another, with me offering assistance as necessary.

Gloria: I want you to know that I love you very much and I am so scared that we have gotten completely off track of our mission. Would you please tell me what you think about that?

Soul: I think you are right. I have felt pretty much on my own for a long time. And we haven't talked to God about our mission since you were a little girl.

Gloria: I know. And I'm sorry about that. Would you please tell me what you remember about our mission?

Soul: Do you remember when we met with our spiritual overseers before we came into this life? They told us that we had a special gift for helping people to feel close to God. And that was what we were to be doing in this life. And you used to do that when you were a little girl, do you remember?

Gloria: Yes, I remember telling my mother that God loved us and would help us. And then she would tell it back to me. And I liked to hear her say it especially when we had such a hard time after daddy died. We prayed together that daddy would be with the angels and that someday we would all be together again.

Soul: Yes, those were the good times. We were close to God and to each other. And even in high school, we prayed a lot and felt our closeness to God. I think everything changed when you went away to college.

Gloria: That's true. I had to work really hard in college to make my grades and after I graduated, my colleagues at work weren't interested in spirituality.

Soul: I know. That's when you stopped talking to me. And that was very hard because I couldn't help you anymore. It's been a long time since you talked to me about God.

Gloria: I am really sorry. Can you forgive me? I want to get back on track spiritually.

Soul: If you really mean that, the first thing we have to do is get back to praying on a regular basis. God has always helped us when we asked for his help.

Gloria bowed her head, "Dear Heavenly Father, I ask for forgiveness for ignoring my prayers for so long. And I am asking for another opportunity. Please guide me so that we know the next step to take."

She remained with her head bowed for some time and then tears began streaming down her cheeks. I prayed silently with her and waited until she was ready to share her experience.

Gloria put her arms around herself and whispered, "I love you and thank you, beloved Heavenly Father. And I love you, my dear soul. Thank you for being who you are."

After a time, Gloria dried her tears and smiled. "Well, that was really something! I am so relieved to know that God still loves me. And I'm not going to waste a lot of time berating myself for not doing this sooner. I'd like to share what happened."

Gloria went on to tell me that she had felt a brilliant white light around her and it was like she and her soul were one with the love of the angels and God the Father. She said ever since her daddy died she had felt distanced from God and she realized now that she had blamed God for taking her father away.

During her meditation, Gloria realized that she had been resentful toward God and had chosen to focus on her studies and college life instead of her spiritual life. Now she understood it was simply her father's time to go and she had been given what she needed to fulfill her own mission.

When Gloria had this realization, she asked God to forgive her for her resentful attitude and to give her another opportunity. And she felt flooded with God's love. That was when the tears came. They were tears of joy and release.

Gloria also told me that while she was communing with God and the angels, she and her soul agreed that they would focus on their walk with God and not allow themselves to be derailed. As she put it, "I can't believe how much better I feel.

God loves me and my soul, and we are going to make it Home!"

As you can see, Gloria did this session on her own with my prayers and an occasional comment to assist her. She had definitely made her peace with God and with her soul. She still calls me once in awhile or comes in for what she calls a "spiritual check-up." She prays and talks with her soul on a daily basis. And she rejoices that God has blessed her so richly.

### *"Do You Love Me More?"*

Many are the stories, fables and operas that present the drama of twin flames and many are the lessons for the soul. In my practice as a spiritual psychologist, I have also seen the real life dramas that occur when someone recognizes his or her twin flame. What has impressed me most about twin flames is the inner tie that seems to draw them together from all over the globe.

Sometimes they are meant to be together in this life, and sometimes they are simply meant to love one another from afar because one or the other is married or has a particular mission to fulfill in another part of the world. In most cases, twin flames ultimately come to realize that they are being tested spiritually. I believe God is saying to them in the midst of life's trials, "Do you love me more?"

Twin flames, like the rest of us, have karma with one another and with other people. This may necessitate loving each other from a distance in this lifetime while they behave lovingly toward those with whom they are balancing karma. Sometimes this is very difficult but the joy of reunion once the karma is balanced is the bliss of oneness in the most sacred sense.

I have had several clients who have helped me to

understand the intensity of the twin flame relationship. I will share with you one of the more challenging situations I have seen. I will refer to the twin flames as Bryan and Sandra and to Sandra's husband as Jeff, none of which are their real names.

I received a phone call from Bryan, a handsome middle-aged man, who said he wanted to talk to me about twin flames. During our first session, Bryan told me that he was hurt and angry with Sandra, a woman he had met several months before. He said he knew she was his twin flame and that she had rejected him.

When Bryan told me what had happened, I understood why Sandra had refused his advances. Bryan had recognized Sandra as his twin flame during a business meeting, which she had attended with her husband. His immediate inner reaction was anger that she was married to another man. "Why didn't she wait for me!" was his angry complaint despite the fact that Sandra and her husband Jeff had been married a number of years before Bryan entered the picture.

Bryan called Sandra and asked to meet her for lunch to discuss a matter that was of concern to him. During lunch, Bryan told Sandra he recognized her as his twin flame. He said she would not admit it but he could see the recognition in her eyes. Instead, she told him she was happily married and she had no intention of dissolving her marriage or deserting her children.

Bryan flatly refused to understand why Sandra would not consider divorcing Jeff. He kept pressing his point about twin flames, and Sandra continued to be firm in refusing to consider a relationship with him. He finally got up and walked out on Sandra in a fit of anger. He cancelled his next appointment with me because he said he was too angry to discuss what had happened.

Sandra called me because Bryan had told her he was seeing me as a therapist. She told me she did not expect me to tell her anything about my sessions with Bryan but she wanted me to know that she had recognized Bryan as her twin flame the moment she met him. However, she was in no way going to encourage him. She explained that she loved her husband and that for her a marriage commitment was for life. She also said that she had a strong inner sense that she and Bryan were not meant to be together as man and wife this lifetime.

Sandra added that when Bryan stalked out of the restaurant she knew she was absolutely right about not being together in this life even though she had felt a strong pull and his angry response hurt her feelings. She also told me how much she loved her husband, Jeff. She believed they were soul mates and that they were balancing karma together by raising the children they both love dearly. She feared Bryan would throw his life away because she would not divorce her husband and marry him.

Sandra told me she would take her sorrow to God in prayer and content herself in being a loving wife and mother. As she said, "I love Jeff and the children and I intend to be true to my marriage vows. I pray that Bryan will get it through his head that I have no intention of getting a divorce. At least he had the good sense not to tell Jeff about this situation. Jeff is such a good man and a wonderful husband and father; he would be heartbroken."

She added, "I believe that if Bryan and I pass our tests in this life we will be together in the heaven-world. And that's probably the reason we met this time around." Sandra also told me that she knew her mission in this life was to balance her karma by loving the man she married and doing her part to raise their three children.

You might be wondering, "What happened to Bryan?" Bryan stopped therapy shortly after he realized that Sandra was not going to change her mind. He spent weeks being furious with her and angry with himself for pushing the situation.

Even the prayers of one's twin flame and the assistance of a therapist cannot heal an individual who insists on being his own worst enemy. My prayer for this dear man was that he would come to realize that he was being tested on his love for God. As the scriptures say, "Thou shalt have no other gods before me."

Bryan eventually realized that core anger was his Achilles heel and called for another appointment. In the course of the session, he told me that he had prayed to God for understanding. He had a powerful spiritual experience in which he realized that if Sandra had divorced and married him, his anger would have ruined the relationship. And neither of them would have fulfilled their mission in this life.

Bryan prayed for forgiveness and another opportunity. And he began to work hard in therapy. Over time, he discovered that his anger was rooted in fury at the fallen angels, whom he held responsible for separating him and Sandra in the first place. Once Bryan understood the root of the problem, he did the necessary psychological and spiritual work to let go of the anger and resentment.

Bryan decided to get on with his life and make good karma to bring to the table in the heaven-world. As he told me, "I realize that loving and trusting God is my first priority. If I do my spiritual work and balance the karma I've made, I believe God's grace will bring us together and that will be a great day!"

When I raised a questioning eyebrow, he added, "I know that Sandra and I may never be together in this world, but I will keep her in my prayers and I believe we will be reunited in the afterlife. She is a beautiful soul and I am proud of her for sticking to her guns.

"For me, I promised God that I'm going to focus on my relationship with him and on balancing my karma. I'm going to turn that anger into inner power so that I can mobilize the strength to do what's right whatever the circumstances. I have faith that if I do that and keep on doing my prayers and following God's direction, I will fulfill my mission in this life."

Bryan's actions have been as good as his promise, and he laughingly told me he was certain his guardian angel was mightily relieved. I was relieved also because the ascended masters teach that there is nothing more painful to the universe than discord between twin flames. That is because of the tremendous power inherent in the twin flame relationship, which can be mobilized for good or ill.

Whether or not we are together with our twin flame in a particular lifetime is not the point in the long run. The goal is to fulfill our soul's mission on earth and to win the victory of the ascension. Instead of dwelling on a reunion with our twin flame, we can draw upon the spheres of light in our causal body* to balance our karma, do good works and fulfill our mission on earth. We do this through prayer and invocation, obedience to the laws of God and service to life. And by a continuous striving to be wise, compassionate and true to our Higher Self.

---

*The causal body consists of interpenetrating spheres of light surrounding the I AM Presence at spiritual levels; the color bands of the causal body contain the records of the virtuous acts an individual has performed to the glory of God and the blessing of man during his or her incarnations on earth.

Regardless of our circumstances, we can choose to love our family, friends and neighbors and to follow the Golden Rule, "Do unto others as you would have them do unto you."[58] In doing so we bless others and make good karma, which helps us to reunite with our twin flame in accordance with God's timing.

### *Aïda: A Classic Story of the Love of Twin Flames*

The opera *Aïda,* a classic story of the love of twin flames, is based on a story written by Egyptologist August Mariette with the libretto by Antonio Ghislanzoni. Curiously enough, this famous opera was written in 1869 to honor the opening of the Suez Canal. Why? The ruler of Egypt was looking for an exciting way for Cairo to celebrate this achievement. He ordered the building of a world-class opera house and commissioned Giuseppe Verdi to compose a premiere opera.

Verdi agreed to compose the music and insisted that the costumes and sets be produced in Paris to ensure the best possible quality. Unfortunately, *Aïda's* debut was delayed by world affairs when in July of 1870 the French declared war on Prussia. As the conflict raged, the production was held hostage in Paris and the Cairo Opera House opened with a performance of *Rigoletto.* It would not be until December 1871 that *Aïda* finally premiered in Cairo and shortly thereafter at La Scala in Milan.

The opera setting is in Egypt. One of the most popular and elaborate operas of all times, *Aïda* has been performed in every major city throughout the world. This opera with its magnificent "Triumphal March" is a favorite of music lovers everywhere.

## *ACT I*
### *Scene 1: A Great Hall in the Royal Palace at Memphis*

Ramfis, high priest of Egypt, tells Radames, the captain of the Egyptian guard, that the Ethiopians have invaded Egypt and that the goddess Isis will decide who is to lead the Egyptian armies. Hoping that Isis will choose him, Radames dreams of returning victorious and freeing his beloved Aida from her lowly position as a slave of the Egyptian princess, Amneris. He sings of her in the beautiful aria, "Celeste Aida."

Amneris, herself in love with Radames, enters. Hearing his song and observing his elation, she suspects that the ardor in his singing has to do with more than military glory. When Aida appears, Amneris' fears are realized. As the three sing together, she detects the strong feelings between Aida and Radames.

The king enters with the high priest Ramfis and various officers. A messenger tells of the devastation of the Ethiopian armies under their king, Amonasro. At mention of his name Aida exclaims, "Mio padre! (My father!)" But her exclamation is not heard by the Egyptians who do not know of her royal birth.

The Egyptian king announces that Isis has chosen Radames as head of the Egyptian armies. As the king leads a battle chorus and Amneris exhorts Radames to return victorious, Aida echoes their words with a foreboding sense of the tragedy to come. She is torn apart by her love for Radames on the one hand, and her loyalty to her father, her country, and her people on the other.

### *Scene 2: The Temple of Vulcan in Memphis*

The high priestess and priestesses chant an invocation to the deity Phtha, to which the priests respond. The sacred dance of the priestesses then begins. Radames is led in and Ramfis places the sacred sword in his hands. Ramfis invokes the aid of the gods in protecting Egypt.

## ACT II
### Scene 1: A Hall in the Apartments of Amneris

Radames has been victorious and Amneris watches Moorish slaves dance for her as she is attired for the triumphal feast. When Aida enters, Amneris is determined to find out whether her jealous suspicions are justified. She tells Aida that Radames has been killed in battle, leading Aida to reveal her love for him. Then Amneris scornfully tells her that he is in fact alive.

How dare a lowly slave presume to rival the Egyptian princess herself in love! Their duet is joined in the background by the battle song heard previously, sung in the distance by the returning warriors. Aida, left alone once again, implores the gods to pity her.

### Scene 2: An Avenue to the City of Thebes

The king and Amneris arrive in state. After a chorus of praise and thanksgiving to Isis and the king, a grand march opens with a resplendent procession. Radames enters; the king greets him and orders Amneris to place the victor's crown on his head. He tells Radames that he can have any wish he desires. The Egyptian slaves then appear. With them is Amonasro, unknown to the Egyptians as the Ethiopian king.

Aida recognizes her father at once and embraces him. But Amonasro cautions her not to betray his rank. Amonasro then tells the Egyptians that the Ethiopian king is dead and pleads for the lives of the prisoners and slaves. The

Egyptian people support his plea, as does Radames, who requests the slaves' freedom as his reward.

The king releases all but Amonasro and Aida, who, at Ramfis's insistence, are retained as hostages. He then presents Radames with Amneris' hand, leaving Aida and Radames in despair. The final ensemble expresses the jubilation of the people and the diverse reactions of the individual characters.

### *ACT III*
### *Scene 1: A Hall in the King's Palace*

Amneris is alone, near Radames' prison, after he has been labeled a traitor for secretly asking Aida to be his bride after his next victory and then revealing to Aida the Egyptian army's plan to attack Ethiopia. Although deeply hurt, Amneris sends for Radames, offering to save him if he will renounce Aida. He steadfastly refuses.

Proud and despairing, Amneris lets him go to his doom. In increasing distress, she overhears his trial. He offers no answer to the charges of Ramfis and the priests, and he is condemned three times as a traitor, then sentenced to be buried alive. In an impassioned outburst, Amneris curses the priests for their cruelty.

### *Scene 2: Upper floor, the Temple of Vulcan*
### *Lower Floor, a Tomb*

Radames is buried alive. He turns his final thoughts to Aida, who emerges from the shadows, having entered the vault to share his fate. Radames tries in vain to dislodge the stone that locks them in. Bidding farewell to life on earth, the lovers greet eternity, as Amneris, in the temple above, prays to Isis for peace.

### *Aïda as a Story of Twin Flames*

We can view the opera *Aïda* as a story of twin flames whose love has drawn them together in a karmic predicament for which there is seemingly no earthly solution. Aida's choice to enter the valley of death with her beloved rather than to be separated portrays the depth of the love of twin flames.

This drama of human tragedy is illustrative of the trials and temptations of the soul's journey in time and space. As long as good and evil exist, the soul must make choices and hopefully choose wisely. Were this a real-life story, Radames and Aida would likely reembody to fulfill the mission of each one's soul, since opportunity was cut short in that lifetime.

Many twin flames choose to embody on earth to fulfill a special mission. According to the teachings of the ascended masters, twin flames become separated due to wrong choices and the resulting karma. They are called to balance their karma and fulfill their mission on earth so that they may be reunited for eternity in the heaven-world.

Whether or not we know who is our twin flame or encounter him or her in this lifetime, fulfilling the mission of the soul needs to be our highest priority. If we are not certain what that mission is, we can pray for illumination and guidance. And we can determine to be true to our Higher Self in every endeavor.

Life on planet Earth has always been a challenge, and we continue to live in tumultuous times. The battle of good and evil is as rampant today as it was when *Aïda* was composed. The difference is that the battle is no longer restricted to a few countries; it now occurs worldwide.

## *The Mix of Good and Evil*

How are good people to know what the right choice is in situations that are a mix of good and evil? Many people face that dilemma today. Rarely is one person completely right and another completely wrong. Given that fact, I believe the best course is to pray for divine guidance, to act in accordance with principle and honor, and to endeavor to be true to the Higher Self.

What if we make a mistake? We can make it a point to acknowledge the mistake, correct it quickly and figure out how not to make the same mistake again. And we can apologize if our error has created a problem for other people.

When self-correction becomes a daily habit, we make fewer mistakes because we are being watchful rather than cruising along unthinkingly. We also make more friends and fewer enemies. And we feel better about ourselves because we are synchronized with our Higher Self.

There is no greater sorrow for the lightbearer than knowing that one has given in to the wiles of evil and not been true to one's Higher Self or to God. And it is a daily test in today's world. Some form of evil seems to be rampant almost everywhere. Whether it reveals itself through terrorism, torture, murder or vengeance or in attitudes of hatred, deception and the degrading of other people's character, evil is a major problem for the civilized world.

We all face the temptation to shade the truth, to react to an attack with a snide remark, to assume the worst about a person who hurt us or to coat nasty retaliation with sugary insincerity. Yet when we harbor hateful thoughts or spout words that degrade other people, we compromise who we are as souls of light, sons and daughters of God. And then we have a hard time forgiving ourselves for behaving in a manner that we ourselves do not respect. What do we do when we realize that we have fallen into this human trap? We call upon the Lord and ask for forgiveness.

God is infinitely forgiving when we are truly penitent because he loves each and every one of us. And our guardian angel is but a prayer away. So, if we are wise we will decide to do a turnaround of any negative intentions, thoughts or actions. And we will choose to live as if we were one with our guardian angel.

### *The Challenge of Forgiveness*

What do we do when friends or colleagues refuse to forgive us and continue to see us in a negative light? It is important to realize that we can do little to change the opinions of others because real change always comes from within. Sometimes we have to content ourselves with doing the best we can and choosing to be nonreactive to the negative behavior of other people. Although this is not easy, it is a form of self-discipline that ultimately creates a sense of inner peace.

Genuine forgiveness is important in strengthening our sense of inner peace. If we would be truly peaceful, we need to forgive others, including those who hurt us. We can remember Jesus' words on the cross, "Father, forgive them, they know not what they do." And we can strive to walk in Jesus' footsteps and nurture the light of forgiveness within ourselves.

Many people discover that forgiveness is as great a blessing, or perhaps more, to the one who forgives. Why is this? Forgiveness propels us into a higher consciousness that is peaceful and has insight into the propensities of human nature. Thus, the one who forgives receives the blessing of alignment with higher consciousness.

I believe it is good to pray for resolution in troublesome relationships, while acknowledging that everyone has free will. I also believe it is helpful to understand that people may not know how to forgive. They may have been so wounded by situations in their own life that they have developed a habit of being on guard and looking with a jaundiced eye at the actions of others. Perhaps if we knew the details of their lives we would better understand why they find it difficult to forgive.

Whether or not other people forgive us, I believe it is enlightened self-interest for us to forgive them. Why? In order to forgive others we are called to identify with our higher values, to look at all sides of the issue and to admit any wrongdoing, including our own. And that requires total honesty on our part, which can be both a challenge and a blessing.

## *Transformation in Consciousness*

When we decide to forgive, we realize that forgiveness necessitates a transformation of consciousness. We cannot forgive when we are seething with anger or holding a grudge! In order to outwit the human tendency to retaliate, we need to align our consciousness with the Higher Self. Otherwise, the human self will take the easy way out. And that means blaming the other guy.

So, we do our prayers, ask God to guide us and ask ourselves, "What would Jesus do? What would my favorite saint do? What would my Higher Self have me do?" And we do our best to behave accordingly. Once we get used to congruency with our higher consciousness, we feel good about ourselves because we are in sync with our inner identity as sons or daughters of God.

Identifying with higher consciousness becomes an ongoing process because outworn elements of habit and accompanying lower vibrations may surface when we least expect them. This is a good reason to form a regular habit of meditation, prayer and decrees, which helps us maintain our vibration at a higher level.

As we continue our spiritual practices, we find ourselves increasingly more comfortable with the higher vibrations of Spirit than with the lower vibes we are discarding. As we transcend the foibles of our human self, we identify more with our Higher Self. And we experience the beauty of our soul and spirit. This grand exchange heralds a gradual transcendence into higher levels of being and ignites a sparkling fire of happiness in our heart.

# 7

# Intuition and Intention

*If ye have faith as a grain of mustard seed,*
*ye shall say unto this mountain,*
*Remove hence to yonder place; and it shall remove;*
*and nothing shall be impossible unto you.*

—JESUS CHRIST

*I*ntuition and intention are avenues for strengthening our faith and achieving our goals, particularly at the level of the soul. Intuition is a sudden hunch or insight that seemingly comes out of nowhere yet is rooted in the superconscious. The intuitive sense includes our spiritual awareness, our higher instincts and our connection with the Divine that knows all things.

Have you ever suddenly sensed danger just before a dangerous situation occurred? This is an intuitive response of the mind and body to impending danger. The intuitive response also reveals itself in instinctive physical reactions, such as curling into a protective ball in the face of an inevitable automobile crash.

In a positive sense, intuitive body wisdom surfaces in the way we respond to the rhythm of music, particularly folk music or music from the early 1900s. Who can resist tapping a foot to an Irish jig or an old-fashioned square-dance tune? At times when clients are troubled about a difficult situation, I suggest that they lift their spirits and allow intuitive ideas to come to mind by dancing with themselves. It's fun and a great way to get intuitive ideas to surface.

Spiritual intuition originates in the realm of Spirit and the Higher Self. We access our spiritual intuition by connecting with the Higher Self through prayer, meditation and striving to fulfill the mission of our soul. And the more we exercise spiritual intuition the more we feel a sense of oneness with the Higher Self and realize what we need to do to fulfill that mission.

When we apply intuition in our daily life, we learn to trust intuition as a guide. We explore realms of time and space that we do not encounter when we rely solely on human thinking and planning. I believe intuition is God's way of guiding us in the physical realm if we allow him to do so.

We strengthen our spirituality and faith in God when we pray, meditate and read the scriptures. The Word of God comforts the soul, connects us with our Higher Self and helps us stay focused on our divine purpose and how we can fulfill our calling. When we pray for guidance, meditate on our inner experience and see positive outcomes to our actions, our faith is strengthened.

### Cultivating a Sixth Sense

We sometimes say, "That must have been some kind of a sixth sense." What do we mean by that? The sixth sense is what some people call a hunch and others refer to as a "gut feeling." It is an active aspect of intuitive intelligence that translates hunches and gut feelings into useful information.

I sometimes suggest to clients that they cultivate their intuition and see if it proves helpful in decision-making. Trust your intuition in a benign situation and see what happens. If your intuitive response produces a productive outcome, you begin to trust it. If your intuition produces questionable results, you can couple it with the analytic mind. In this way, you examine your own process and test out your level of comfort with intuitive decision-making. If you feel more comfortable analyzing problematic situations, you may prefer to try out solutions in your mind.

I suggest taking a moment to reflect on a particular decision you would like to make and trying it out as if you were examining a new car before buying it. Ask yourself, "Can I afford it? Does it fit who I am? Will it meet my needs? Am I comfortable with it? If not, why not?"

As you ask yourself these questions, a variety of thoughts or images will likely come to mind. Since they all relate in some way to the decision you want to make, take a moment to write down what these thoughts and images mean to you. And pursue whatever comes to mind.

Until you feel comfortable finalizing your decision, I suggest that you continue to reflect on the pros and cons. Once you have considered all of these aspects, you will be ready to make a decision. Whatever you decide, you will have the comfort of knowing you passed your decision through a number of levels of consciousness instead of acting in haste.

Prayer, reflection and self-questioning are good ways of confirming our intuition, of testing its accuracy. In my own work, both in my practice and in my writing, I find a combination of prayers, intuition and analytic thinking invaluable.

Logical analysis of a problem as it presents itself coupled with prayers for guidance and a review of our thoughts and emotions promotes understanding and equanimity. Equally important is the ability to recognize and pay attention to any underlying sense of discomfort within ourselves or in our interaction with other people. This is where intuition and ability to empathize is often vital to resolving a problem.

Addressing the subtleties of a dilemma, including one's subconscious or unconscious thoughts and feelings, is often key to resolving disturbing situations. In my work as a clinical psychologist, in-depth exploration is invaluable in helping a person to resolve painful emotions, gain a more objective perspective and take constructive action in a difficult life situation.

### *Intention Helps Us Fulfill Our Goals*

Another important aspect of goal attainment is intention, which is more concrete than intuition. Intention means having a definite purpose in mind. Intention refers to a plan, design or a commitment to a specific goal and connotes making the effort to achieve it.

Philosophically, intention is the orientation of the mind toward a particular object or goal. For example, we might ask ourselves, "What is my intention in pursuing a particular goal? Or pursuing spirituality? Or studying the soul?" Our answers reveal to us the focus of the mind toward that goal or interest.

Intention is mindfulness, purposefulness, in contrast to its opposite, mindlessness, in which the mind flits here and there with no particular purpose. Clarifying one's intention and sense of purpose is extremely helpful in setting and achieving necessary goals and fulfilling the spiritual destiny of our soul and spirit.

All of us have come into embodiment to fulfill the destiny of our soul, and this means balancing karma and pursuing our spiritual mission as well as whatever we do in an outer sense to keep body and soul together.

People often ask, "How do I know what my mission is?" The answer comes through prayer and attunement to the prompting of the Higher Self. Whatever is pleasing to God, uplifting and constructive to life, compassionate and helpful to others in some way relates to the mission of our soul.

When we center ourselves in our higher aspirations and determine to relate to others with loving-kindness and helpfulness, we please God and attune to our mission. That mission always includes being true to higher values and choosing to be gracious to those whom we meet on the road of life.

All of this implies fulfilling the intention to identify with our Higher Self and choosing to outwit the lower aspects of human nature, including the tendency to moodiness, being unpleasant or wanting to get even with people who are unpleasant to us. When we determine to be true to our Higher Self in problematic situations and succeed in doing so, we accelerate in achieving higher consciousness. And we feel a sense of inner joy and happiness.

### *Pursuing Cosmic Intention*

In a discourse delivered through Mark Prophet about the problematic nature of human moods, the ascended master Lord Lanto addressed the tendency for all of us to identify with the lowest common denominator of human behavioral patterns and contrasted this with the course of highest love and cosmic intention.

Lord Lanto's instruction is timely for all who are striving to maintain higher consciousness in the midst of today's complicated and often frustrating life situations:

> The course of the highest love, as it meanders through the personal labyrinth where self-identification has created its own canyon walls, is naturally restrained to conform to the confinements of the self. Yet it must be borne in mind that the highest power is the highest power, the highest love is the highest love and it is able to overflow the banks of self-imposed limitation and to inundate the soul with the purifying energies of the Holy Spirit.
>
> The tendency of people to identify with the lowest common denominator of human behavioral patterns, whether their own worst deeds or another's, is contrary to divine principle. Therefore to dare and to do must still be the fervent cry of the man of the Spirit who would advance over all obstacles including his own self-woven shrouds of negation. Once and for all the soul cries out, "I want to be free!" But with each new challenge it seems to be confronted with an impenetrable door whose mysterious face will not yield to the hungry and thirsty traveler.
>
> In reality, the time and tide that wait for no man are vehicles of divine opportunity. When a balanced understanding of divine love and life is maintained during periods of personal struggle and social upheaval, the fiery intensity of cosmic intention is able to burn through the obstacles in self and society without scorching the evolving consciousness of men.

But this is true only when the disciple is able to stand aside. Carefully balanced on the razor's edge of pure reason, he is able to keep the flame on behalf of many innocent souls. He is in the world but he is not of the world, and from this vantage point he perceives the need to defend his cosmic rights against the forces, which would defraud him and all mankind of their divine inheritance. He knows that the strength that is sufficient for the day will be forthcoming through his simultaneous invocation of the assistance of heaven as a humble servant-son.

Man who dares to do the will of God ought not to dare without meekness. "For the meek shall inherit the earth."[59] The type of meekness of which we speak is that quality of graciousness, which is manifest in those who know the source of their strength and use their knowledge not against other parts of life, but for the emancipation of all.[60]

## Balancing Love and Discernment

Wherever we are, a major key to balancing karma is to love others as we would want them to love us. We can ask our Higher Self to help us cultivate loving intention and an intuitive awareness of the needs of others. When we couple these together, we are better able to behave lovingly. Sometimes it may be as simple as listening attentively to another person's story. And at other times, we may be called to lend a helping hand. As we practice loving intention and intuitive awareness on a daily basis, we find it natural to extend the love of our heart to friends, loved ones, neighbors, colleagues and all we meet along the road of life. We can offer that love in little ways: through a simple "hello" or "good morning," a smile or a word of encouragement, a helping hand, a loving pat on the back. And we can choose to behave lovingly even when others do not return the favor.

Sometimes a loving word or gesture on our part is rejected because the person on the receiving end is distracted or burdened by their private sorrows or the effluvia of the world. Others may be shy and cautious and reject love because they have been wounded in the guise of love. They may react to loving-kindness as if it were a control technique. And with those who are angry or volatile, a loving gesture may very well produce agitation, irritation and a quick rebuke.

Therefore, it is important to exercise discrimination and to balance love with discernment. When we attempt to be loving and kind to others and are misunderstood or rejected, we do well to step back and privately pray for the angels to give them love and comfort and soothe their pain.

We also do well to ponder the classic words of Shakespeare. They are as apt today as they were in his time:

> To be, or not to be; that is the question:
> Whether 'tis nobler in the mind to suffer
> The slings and arrows of outrageous fortune,
> Or to take arms against a sea of troubles,
> And by opposing end them?[61]

Since we are unlikely to change the mind of anyone whose mind is already made up, we comfort ourselves by realizing that we did the best we could. We strive to refine our discrimination and discernment. And whatever challenges we encounter, we choose to keep our heart open and the faucets of love flowing. Many of our problems melt away when the love of the inner Christ and Holy Spirit flows through us without reserve.

## Love That Has the Courage to Be

While we do not need to love human imperfection, we can love the soul, including our own soul, who is on the path of becoming whole. And we can ask the angels to give comfort and solace to those who are suffering, discouraged or caught in the trap of karmic circumstances.

The ascended master Serapis Bey tells us:

> Love must radiate from within the heart to the entire being. For even in the case of loved ones, when you give love with intensity and the loved one is dealing with karmic patterns or the effluvia of the world or the burden of the day—that loved one may not receive that love, may even reject it or become irritated by it, because the very substance untransmuted on the surface of each world may easily become agitated by the intense love of the Christed ones and of the heart chakra. Therefore, do not be dismayed, do not be offended, do not be hurt in your loving.
>
> If the devotees of the ascended masters would meditate upon love and expand their capacity to give love wisely with a pure discrimination of the heart, you would find a great expansion of this activity. For the Great Central Sun Magnet is the magnet of Cosmic Christ Love.
>
> Therefore, a bit of advice from Serapis tonight: Look at your own momentums. Have you left off loving life because you are habituated to the rejection of your love? Have you, therefore, made the mode of your daily life not to give love out of concern for being rejected?
>
> Blessed hearts, it is not a wise use of love to simply allow it to flow and then be abused. Love, wisely given, is a sacred transfer of a pearl of light from your heart to

the heart of the beloved, the friend, one in need. From the purest center of your Christ consciousness, send love to the purest center of those who are the children of God. And then you will never leave off loving—loving life free!

And when you reinforce your life with calls to the Archangels for protection, with a tube of light,* with calls to Astrea for the binding of the demons and discarnates that would steal your love and misuse it—when you do all of these things that you have learned and then meditate on greater and greater love, you will find that you will begin to feel like a new person, that the fuller expression of your own self will be the fruit of your loving others with this perfect Love.

With the transfer of the pearl to the heart of Christ in loved ones, the very warmth of the heart opens the pearl and releases the fragrance and the fervor of devotion for God. Thus, El Morya has taught: *Guard the heart!* And I would say: Guard the sendings of the heart! Guard the love of the heart! Guard the magnet of the heart!

Many of your problems of human habit will melt away when the creative fires of Love of the Holy Spirit flow forth from you abundantly and without reserve. You need not love human imperfection, but you ought to love the soul on the path of becoming whole. Therefore, give comfort to the soul in need of comfort.

The soul that has need may be the soul that is not perfected in love. Therefore, judge not—but give. And in your giving, be the healing of all life. Thus, I welcome you to Luxor for advanced training in the steps of the Master's walk with his disciples.[62]

---

*See Alchemical Energy Formulas, pp. 249–59.

## *Applying Spiritual Concepts*

Let us look at some of these spiritual concepts and how we might apply them in our lives. Many people have suffered rejection from friends, family, neighbors, fellow workers, supervisors or employers. Some people nurse wounded feelings for years without resolution. Others become angry and judgmental towards those who have rejected them. Which is worse?

From my own experiences and those of my clients, I have concluded that nursing our wounds or becoming angry and judgmental in the face of the insults simply adds to the pain. As we revolve the details of how we have been hurt, we reactivate the pain and intensify our wounded feelings.

What is the solution? I believe it is to extend the forgiveness of the heart even if the person on the receiving end is unaware of it or refuses to accept responsibility. And in order to do this we need to deepen the love of the heart.

We do this by loving God, by reminding ourselves that God loves us and by choosing to behave lovingly even when provoked. It also helps to remind ourselves that being true to our Higher Self is first priority and that the soul we most need to save is our own.

In my work, both spiritual and psychological, I am continually reminded that *love* is the universal solvent of pain and distress. Often when we feel hurt or resentful our soul is in despair and in need of love and support. I suggest that my clients put their arms around themselves and give their soul a loving hug. This is a way that we can comfort our soul and generate a spirit of love.

I teach my clients to dialogue with the soul to discover the deeper roots of their emotional pain. When they begin to dialogue with their soul, people often discover that their own self-rejection and the resulting pain of isolation is the major cause of their soul's pain.

I have found that the best remedy is to replace self-rejection with love and acceptance, so I remind my clients that God loves each of us unconditionally even as we love our children. And I explain that we can experience the current of divine love if we ask God's forgiveness for our mistakes, forgive ourselves our shortcomings and love ourselves as God loves us.

One way we can start loving ourselves is to kneel at the side of our bed each night to pray for loved ones and to thank God for the blessing of life and opportunity. Our prayers of gratitude place us in a receptive posture to welcome the return flow of God's love, which restores hope and trust in our soul and spirit.

### The Power of Love and Grace

Quaker philosopher Rufus Jones believes that all of us play a part in the working out of divine purpose, which is love, and that prayer can make us powerful channels of divine intent.

He writes:

> Atoms can reveal mathematics. Flowers and stars and mountains and sunsets can reveal beauty. The biological order can reveal life in its ascending series. Historical events can present a dramatic story that expresses and vindicates a moral order. But it is only through a concrete person who is divine enough to show love and grace in consummate degree and human enough to be identified with us, that we can be assured of love at the heart of things.[63]

Jones also refers to the *Satyagraha* of Mohandas Gandhi, saying:

> The soul-center of a pure, sincere person becomes, in Gandhi's view of life, a fountain of love and truth and wisdom, and when it keeps its selfish desires and its individual aims in complete abeyance so that the stream of life is pure, all the strength and love and truth of God flow through the soul of the person of that type. The soul becomes, in fact, a channel of the infinite Reality and an extraordinary center of energy.[64]

## Healing the Pain of the Soul

Here is an example from my files of how divine love can heal the pain of the soul. Melanie, a client, felt she had good reason to be depressed because the man she loved had rejected her and broken off their engagement. She went over and over it in her mind and she could not seem to move on with her life.

In her therapy sessions, we discovered that although Melanie is an accomplished musician, a loving person and has a number of caring friends, she did not love herself. And the rejection by her loved one was evidence in her own mind that she was basically flawed.

When her friends tried to comfort her by telling her she was a good person, she thought they were just telling her what she wanted to hear. She avoided her friends and dug herself into a deep ditch of despair.

I suggested that she dialogue with her inner child or her soul to discover the root of the despair. She decided she might as well try it because nothing else was working. She said that she realized this was more of a soul issue than only the breakup of the relationship.

She began the dialogue.

Melanie: I would like to talk to you, my soul. I think that the reaction to the breakup with Frank is more from you than from me. Am I right?

Soul: Yes, and I feel terrible about it. Frank was the man of my dreams, the one I knew could help me love myself.

Melanie: I love you. Does that help?

Soul: Yes, but it doesn't solve the fact that Frank doesn't.

Melanie: Why is it so important that Frank love you?

Soul: If he doesn't love me, I might as well give up on myself because he's a wonderful person.

Melanie: Why is it so vital for Frank to love you? Isn't it enough that God loves us?

Soul: No, he doesn't!

Melanie burst into tears. She sobbed and sobbed until she cried herself out.

"Melanie," I asked, "Why does your soul believe God doesn't love you?"

"I don't know, but it's something very deep," she replied softly. "Beloved soul, why do you think God doesn't love you?"

Her soul responded, "Because I'm bad, that's why!"

Melanie burst into tears again, but this time it did not last quite as long. And then she continued to talk to her soul.

Melanie: I really want to understand why you think you are bad. I don't love myself but I don't think I'm just plain bad!

Soul: I don't want to talk about it.

Melanie: Please, I really want to help.

Soul: Well, I got mixed up with bad people, and I don't see how God can still love me.

Melanie: When was this? I don't remember being mixed up with bad people.

Soul: You wouldn't unless you remember when I turned my back on God.

Melanie: I always had an uncomfortable vague feeling that something like that happened. Please help me remember so I can help you.

Soul: I didn't want to come into this body, and I was mad at God for not letting me stay in heaven. Last chance!

Melanie: What do you mean, last chance?

Soul: The spiritual advisers didn't exactly say that, but they were pretty definite that I had to get rid of my anger. And look at me; I'm nothing but a ball of anger. It's hopeless!

Melanie: Why are you so angry?

Soul: Well, if you must know, I'm angry that I have to get rid of my anger!

Melanie: Oh boy, Dr. Barrick, help!

I entered the dialogue and spoke softly to the soul. I asked her why it was so scary to get rid of the anger.

There were several minutes of silence while Melanie and her soul digested the question.

"How do you know it's scary to me?" her soul finally asked.

I responded, "Because I know Melanie and she is you in this life. And she's scared of her anger. And anger is usually a cover-up for some kind of vulnerability. I'm guessing that your vulnerability is fear. Am I right or wrong?"

Melanie burst into tears again. After a few minutes, she dried her eyes and we went on with the dialogue.

Her soul said, "Well, you're right, and I don't know how to get over that. I've been scared for a long time, and my biggest fear is that I won't get home to God."

"Do you realize that God loves you?" I asked.

"I don't see how he can," was the despondent reply.

"It seems to me that Melanie is a lovable person, and I don't see how she can have a soul that isn't lovable," I answered.

Melanie was quiet for a time, and then she said, "I think my soul is digesting that. And I am, too. Do you really think we are lovable?"

"Yes," I responded. "I do. And I think that if you started behaving lovingly toward yourself, you would begin to believe it."

Melanie smiled through her tears. "You got me on that one. I haven't been behaving lovingly toward myself ever since Frank rejected me. You know, I think I took that as if God was rejecting me. And when I got angry with Frank, I thought for sure that God would reject me. But then you threw me a curve by telling me God loves me. Do you really believe that?"

"Yes," I responded. "Because God loves all of us as his children, and he doesn't get angry just because we get angry. I believe that God wants you to be the loving soul that you really are. And that means replacing your anger with inner strength."

"How do I do that?" Melanie asked.

I silently asked God for help and shared with Melanie what came to me. "I suggest you ask God to heal the hurts that fuel your anger. And I also suggest you offer your soul a large dose of love mixed with an equally large portion of inner strength and behave as if you had already digested it."

Melanie closed her eyes. When she opened them, she smiled a little. "I feel better and so does my soul. I think you're right. I don't do a very good act with anger because that's not who I really am. I think it's a way I try to protect myself."

"That's a great insight," I responded. "What did God tell you when you were praying for him to help you?"

"He said that the way to develop inner strength is to be true to myself, my Higher Self, and to ask him what to do when I feel scared," Melanie responded.

"Are you willing to do that?" I asked.

"Yes! I'm sick and tired of being grumpy and depressed and waking up with a wet pillow!" Melanie exclaimed.

I couldn't help but chuckle, and Melanie did too. Laughter born of insight is an excellent replacement for anger.

Melanie started doing a serious turnaround, both spiritually and psychologically. She started a regular regime of prayer and talking to God. And she agreed to talk to her soul several times a week so that she would stay on track.

She decided that part of the anger was pent-up energy that needed expression. She joined a health club where she could get regular exercise. And when she felt herself getting angry, she would go for a run because, as she put it, "I can't be angry and run at the same time!"

Once she felt the anger dissipating, she would return home and do spiritual work to raise her consciousness. If the anger came up on a day when she could not go outside, she would run in place in her living room. She told me that worked well, too.

Gradually, Melanie developed a momentum on inner strength instead of sinking into anger or despair. As she told me during her final therapy session, "I love feeling my inner power! It's a much better way to handle life than sulking or exploding in anger. And my soul agrees with that little analysis!"

## *Affirming Our Spiritual Identity*

I believe that it is important for all of us to affirm our spiritual identity on a regular basis because it is so easy to become cynical or despairing about the troubled world in which we live. World events make it all too easy to dwell on the worst in other people as well as in ourself. We tend to get caught up in the negative dramas and forget that we are spiritual beings on an earthly journey and that we have a special mission to fulfill.

When we heed the intuitive prompting of our Higher Self and choose to be kind and loving to others, we affirm our true identity. When we center in our heart, we can behave lovingly even when other people are unkind. I believe that every intentional act of kindness and thoughtfulness does have a positive impact whether or not others acknowledge it.

Sometimes people who are preoccupied by a difficult life situation do not immediately respond to a kindness. Yet we have sent the vibration of love and kindness to them and at some level their soul and spirit are heartened. I have had clients tell me that even though they did not respond to someone's thoughtful gesture because they were so upset they were comforted inwardly and have always remembered that person with fondness.

I always encourage these people to let the other person know how much that gesture meant to them. They will feel good and the other person will be encouraged to continue being thoughtful even when people do not immediately respond. Simple thoughtfulness is a true blessing to the giver and the receiver. And as we practice it on a daily basis, we increasingly identify with our inner spiritual nature.

Each of us is called to be true to our Higher Self and to

fulfill our spiritual mission, a mission that is unique to our soul and spirit. And we can do this when we determine to unite with our Higher Self and love God with all our heart and soul. In a very natural way, our love for God transforms our human self and we find ourselves making a positive difference in the lives of family, friends and people we meet in our daily activities.

## Affirmations for Soul and Spirit

Affirming our higher nature on a daily basis can strengthen us and help us pursue the highest intentions of our soul and spirit. When we give affirmations we also remind ourselves we are sons and daughters of Father-Mother God. We reinforce our inner realization that no matter what our outer appearance may be, inwardly we are souls of light on earth for a heavenly purpose!

I suggest giving prayers and affirmations on a daily basis, coupling them with meditation on God's light and love as we ready ourselves for sleep or awaken in the morning. This form of worship is particularly helpful when we feel downhearted or at a loss for an answer to some knotty problem in our life.

When we commune with God and the heavenly hosts in this way, we visualize love and light all around us flooding our mind and heart, body and soul. The light of God raises our consciousness to higher levels, and the radiance of God and the intercession of the angelic hosts often bring insight and resolution to seemingly impossible human problems.

The sense of bliss we feel as God's love multiplies the love of the heart and uplifts our soul and spirit is beyond mere words. My prayer is that as we nurture our own soul and spirit and look upward to the heaven-world, we also choose to be a positive influence for those we meet along the road of life.

As we offer our prayers and affirm the light of God in soul and spirit, we raise our consciousness and vibration. And we ready ourselves to return Home to the heaven-world—in accordance with God's timing and the fulfillment of our divine plan. To this end, the ascended master Kuthumi, the master psychologist, has given his students the following "I AM" affirmations:[65]

### I AM LIGHT!

I AM Light, glowing Light,
Radiating Light, intensified Light.
God consumes my darkness,
Transmuting it into Light.
This day I AM a focus of the Central Sun.
Flowing through me is a crystal river,
A living fountain of Light
That can never be qualified
By human thought or feeling.
I AM an outpost of the Divine.
Such darkness as has used me is swallowed up
By the mighty river of Light which I AM.
I AM, I AM, I AM Light;
I live, I live, I live in Light.
I Am Light's fullest dimension;
I AM Light's purest intention.
I AM Light, Light, Light
Flooding the world everywhere I move,
Blessing, strengthening and conveying
The purpose of the kingdom of heaven.
AMEN

# 8
# Consciousness and Spirituality

*Live near to God, and all things will appear little to you
in comparison to eternal realities.*

—ROBERT MURRAY MCCHEYNE

My spiritual journey propelled me into my work as a minister and clinical psychologist. The more I focused on spirituality, the more I accessed higher consciousness. Today I find higher consciousness and spirituality to be thoroughly intertwined with my psychological techniques. For this, I am grateful!

Over the years, I have come to understand the "I AM Presence" as an expression of infinite reality and truth. When I am aligned with that state of consciousness, I find myself not having to think about what I will say next. An intuitive response comes to mind without my thinking or planning what I am going to say. And my clients respond accordingly.

When the mind and heart are focused on God, an insightful question, a helpful response and in-depth clarification occur without conscious deliberation. And that prompts me to realize anew that God is truly the divine therapist working through the consciousness of the practitioner and the client.

### *The Desire for Enlightenment: A Case Study*

As we have seen, at times clients may dialogue between two aspects of themselves in order to clarify their thoughts and feelings. They do inner child work or soul work depending on the way they describe it, e.g., "me and myself at a younger age" or "me and my soul."

I remember Wayne, a man in his sixties, who entered therapy, as he put it, "to achieve higher consciousness." He explained that financial crises were his Achilles heel—no matter how much he prayed, he would "get down in the dumps" over money.

He said, "I don't want to be constantly upset about money, no matter how much I'm making. But as soon as I have a slow month, that's all I'm thinking about—money, money, money!"

I asked, "Have you always been this concerned about your finances or is this a more recent development?"

"I think I've always worried about it but it's getting worse as I get closer to retirement age," he replied. "I can't retire yet because I wouldn't have enough income."

"Do you have any kind of retirement plan?" I asked.

"Yes, but it means tightening the belt," Wayne responded, "and I think my soul is even more upset about that than I am."

I suggested, "Why don't you ask your soul about the upset?"

Wayne sighed, "Okay, I thought that was what I needed to do and that's why I made the appointment."

"All right," I replied, "Why don't you close your eyes, meditate upon your soul, and ask her what she is upset about?"

Wayne was quiet for several minutes. Then he opened his eyes with a puzzled look on his face. "I don't quite get it," he said. "My soul seems to think the energy technique might help me understand."

"Well, why don't we take her at her word?" I replied. "The bilateral brain stimulation will help process whatever is going on. Let me know when you want to stop and talk."

We took the initial measures and began the bilateral brain stimulation. After several minutes, Wayne signaled that he wanted to say something.

"My soul believes that money is our safety net," Wayne reported.

I encouraged Wayne to dialogue with his soul out loud so that I could help as necessary.

"Why is money your safety net?" Wayne queried.

"If we have money, we can protect ourselves," his soul replied.

"Protect us from what?" Wayne asked.

"Protect us from rack and ruin," his soul responded.

Wayne looked baffled so I suggested, "I'm going to continue the bilateral brain stimulation and I suggest that you ask your Christ Self to help you understand what your soul means."

Wayne closed his eyes again and we resumed the bilateral brain stimulation. I prayed silently for divine direction for Wayne and his soul. After several minutes, Wayne signaled me to stop.

"Now I understand," he said with tears in his eyes. "I remembered a lifetime when I lost everything, became destitute and ended up dying of starvation. I think my soul is afraid it will happen again."

"No wonder she is upset," I responded. "I suggest that you put your arms around yourself and comfort your soul. Let her know that you understand her pain and that you have no intention of losing everything and becoming destitute again. And ask your Christ Self to help her understand."

We resumed the bilateral brain stimulation and it was a while before he signaled me to stop. When he did so, he was much more at peace.

"What happened?" I queried.

"I did what you suggested and had an amazing experience," he responded. "My soul was beginning to calm down. When I asked our Christ Self to help us, we were enveloped in brilliant light. It's absolutely the most blissful experience I have ever had. And we are going to trust God from now on."

"That's a wonderful resolution," I responded. "Let's check out any level of upset."

Wayne closed his eyes and meditated on the scene we had started with. "It's a zero," he announced with a grin.

"Great!" I replied. "Now that it's neutralized, what positive affirmation do you want to connect with the memory of that lifetime?"

"I am one with my Christ Self and I am moving on," Wayne smiled.

He gave the affirmation fourteen times as he connected it with the memory of the past life. When he opened his eyes, he said, "That's really true. I am one with my Christ Self and I am moving on! And my soul is at peace."

"Ask yourself, how true is the affirmation, on a scale of 1 to 7, when you remember the past life scene," I suggested.

Without hesitation, Wayne announced, "It's a 7!" That

meant it was completely true. We shook hands and ended the session.

This resolution of consciousness at the level of the soul was exactly what Wayne needed. He continued therapy until he could maintain and deepen his sense of inner peace even in the face of financial difficulties. And he smilingly told me that money is no longer his god and he is doing just fine on his retirement income.

## Action Based on Higher Principles

Most of us agree on a few basic principles: Preserving life is important, upholding one's honor is important, and diplomacy and arbitration are the best means of resolving our differences.

Yet, beyond a statement of higher principles, we also need enlightened action. We need to stand together to confront evil and uphold what is good. We need to stop nit-picking one another and agree to disagree instead of giving in to hatred or violence. And, above all, we need to uphold the spiritual principles of Jesus, Gautama Buddha and all of the enlightened ones who have gone before us.

In order to do all of this we choose to access our superconscious mind, the mind of our Higher Self, our Christ Self, our Buddha Self. At the level of the superconscious mind, we contact our ideals, our faith, our intuition, our inspiration, our higher wisdom, our sense of honor and destiny and the remembrance of our spiritual mission. From that perspective, we can make wise decisions and take positive action.

At the level of the conscious mind, we can focus on spiritual precepts, constructive concepts, positive and creative ideas and logical analysis when making decisions. We can choose to hold our negative emotional reactions in check. We can decide to honor the best in people instead of revolving their faults and to uphold with honor what we have been entrusted by family, neighborhood, church and professional colleagues. We can determine to be practical at the same time that we take constructive action.

When it comes to the subconscious mind, we can choose to pay attention to what is going on just beneath the surface of our conscious thoughts and feelings and note any tendency toward negative, narrow-minded or pedantic thinking. We can correct ignorance with information and the habit of revolving old hurts and opinions with forgiveness. And we can determine on a daily basis to correct the tendency to be unkind, inharmonious or hateful.

We can take to heart the words of Walt Disney's Thumper, Bambi's friend, and remind ourselves, "If you can't say something nice, don't say nothing at all!" If this creates a twitch of a smile in the corners of your mouth, that's good. Sometimes a touch of humor is all we need to break the spell of unkindness.

The unconscious correlates with the physical body. We need to tend our body with respect and pay attention to proper diet, exercise and cleanliness. And we can ask our Higher Self to bring to our conscious awareness any hidden flaws that we need to correct.

Once we do that, we need not be surprised if hidden flaws surface when we least expect them nor be dismayed if friends or loved ones point them out. We can decide to be grateful for the reminder because once we recognize a flaw in character or a negative aspect of behavior, we can choose to transform it.

Prayer is particularly helpful, along with the determination to heal our flaws and to develop new habit patterns.

God helps us to heal the errors inherent in the human condition when we do our part to correct them.

## *Looking in the Mirror of Self*

What we see in others is always in some way a reflection of ourselves, both the superior and inferior elements. If we value a superior quality in another person, we also either have or respect that quality or we would not notice it in another. If we are annoyed by an inferior quality in another person, we do well to reflect on how we may have that same quality in ourselves.

Seeing a reflection of one's negative qualities in another person is typically very upsetting, while noticing the positive aspects may be quite reassuring. Thus, all of us revel in companionship with people who reflect our best self, our constructive hopes and dreams. And we tend to turn off to people who reflect the problematic and reactive aspects that we harbor in our worst self, our destructive or negative self.

The negative dimensions of self frequently operate at subconscious or unconscious levels because most people prefer not to admit them at the door of conscious awareness. However, it is only when we dig them out and expose them to the light of truth that we can transform those negatives into positives. I have had clients who have chosen to go through this process because they really want to identify with their goodness instead of the temptations of "badness," their virtues instead of their flaws.

## *Steve and the Gang*

I remember Steve, who had joined a group of guys because he thought it was fun to do mischief. At first, the gang was only an annoyance to other people. Then the gang started hurting people who gave them any back talk. This prompted Steve to enter therapy.

He told me he did not want to hurt people. He had gotten in with the gang because he was a practical joker and that is what he thought they were up to. When he saw them beat up a man who did not appreciate the joke and threatened to go to the police, he was horrified but afraid to show his reaction.

Now he did not know how to get out of the gang without having them turn on him. As Steve said, "They are capable of really hurting people who turn on them. If I had known that, I would never have gotten in with them in the first place. And now I'm afraid it's too late!"

We talked about the fact that he had been drawn to that gang because it mirrored his own desire to create thrills and excitement. And we talked at length about Steve's alternatives and the potential repercussions.

The more Steve talked about the gang, the more certain he was that he had to get out before they demanded his involvement in illegal activities. He was afraid to go to the police for help because the gang would find out and beat him up. He did not think they had ever killed anyone but, as he put it, "They can do serious damage to a guy."

Steve was changing jobs at the time and had an out-of-state possibility, which was an answer to his prayer. He excused himself from gang activities by telling them he had to prepare for the job interview. He focused on updating his résumé and getting ready for the out-of-state interview. And he asked God to help him exit the gang without incident.

Fortunately, all went well with the interview and Steve was offered the job. As Steve told me, "It's like a grace that's being extended to me because I did a turnaround. I just want them to be stopped before they hurt anyone else. I'm going to clue in a friend I have in the police department."

Steve told his friend about the gang's activities before he left for his new job. And it was a good thing that he did. The police had been watching the gang and were planning to bust them as soon as they had the opportunity.

The police department gave Steve immunity for informing them about the gang's plans for vandalizing a local business. He left town, the gang was busted, and a very relieved Steve called to tell me the news.

He said, "You know, I think my guardian angel must have been watching over me so that I got out of that gang. I've learned a lesson I'm never going to forget. And I'm never going to forget that mirror thing you taught me about.

"You can't just hang out with people for the thrill of it and not get seduced by it, even when you know it's wrong, because you've got a part of yourself that is just like them. I'm one lucky guy to have learned my lesson and done a turnaround before it was too late! I just hope I haven't made too much karma by being in the gang even though I never participated in roughing anybody up."

I told Steve, "I think the fact that you turned over a new leaf, did your prayers and gave the police the information they needed to bust the gang stands in your favor. And I think you have learned an important lesson, that what you are attracted to is a mirror of some part of you—in this case a potentially criminal aspect of your consciousness."

I added, "I believe you need to ask God for forgiveness and to make a vow to your Higher Self that you will never flirt with evil again, no matter how exciting it might seem to be."

"Yes, ma'am!" was Steve's response. And he has been true to his word. He is fortunate to have been able to make a turnaround and start a new life. I think Steve's Christian upbringing and knowing that God answers our prayers was a big part of his successful turnaround.

## Redeeming Dark Thoughts and Motives

All of us can make a conscious decision to expose our dark thoughts and motives to the light of day and to redeem them. This process takes courage, an ongoing dedication to integrity and the constant outwitting of the dweller-on-the-threshold, who will take advantage of every opportunity to devil us into negative behavior. The pursuit of truth and oneness with the Higher Self is both heartening and reassuring to the soul and spirit.

There is nothing more distressing to the soul and spirit of a lightbearer than being untrue to our Higher Self. When we choose negative attitudes, thoughts or behavior, we are expressing the lowest levels of our consciousness. We are ignoring the values of our Higher Self and giving in to the dweller-on-the-threshold. By so doing we demean our soul and spirit and create a momentum on wrong motive, which leads us to ignore higher principles and to be subtly dishonest with ourselves. Consequently, we create a habit of negative behavior, which breeds a sense of inner dismay and leads to more negative behavior and self-destructive practices.

When we acknowledge the shadow, the unredeemed elements of our consciousness, we neutralize the polarity of duality.* And we begin to realize that all that is Real is one with God. As we do so, we begin to discern human good and evil and to align ourselves with God-good. I believe this is the meaning of Jesus' teaching to his disciples:

---

*Duality, as used here, refers to the doctrine that there are two mutually antagonistic principles in the universe, good and evil.

No man, when he hath lighted a candle, putteth it in a secret place, neither under a bushel, but in a candlestick, that they which come in may see the light.

The light of the body is the eye: therefore when thine eye is single, thy whole body also is full of light; but when thine eye is evil, thy body is full of darkness.

Take heed, therefore that the light which is in thee be not darkness.

If thy whole body therefore be full of light, having no part dark, the whole shall be full of light, as when the bright shining of a candle doth give thee light.[66]

Jesus' eye was single. He did not see the world in terms of polarity but from the whole-eye vision of God.

## *Claiming Higher Consciousness*

When we see flocks of birds flying overhead or herds of animals in fields or forests, we notice that they live and move together peacefully for the most part, unless it is mating season in which there is some dueling for position.

As lightbearers, we are called to cultivate a similar spirit of brotherhood at the same time that we plumb the depths of our soul and seek to unfold higher consciousness. Jesus told us, "Love thy neighbor," and if we study the major themes of the different religions in the world, we find a common thread of brotherhood, of loving one another, serving one another, being honorable toward one another.

Whether we follow the teachings of the Bible, the Qu'ran, the Bhagavad-Gita or the Buddhist scriptures, we find similarities in philosophy that are quite simple. All of them teach that it is good to love one another, to be kind, to be sincere, to be patient, to serve the best in one another. Why did the great teachers come to teach us these simple truths? Because while these precepts are simple in concept they are difficult to live by.

The ascended master Djwal Kul gave this instruction to his students:

> In many an Oriental rice paddy there stand blessed ones with feet bared and immersed in the chilly waters, as they endeavor to render their service which enables at least some of the teeming millions of lifestreams there to have their daily (and so much needed!) bowl of rice. These who do so serve enjoy to the full the warmth and comfort of the sun upon their bodies, all the while enduring the discomfort of the chilly waters which numb their lower limbs as they work.
>
> Now, as the light and warmth of the sun comfort the worker in the rice fields, so do many basic and elemental Laws of Life which have been revealed and accepted from all the great religions and philosophies of the world enable the average mind and consciousness to find certain peace and contentment—just in the considering of the simple aspects of Deity—i.e., the concept of heaven, God and his Son, the saints and the angels.
>
> However, as the lifestream begins to reach out for a more complete understanding of real truth (which begins to reveal to the seeker the expanding knowledge of Divine Law, as well as revealing the limitlessness of the realms of heaven and those who abide there), some of that "first born" happiness and spiritual elation which came with the first finding of truth may seem to take flight.
>
> This widening panorama—the increasing knowledge of truth, the necessity of bringing one's world into line with the Divine Law of balance and the limitless expanse of the realms above the human—all of this

seems at times to "overwhelm" the new student on "The Path." After such a stretching of his spiritual vision, he is inclined to long for the simple "bowl of rice"—the primary ideas of just God, heaven and the angels which may have comprised his original consciousness of Deity in this embodiment.[67]

I believe that most of us have the opportunity to live our higher precepts. However, we often do better with people we scarcely know than we do with our own families. Perhaps we get to know one another too well within the family circle. And yet, the family can be a profitable field in which to plant seeds of good and harvest higher consciousness.

Have you noticed that when you feel peaceful and happy, your family seems more peaceful and happy? I believe that is because when we send out good vibes we quicken similar vibes in other people. In keeping with the old saying, "Like creates like," we benefit our family and friends when we choose to cultivate good vibes.

How do we do this? We pray, we thank God for our blessings, we ask God to help us identify with our Higher Self. And we reflect on the blessings we have. If we are having a difficult time, we pray for illumination so that we can find a way to address the problems in a positive manner.

We create good vibes when we ask God to help us take the high road in every situation, to grant us the wisdom to pass our daily tests, the grace to handle disappointments courteously and the courage to express generosity in interactions with others.

We make more good vibes if we proceed as if our prayers had already been answered. We thank God for every blessing, we strive to pass our tests, we cultivate grace and courtesy and choose to be kind and loving to others—no matter how they act toward us.

I have found that when I do my part the universe contrives to make up the difference. I am often amazed at the shift in my outlook on life when I pray for God's help. Then I remind myself of the old saying, "If you are amazed at the love and grace of God, the thimble of your consciousness is too small!"

Ask yourself, "What is the size of the cup of my consciousness? Is it a thimble or a cup or a barrel?" If it is only a thimble, by choosing to treat others with love and kindness you not only fill the thimble but also a cup or a barrel. I believe that the angels pour out all of the love and grace of heaven when we ready ourselves to receive it. It's really all up to us!

## *Desire for Enlightenment: A Case Study*

I remember a lovely older woman who in her young adulthood had been quite worldly. She entered therapy to resolve her concern about what she now considered to have been "many mistakes," including sexual encounters outside of marriage.

Sylvia related her mistakes with a genuine sense of sorrow that she had so misused the sacred fire. Although she had prayed for forgiveness and forsaken her sexual escapades many years before, she was worried that she would not be able to make her ascension at the end of this life.

She asked me, "Do you think God has forgiven me?"

"God forgives us when we are honestly penitent and change the behavior," I replied. "I think the most difficult part is forgiving ourselves."

Sylvia responded, "I know that's true, but I still feel really bad about it. Do you think it would help me to do the

EMDR work on it?"

"Yes, I do," I responded. "If you are ready to let go of those records, the bilateral brain stimulation will help you do that. I truly believe that God forgives us when we pray for forgiveness. And I also believe that God wants us to forgive ourselves, learn our lessons and move on."

"Okay, I'm ready," said Sylvia. "I want to be done with this business of condemning myself."

"Why don't you focus on the moment that you still feel the most upset about in those sexual encounters?" I suggested.

Sylvia was thoughtful for a few minutes before responding. "I know what I want to focus on—it's the moment when I realized I had to turn my life around. I had just gone through another affair, which ended badly, and I was feeling terribly sorry for myself. And it's as though an inner voice said to me, 'Well, haven't you had enough of your mistakes and tears?' I was so ashamed of myself that I didn't even answer. I just cried and cried."

"That must have been a real wake-up call," I responded. "Let's go with that."

We took the initial measures and the level of her emotional upset was 10, extremely upset. She was still maximally distressed about that period in her life, which she had been revolving at a subconscious level ever since.

Sylvia focused on the moment when she had felt so sorry for herself, and we began the bilateral brain stimulation. Sylvia soon became quite agitated and I encouraged her to stay with it. She did so. Several minutes later, she signaled that she was ready to stop and talk.

She said, "I realize that I've been punishing myself by revolving this shame stuff. And I don't think that's very smart. Would you say a prayer for me?"

"Of course," I responded. I prayed to the angels of forgiveness to assist Sylvia to forgive herself and to be able to move on.

We continued the EMDR processing and Sylvia experienced a combination of grief and relief. When she signaled that she was ready to stop and talk, she said, "Well, that was really something! I realized that God was pouring out the grace of heaven upon me and I was so buried in my grief that I didn't perceive it. I can't believe I was so dense."

"Focus on that," I suggested and we continued. Sylvia went through tears and laughter as she began to see how she had held on to her human errors by revolving them, instead of simply accepting the forgiveness that she had been praying for.

"What a scene!" she exclaimed. "Let's stop for a moment."

Sylvia ruefully explained how she had decided she was not worthy of forgiveness and had continued to punish herself. "God forgave me. Why can't I forgive myself?" she exclaimed.

"Ask yourself that question," I replied. We resumed the process and she grimaced to herself but did not signal me to stop.

Several minutes later, she gave a big sigh and said, "Okay, let's stop."

"What is happening now?" I asked.

"Would you believe I was just being prideful and stubborn? I was playing God with myself. I flashed back to another lifetime when I had done the same thing and ended up making myself miserable until I died. What a waste!"

"How do you feel about it now?" I queried.

She answered with a little smile, "Actually I feel better because my soul told me she was sick and tired of revolving all of this junk and I had better let it go! So I did."

"Good," I responded. "Let's check on how we are doing. Remember the scene we started with and tell me how upset you feel about it now."

Sylvia was quiet for a moment or two. Then she said with a sigh of relief, "I don't feel very upset at all. I was kind of searching to see if that would change. But it didn't. I'd say I'm down to a 1 or 2."

"What's making it a 1 or 2?" I asked.

"Stubbornness," was Sylvia's immediate response.

"Okay, I suggest you focus on stubbornness," I replied.

After a brief set of bilateral brain stimulation, Sylvia opened her eyes and laughed. "Well, that was something. My soul told me, 'Okay, I'll give it up. I don't really like being stubborn.'"

"Good!" I replied. "What degree of upset do you feel now when you remember the scene we started with?"

Sylvia declared, "It's a big round zero!"

I responded, "Great! Now let's couple a positive affirmation with that scene. What would you like to affirm?"

"I love my soul and we are free!" was her quick response. She gave that affirmation fourteen times as she remembered the original scene. When she had finished, Sylvia thanked her soul for doing a turnaround.

Sylvia called a few weeks later to say that she felt like a new person. She also said that she was communing with her soul on a daily basis and her soul was at peace.

## Climbing the Ladder of Attainment

When we make in-depth soul-searching a regular practice in our life, we begin to refine our character and mobilize compassionate behavior. In this way the outer self, the self we show to other people, gradually becomes more and more an extension of the Higher Self. And we find ourselves on a higher rung of the ladder of attainment.

When we realize that the way we perceive other people is typically a projection of a part of ourself, we are on our way to neutralizing the polarity of duality and to experiencing oneness with God, oneness with the Higher Self and oneness with the universe.

As long as we see other people through the lens of our own consciousness, we cannot be totally objective in our perspective of them. If we would see beauty and wholeness in others, we do well to cultivate beauty and wholeness within ourself. To do this, it is necessary to discard or redeem the inferior elements of self. The more we cultivate this divine exchange, the more real we feel. And the more we touch the reality of oneness with God.

We realize that negative thoughts and projections are an expression of duality. They reveal more about the consciousness of the perceiver than whatever is being perceived. We are dualistic beings until we become Self-realized and have the singularity of the third eye, the eye of the Divine One. This is a goal for every lightbearer.

All of the great adepts and spiritual teachers reached their level of attainment through a one-pointed focus on God. They did it in different ways—some through meditation, others through spiritual intercession, others through simply giving glory to God for all goodness. One way or the other, the Great Ones learned to keep their mind and heart on God. When we choose to follow their example, we bless our own soul and those we encounter.

# 9
# Discernment of Good and Evil

*You can't turn off the darkness,*
*but you can turn on the light.*

—OLD SAYING

As we strive to keep our mind and heart on God we are called to discern good from evil. This is no small task today because the energies of good and evil are so convoluted that it is often difficult to tell which is which.

We can benefit from instruction Mark Prophet gave to his students about this dilemma.

He said:

> Beloved ones, mindful now of the cherished words of the Psalmist of old, "Yea, though I walk through the valley of the shadow of death, I will fear no evil: for thou art with me; thy rod and thy staff they comfort me," I would speak of the insidious mechanical grids and forcefields which exist invisibly but subtly in the planetary atmosphere....
>
> The lovely sweet earth upon which God has bestowed so much abundance has become a treacherous abode in

many unexpected places, for the very atmosphere itself has been charged with large floating grids or forcefields embodying crosscurrents of human thought and feeling. And the conflicting harmonic rate of vibration of these fields is such as to bring about great discomfort to elemental life as well as to mankind. . . .

As you know, precious ones, whenever an individual uses energy, and this always occurs whenever thought or feeling is exercised, the energy itself is not destroyed even after passing through the nexus of consciousness where qualification with bane or blessing occurs. Hence, energy is continually being released by all of mankind into the atmosphere.

### The Law of Harmonics

Now, because of the law of harmonics dealing with affinities, like seeks out like; and therefore, a strengthening occurs in the strata of misqualified energy as well as in that of properly qualified energy as line upon line of similarly qualified vibrations are added thereto.

Many have noted that in spiritual places, temples, and churches they can receive a greater inrush of peace than in the busy streets and businesses of the outer world; contrariwise, when entering into places qualified with feuds or destructive and trivial passions, mankind are often ensnared in feelings which do not sustain the vibratory action of God-happiness and peace. . . .

### Floating Grids and Forcefields

There do exist, then, in the atmosphere throughout the entire planet, floating forcefields or grids containing the scapegoat energies of mankind's wrong thought and feeling. These abide in larger quantities in the so-called ghettos of the large cities and such places as are rampant with the ravages of crime and poverty. Yet I can recall but few spaces upon the landed area of the earth where these large forcefields do not occasionally drift to bring about potential destruction where taken in. They are like floating minefields in the sea. Insidiously existing beneath the level of visibility, they drift to affect the unwary of mankind and to bring about results little dreamed of by most contemporary men....

I cannot deny some of them, by reason of size and density patterns, are particularly lethal and hence deadly to those who are unsuspecting and therefore unprotected against them. Just as a cloud will cover the face of the sun preceding a storm, so in many cases a sudden feeling or drop in the level of happiness or well-being will indicate the presence of such an invisible forcefield.

### Two Simple Defenses

There are two simple defenses available to mankind against these unseen pitfalls. One is to recognize that mobility can soon bring an individual into an area out of the center of the thrust; hence, many times a distance of one or two miles will give absolute safety. At other times, for various reasons when individuals cannot conveniently flee the invaded area, they can make mighty application to the Godhead, to the cosmic beings and the ascended masters, including beloved Jesus and Archangel Michael, for spiritual assistance in moving these forcefields away or transmuting them into light.[68]

## *Turn on the Light!*

In keeping with Mark Prophet's instruction, we need to be aware of the subtlety of darkness and do our best to discern it, particularly when it is cloaked in shades of gray.

Prayer and invoking the light are of major assistance in right discernment.

When life gets tough, I think of the old-fashioned revival hymn that had a refrain something like this, "I'm going to turn on the light!" And I think of that when I contemplate the complicated problems of our times. No matter how dark it may seem we can turn on the inner light—the light of illumination, the light of hope, the light of the Christ, the immanent presence of the Divine.

Where is the darkness on a bright, sunny day? Where is the darkness in a saint like Mother Teresa? Where is the darkness when people are upholding honor and virtue? The answer to each question is the same: In the light, darkness no longer exists!

Honor and virtue are qualities of lightbearers, people who honor the light of God. When we identify with the light of God, darkness has no power. We think about this when we are doing our daily choices. We ask ourselves, "What would Jesus do? What would Buddha do? What would my Higher Self do?" And we behave accordingly.

What if we don't feel like it? That is when we remember that "not feeling like it" may be coming from the dweller-on-the-threshold lurking just beneath the surface of consciousness. That dweller is sure to pop up when we hesitate to do what is right, ponder the lesser of two evils or choose expediency rather than higher principles.

Thus, we are wise to determine whether an action we are contemplating will be a step forward or backward on our spiritual path. And we need to consider the impact on other people. If we are convinced it will be benign or positive, all well and good, but often a seemingly innocuous action impacts other people in a hurtful way. In that case, we have made karma with those people, which we must balance sooner or later.

## Teachings of Jesus: the Beatitudes

Many of my clients find it helpful to remember the words of Jesus Christ to his disciples. As recorded in the Gospel of Saint Luke, before Jesus chose his twelve disciples he went to a mountain and prayed all night. In the morning, he called his followers together and chose twelve whom he named as his apostles.

Following that action, he came down to the great multitude of people who had come to hear him and to be healed. And without concern for saint or sinner, Jesus healed them all. He then gave instruction to his disciples, and that instruction came to be known as the beatitudes.

The Gospels of Matthew and Luke contain these teachings from what is known as the "Sermon on the Mount." I believe they are as apt and timely for civilization today as they were for Jesus' disciples two thousand years ago.

### Beatitudes: Gospel of Matthew

And seeing the multitudes, he went up into a mountain: and when he was set, his disciples came unto him:

And he opened his mouth, and taught them, saying,

Blessed are the poor in spirit: for their's is the kingdom of heaven.

Blessed are they that mourn: for they shall be comforted.

Blessed are the meek: for they shall inherit the earth.

Blessed are they which do hunger and thirst after righteousness: for they shall be filled.

Blessed are the merciful: for they shall obtain mercy.

Blessed are the pure in heart: for they shall see God.

Blessed are the peacemakers: for they shall be called the children of God.

Blessed are they which are persecuted for righteousness' sake: for their's is the kingdom of heaven.

Blessed are ye, when men shall revile you, and persecute you, and shall say all manner of evil against you falsely, for my sake.

Rejoice, and be exceeding glad: for great is your reward in heaven: for so persecuted they the prophets which were before you.[69]

### Beatitudes: Gospel of Luke

And he lifted up his eyes on his disciples, and said, Blessed be ye poor: for your's is the kingdom of God.

Blessed are ye that hunger now: for ye shall be filled. Blessed are ye that weep now: for ye shall laugh.

Blessed are ye, when men shall hate you, and when they shall separate you from their company, and shall reproach you, and cast out your name as evil, for the Son of man's sake.

Rejoice ye in that day, and leap for joy: for behold, your reward is great in heaven: for in the like manner did their fathers unto the prophets.[70]

## *The Importance of Civility*

I believe Jesus' teachings are relevant for all who seek to act with civility, a quality much needed in the world today. The dictionary defines civility as polite behavior, meaning behavior that shows refinement, courtesy, consideration and tact. These qualities create receptivity to one another's ideas and an open door to negotiating differences.

To cultivate civility, we interact with one another politely and respectfully. And if we couple civility with compassion, we add the healing balm of tenderness and mercy. I believe that to heal a world steeped in pain and suffering we must relate to one another with civility *and* compassion.

We refine our expression of civility and compassion by treating other people the way we want to be treated. This means extending loving-kindness, tolerance and understanding to others and doing our best to make amends when we make mistakes. And it means extending forgiveness to those who trespass against us and pray that they mend their ways.

When this kind of behavior becomes the norm in a group of people, we create community. This is in keeping with the spiritual meaning of the word "community," which is "come ye into unity." Unity means that we can disagree with one another in a respectful and truthful manner. A higher truth may emerge by talking through disagreements. I believe unity is at its best when good people unite in a common cause to support what is truthful, wise, compassionate and constructive in purpose.

Thus, when faced with a problematic situation, we are wise to ponder, "What is it I really want to achieve here? What higher standards do I want to uphold? What does that mean in terms of how I want to conduct myself?" As we contemplate our answers to these questions, we clarify our motives and intentions. Only then do we decide what action we want to take.

When we clarify our motives and intentions and match them with higher standards, our subsequent actions will likely reflect both civility and compassion. If despite our best intentions we find ourselves in the "heat of a battle" in the problematic situation, we will be able to maintain our attunement and make wise decisions.

Once we set our course of action there is another vital

step, which is to confirm our goals and intentions with the Higher Self. We center in our heart, pray to our favorite saint or meditate on the light and ask our Higher Self, "Am I being true to myself and to my God? Am I in the right vibration? Am I congruent with right intention? Am I setting the right goals? Am I making the best decisions? Am I taking right action?"

I suggest writing down your answers to these questions as you receive them intuitively during your communion with God. It is all too easy for divine direction to slip away from us once we return to our everyday life and interaction with other people. However, when we write down our understanding immediately following our communion with God, we find it relatively easy to follow through with appropriate action.

Once we have taken action, we check in with ourselves again, "Am I at peace with the way I handled the situation?" If so, we know we did the best we could. If not, we analyze the process and make notes of what we will do differently the next time around.

If we have not handled the situation to our satisfaction, the mistakes may be attributable to the not-self, the conglomerate of underlying negative motives, attitudes, thoughts, feelings or impulses. When the not-self surfaces unexpectedly, it is often difficult to behave in a positive constructive manner.

We outwit the tricks of the not-self by choosing to correct our mistakes and apologize for any inappropriate behavior. Here is an example of a young man who came face to face with his not-self in a challenging situation in the business world.

### *Civility and a Corporate Deal*

Bruce, a client of mine, learned about the tricks of the not-self when he was assigned to work with a valuable client who was known for his volatility. Bruce bungled a negotiation with the client by losing his temper when the client insulted his ego.

As Bruce told me, "This guy acted like I didn't know what I was talking about. He kept reminding me of facts and figures I already had in mind, like I was some kind of a new kid on the block who didn't have his act together."

"How did you handle that?" I asked.

Silence for a long minute. I could see that Bruce did not want to talk about his mistake and yet that was why he had come in for a session. So I just waited.

Bruce finally muttered, "Well, I lost my temper, which was stupid. And then it went from bad to worse. He walked out on me, and I'll have to do some fancy footwork or I'll lose the deal."

"Is there any way you can mend fences?" I asked.

"Sure, if I eat crow and let him lord it over me!" Bruce grumbled.

"Bruce, you didn't come in just to complain about this guy, no matter how insulting he might have been. Have you thought about what you might do to resolve the situation?" I asked.

Bruce was silent before responding, "Yes, I've thought about it, but I've got to get past being so mad at him. Can you help me with that?"

"I'll try," I responded. "Let's take a look at what you're mad about. It sounds like you were ticked off because he was reminding you of what you already knew. Why did that make you so angry?"

Long silence, but Bruce was obviously thinking about it. "He's actually a lot like my grandfather who lived with us when I was growing up. He second-guessed everything I did, and my parents told me I had to be polite to him no matter what. When I think about it, this guy was very similar. I'd make a point and he would pick it apart. I'd make another one, and he already knew that, et cetera, et cetera."

"Did you ask him what information he needed from you?" I queried.

"Well, no, I already knew ahead of time what he was coming in for, so I had the facts and figures ready for him. And then he sat down and proceeded to tell me what to do. I couldn't even get a word in edgewise!" Bruce was heating up again.

"Whoa, there," I said. "Listen to yourself. Isn't he the client? Aren't you meant to answer his questions and respond to his agenda? It sounds to me like you had your agenda, he had his, and you were ticked off because he wouldn't follow yours. But he's the client. He hired you, not the other way around. Right?"

Bruce was on the edge of losing his temper. I thought I might as well keep going or he would not see how he had triggered the drama. And if he did not get it, he was likely to have to leave the firm. I knew he did not want to do that. So, I reminded him that losing his temper was what had ruined his relationship with the client.

Bruce was silent for a while, both angry and chagrined. He finally responded, "Okay, okay, I get your point. I've always had a problem with my temper and I need to figure it out or it's going to cost me my job. I think you're right about this relating to what happened with my grandfather.

I can't believe I'm still reacting to that but I can see that I am. How do I get out of this mess? Do you think it would help to do EMDR?"

"Yes, I think that's a good idea," I responded. Bruce chose to do the bilateral brain stimulation with the headset so he could close his eyes and get back into the situation with his grandfather.

I prayed for Bruce to contact whatever was triggering his temper reactions and we began the bilateral brain stimulation. After a short time, Bruce signaled he wanted to talk about what he was experiencing.

Bruce had gone back to a time in his teens when his grandfather had disciplined him severely without checking into what had really happened. Bruce had tried to explain but his grandfather did not want to hear it. To add insult to injury, the grandfather told Bruce's parents his version and they would not listen to Bruce's explanation.

That settled it for Bruce, who was already upset about being polite to his grandfather no matter what. He withdrew from the family, made it a point to stay out of trouble even if he was harassed and left home as soon as he was of age. He had little contact with the family from then on, and his parents never understood what happened because he did not explain.

We continued the energy work and Bruce processed a number of hurtful situations that had been sitting unresolved beneath his conscious awareness. He began to feel much more peaceful. When we went back to the scene with the grandfather, his emotional reaction had diminished markedly.

The next time we stopped to talk, he told me, "I've been going through a number of related situations. I can see how that drama with my grandfather set in motion a whole chain of reactions in me, and I never really looked at it. I think when I reacted to my client it was like he was my grandfather all over again. Actually, he just wanted to set the terms, which he had a perfect right to do. Thank God, I'm beginning to see where all of this has been coming from."

We went on with the EMDR session until Bruce felt at peace with himself and with the original drama with his family. The positive affirmation he wanted to connect with the neutralized drama was "I will be true to myself and honorable with my family."

Then we went back to the recent event with the client and checked out Bruce's emotions with respect to that scene. Bruce said there was still a bit of annoyance but on a scale of 0 to 10, where it had been a 10 it was now a 3. I asked him, "What's making it a 3? What's still there?"

Bruce replied, "I behaved like a high school kid instead of a professional."

"Okay," I replied. "Focus on that."

The next time we stopped, Bruce said it was now down to a 1 and he wasn't sure what was still there.

I suggested, "I wonder if you need to ask forgiveness and forgive yourself?"

"I'll try that," Bruce said. "I think you're on the right track."

As we continued the bilateral brain stimulation, Bruce consciously asked God to help him and felt a return current of light, which greatly encouraged him. He thanked God and focused again on the situation with his client. After a period of time, he smiled, stretched and said, "Okay, let's talk about it."

"What happened?" I asked.

"That was great!" he responded. "I visualized being with

the client and apologizing to him, and now I feel okay about it."

"Let's go back to the original scene," I suggested. "How upset do you feel now on the scale from 0 to 10?"

"It's a zero!" Bruce responded with a grin. He was ready to apologize to the client and correct his own behavior.

Bruce was as good as his word; he contacted the client and made his apologies. The client was also relieved. He told Bruce, "I have a temper myself or I wouldn't have walked out on you. Let's shake hands and move on."

When he came in for a follow-up session, Bruce told me he and his client were working well together and his superiors were pleased with the outcome.

Bruce remarked, "Maybe it was a good thing all of this happened. Otherwise, I don't know if I ever would have resolved it because I didn't realize the situation with my grandfather was fueling the whole thing. I'm going to see what I can do to repair that situation. And I'm going to be a hawk-eye about not letting my anger rip. It's simply not worth it!"

Several months later Bruce filled me in on what had happened with his family. He had decided to apologize to his grandfather and his parents and explain why he had withdrawn from the family. Instead of blaming his grandfather, he simply told them that he had not been grown up enough at the time to handle the situation properly. And that he regretted the pain he had put them through.

Much to his amazement, Bruce's grandfather said he had a bad habit of being overbearing and was mightily relieved to make peace. His mother cried with relief and both mom and dad gave Bruce a hug and welcomed him back into the family circle.

Bruce told me, "My only regret is that I waited so long to clear all of this up. Changing my own outlook made all the difference, on the job and in the family. I've learned an important lesson and I'm turning my life around. I'm making it a point to check in with my Higher Self on a regular basis. And if you want to put this drama in one of your books, go right ahead. Just disguise the details and my identity if you don't mind."

I told him, "Okay, Bruce, I'm really proud of you. If I do put you in one of my books, you will likely recognize yourself, but no one else will. May God bless and keep you in his loving care, and congratulations on your turnaround and big win!"

## *The Power of Prayer*

Another client, Joan, came to see me after having a serious quarrel with her business associate. She was angry with herself for making a wrong decision that resulted in losing a client and then getting angry with her associate when she was called on it.

Once we talked it over, Joan realized she had set herself up by not correcting herself immediately when the client challenged her. She said, "I was embarrassed about it and lost my cool. I don't blame the client for walking out.

"I'm going to take your suggestion and build in a 'stop reflex' and practice it in benign situations. Then I'll be prepared for the big ones. I can see that I tend to jump to conclusions and quick action. And that is not good.

"I think that if I excuse myself from a problematic situation, take a deep breath and ask God for guidance, I'll make better decisions. And I'm going to try one more time to make peace with our client. I was wrong and I'm going to tell him so."

Joan called several days later to say that the conversation with the client had gone well. She said, "He's reconsidering his decision, which he admitted he made out of temper. What a big lesson this turned out to be for both of us! I've also learned that it's better to admit and correct a mistake. And that's a lot easier to do if I am attuned to my Higher Self. I'm putting a note on my mirror to remind me."

She added, "I am going to make it a point to pray for patience and discernment in the workplace and in my life. I can see that most of the problems I have are the result of quick judgments in reaction to other people instead of taking a step back and asking God to help me discern the best course of action."

When we pray with love and sincerity we become a powerful conduit for the outpicturing of divine intent. And when we attune to the return current of God's love, we experience a lifting of spirit and a strengthening of resolve—and our soul is raised up in the bliss of divine reality once known and now remembered.

# 10

# Tapping the Wisdom of the Heart

*The power of the heart
conquers (achieves) absolutely everything.*

—EL MORYA

*M*any people agree in principle that the wisdom of the heart is wiser than the mind. Why? Because the mind is usually preoccupied with everyday matters, logical thinking and mental assessment, while the heart is attuned to our higher consciousness, intuitive understanding and the purposes of the soul.

We can transform negative motives, thoughts and feelings by contacting the wisdom of the heart and balancing the threefold flame that burns on the altar in the secret chamber in our heart. Mrs. Prophet has instructed that this inner flame is a source of divine power, wisdom and love.

She taught:

> We draw upon this inner flame every time we take action from the loving, spiritual part of ourselves. It is the fire, the verve, the creative spark that imbues our

finest thoughts and feelings, words and deeds. This flame is spiritual power—the power to change our own lives and ultimately to change the world.

### The Divine Spark Is the Light of the Saints

Your divine spark is the same universal light that has burned in the hearts of the saints, adepts and masters of East and West. The only difference between their flame and our flame is its size and intensity. The more intense the flame, the greater the endowment of light. The greater the light, the more power we have to become living transformers of love.

Like the great revolutionaries of the Spirit, we can increase the size and intensity of our spiritual flame and our empowerment of love. The mystics have given us several formulas to expand that light. Their formulas involve the exercise of heart, head and hand, because we don't expand the flame only through meditation and prayer. We also expand it through the practical application of our heart—the actions we take every day to meet another's need. . . .

### Harnessing the Fires of the Heart

The revolutionaries of the Spirit have discovered how to harness the fires of the heart. Through the white-hot heat of meditation and prayer, we too can release the imprisoned lightning of our heart.

Our meditations in the secret chamber are very private experiences. They start with moving our attention from what's happening around us and going within— "all the gates closed, the mind confined in the heart," as the Bhagavad-Gita says. Christian tradition calls it recollection, withdrawing the mind from external affairs and placing our attention on the presence of God within.

When we go within by devotion and love, we contact the inner flame and commune with the energy that is God. "The little spirit spark of our personal identity is the key that connects us with the Universal," Mark Prophet once said. "[God's] Spirit is the fabric of our world. His energy, his pattern is the only saving grace. We ourselves have to reidentify, reintegrate, repolarize ourselves with that light—and it's got to be done consciously."

### Prayer and Meditation: An Entrance to the Heart

Through prayer and meditation we turn our attention back to the inner light, which is the real source of our being. We become drenched with light—renewed, refreshed and replenished—so we can give more of the light to those who need it. We build up our reservoir of love. As we commune with our Higher Self, who sits on the throne in our heart, we can also access the wisdom of the heart to find solutions to knotty problems.

The mystics advise us to combine our meditations with spoken prayer that comes from a heart on fire with love. For instance, the Zohar instructs, "Whatever a man thinks or whatever he meditates in his heart cannot be realized in fact until he enumerates it with his lips." The spoken word activates the fruit of our meditation upon the Divine and coalesces it in the physical.

Every spiritual tradition has its own beautiful methods for entering the heart through prayer and meditation—from the quiet recitation of sacred words to the dynamic repetition of mantras to the inspired singing of devotional songs, like bhajans.[71]

Thus, we understand that the threefold flame in the secret chamber of the heart is our connection with the Higher Self and with the Father-Mother God, and we align ourselves with the Higher Self when we worship, pray and give mantras and decrees.

Mrs. Prophet taught her students to ask God to balance and expand their threefold flame so that they would be able to be strong, wise and loving in every circumstance, no matter how problematical everyday life might be.

### *Coupling the Heart's Wisdom with Nonattachment*

In today's world, there are many issues, some of which impact us directly. My clients often tell me they feel bombarded or stressed out by problematic situations at home or at work. And when they get caught in a whirl of confusion, they find it difficult to make wise decisions. I offer help through stress-reduction techniques, but I also suggest that they draw upon their spiritual resources.

Sometimes we may simply center in our heart and find peace in that way. At other times, we may need to couple heart-centeredness with nonattachment, the teaching of the Buddha.

Jolene came in for a session to address her reaction to a major quarrel in her family. She was not involved in the turmoil and had done what she could to calm the storm, but several family members were still not speaking to each other.

She told me, "I've done my best to play peacemaker but they aren't responding. I think they actually enjoy making each other mad. And that gets to me!"

I responded, "I understand how disappointing that must be. What would happen if you simply observed what was going on instead of reacting to their quarrel?"

Jolene asked, "How could I do that?"

Since she is a client who is into spirituality, I replied, "I believe you could do it by practicing the nonattachment of the Buddha. If you'd like to try it right now, I'd suggest that you center in your heart and ask Gautama Buddha to help you."

"Okay," Jolene responded.

We were quiet for a few minutes, and then Jolene said, "I've done that. And I'm feeling a bit more peaceful. What do I do next?"

"I want you to imagine that you are one with the Buddha as you bring to mind the situation you have been describing," I replied. "And remember that as the Buddha you are nonattached to what is happening—you are simply observing the situation with compassion. Stay with it for a bit, and then we'll talk about it."

Jolene nodded that she understood, closed her eyes again and entered into her meditation with the Buddha. I joined her in meditation and we were silent for a while.

Jolene opened her eyes and smiled, "I feel better," she said softly. "I feel a oneness with the Buddha and a loving compassion for my family. I realize that they are going through a drama of their own emotions and I can't resolve that for them. And I had another insight, that if I continue to ask Gautama Buddha to help me and my family, I will be helpful to my family inwardly."

"I believe you are absolutely right," I responded. "That's the best gift you could give them because Gautama is such a loving, peaceful being. You can pray for peace and harmony at the same time that you observe with nonattachment."

Jolene left the session relieved and said she would let me know what happened as a result of her continued meditation with Gautama and cultivation of nonattachment.

Several months later Jolene called to tell me that members of the family were talking to each other and that although there was still some tension she was not being drawn into it. She told me, "I'm continuing to practice observing. And it's a joy beyond words to feel the overshadowing presence of the Buddha!"

## Cultivating the Wisdom of the Heart

As we strive to keep our balance in challenging times, we also benefit our soul and spirit by cultivating the wisdom of the heart. Although everyone's experience is unique, when I contact the heart's wisdom I have a feeling of warmth and tingling in my chest. And when I close my eyes to deepen the feeling, I become aware of brilliant light and a sense of inner joy. In this state of consciousness, I feel love and compassion for all life and have insights and realizations beyond my normal state of consciousness.

Intuitively I know what I am to do next or the answer to the question I have been pondering. My mind is clear as a bell and there is a contact with a higher level of consciousness. The answers I receive are wise and logical, and I feel at peace with myself and all life.

However, if I do not immediately make a note of what I have just experienced, the details tend to slip away from me. I realize that I have tuned into a higher dimension in which everything is perfectly clear. When I am no longer tuned into that realm, the details are not that obvious. So, I try to write down my experiences and insights as soon as possible, even if it is in the middle of the night!

Following such an experience, my mind is clear and I am no longer burdened with the debris of the day. I am at peace, my heart sings with joy and I am attuned with my Higher Self. The memory of these uplifting moments helps me handle the daily ups and downs of life and is a comfort to my soul.

The ascended masters teach that the physical heart is connected energetically with the spark of the divine, the three-fold flame of divine love, wisdom and power, in the secret chamber of the heart. They advise us to develop not only intellectual perspective, but also heart perspective.

In her mini-book *Alchemy of the Heart*, Mrs. Prophet gives this instruction:

> Heart perspective is consciously thinking, feeling, acting and breathing through the heart. Whatever you do, even if it's serving someone a cup of tea, it can be an extension of your heart. Heart perspective will change the way you treat others, the way they treat you, and the way you treat yourself. Heart perspective invites honesty and breeds compassion.
>
> A wise monk was once asked by his companions what they should do if they saw a fellow monk snoozing during prayer time. "Should we pinch him so he will stay awake?" they asked. The monk replied, "Actually, if I saw a brother sleeping, I would put his head on my knees and let him rest." That's heart perspective.
>
> When we have heart perspective, we are committed to keeping a warm, open place in our heart where someone who is in pain feels safe to enter. Heart perspective is that creative genius that looks for ways to inject love into every challenge. It inevitably finds a unique and higher solution to a knotty problem....
>
> We have plenty of opportunities to practice heart perspective. In a competitive world where so many people feel compelled to go straight for the jugular vein, we have the opportunity to go straight for the heart. You may be thinking, you may be speaking, you may be feeling, but see yourself doing all of this through your heart until you feel as though it is your heart (and not your

head or your ego or your defense mechanisms) that is thinking, speaking and feeling. This takes practice, but it can be done.[72]

This instruction is practical in our personal life and in the business world. When we relate to friends, clients and colleagues with kindness, we set the stage for compassion and mutual support. And we are more likely to achieve our goals. When we tap the wisdom of the heart and are kind and thoughtful to people we encounter, we soften the harshness that one so often experiences in the world today.

Of course, this does not mean we forget the logic of the mind; we partner mind and heart to address problematic issues. The mind is skillful in assessing facts, establishing priorities, resolving complexities and carrying out logistical details. We tap the heart to cultivate relationships, resolve differences and interact with courtesy and diplomacy.

I believe a partnership of mind and heart is the most effective way of achieving our objectives, whether in business dealings or in our personal lives.

## *Arbitrating Our Differences*

Individuals who are involved in complex situations and difficult transactions often wonder how they can keep their cool and still obtain their business objectives. I usually suggest that they do their best to understand the other person's point of view and maintain a willingness to arbitrate any disagreements.

One of my clients came in for a consultation because he had been caught in the crossfire when his company merged with a larger corporation. Todd had been highly valued in his old company, but now he found himself at loggerheads with a new supervisor after the merger.

Todd told me, "I'm trying to get along with Sam, but it's a real challenge. He insists that I put my reasoning and logistical tactics in writing, which I've never had to do before. And that's such a time-waster. I don't think he trusts me even though I haven't done anything wrong and I've clinched several important contracts. I feel like I always have to watch my back."

"Are other people in your company having similar problems since the merger?" I asked.

"Yes, they definitely are," replied Todd. "Sam has supervisory authority over three of us and we're all under the gun. I don't know if it's worth it to keep trying to please this guy or if I should start looking for another position. I have a good résumé, and a few months before the merger I was contacted by another company. But I'd like to see if I can work something out with Sam before I do that because I like my work and the guys I work with. Do you have any advice?"

"I suggest you sit down with Sam and talk it over," I responded. "Maybe he doesn't realize how he's coming across. If you do decide to have a talk with him, it would be important to be diplomatic as well as straightforward."

"I suppose it's worth a try," Todd responded thoughtfully. "I hadn't considered that he might not be aware of how he comes across."

I added, "If you definitely want out of the situation, I'd say go ahead and give notice, but it sounds like you would like to work it out. That's why I'm suggesting that you put your concerns on the table."

We discussed the pros and cons and Todd went over the points he wanted to clarify. With a sigh of relief, he said, "Okay, that sounds like a reasonable approach. I'm going to try it. I'll let you know how it turns out."

After several weeks, Todd called to tell me that he and Sam had mended fences and he was staying with the new company.

"I was really surprised," Todd explained. "Sam was much more open that I thought he would be. It turns out that he hasn't had that much experience as a supervisor, but when the merger came he was promoted. And that's how he ended up in his supervisory position. Sam told me he was pleased with my work but he needed documentation in order to fulfill his role as the supervisor. That's why he wanted everything written down."

Todd added, "When I explained my view of the situation, Sam was somewhat chagrined that he had created the impression of not trusting me. And he was visibly upset when he asked me if he had come across too strong to any of the other guys and I had to say yes. Anyway, we ended up having a good talk and he's really trying to mend fences. So I'm going to stick around for awhile."

"Hey, that's great!" I responded. "It sounds like you did yourself and the men you work with a big favor by taking the bull by the horns."

Todd laughed and responded, "You're right. I feel pretty good about it. I wanted to let you know how it's been going. And thanks for helping me think it through and encouraging me to be straightforward with Sam. It was the right move. I'll keep you posted on how it goes from here on."

Six months later, Todd called to let me know that he had received a promotion and would definitely be staying with the new corporation. He told me, "I learned a big lesson through this experience—that it's better to stand up and be counted than to opt out!"

So many times, we make assumptions about other people rather than giving them the benefit of the doubt. Todd was pleased that by talking the situation over with Sam instead of putting in his resignation, he had actually done a good turn for Sam as well as benefiting himself and his colleagues.

## *Implementing Higher Principles*

Many people are serious about their higher principles and implementing them in daily life, including on the job. Although this is not the easiest task in today's corporate world, it can be done if a person centers in the heart, thinks from the head and exercises good judgment.

Jeremy, a client of mine, called for an appointment because he was in trouble with his boss for discussing religion with a colleague who had similar interests. Although this occurred during a lunch break, another employee overheard the conversation and reported Jeremy for "proselytizing" in the workplace.

Jeremy had a good relationship with the boss and explained to him that he and his colleague were simply exchanging points of view. However, the boss explained that such discussion was best done away from the workplace. If they wanted to talk about their religious beliefs, they needed to do so at home or in church.

Jeremy told me the story, adding with exasperation, "I guess separation of church and state applies to the lunch hour, too! I decided to come in for a session because I need to figure out whether I want to keep a job where there is this kind of scrutiny."

"How important is the job to you?" I asked.

"Well, it would be a challenge to find one with the same

opportunities and benefits unless I move to a larger city. I think that's part of the problem around here—everybody knows everybody else. And the other factor is that the guy who reported me wants my job. My boss clued me in about that and said that was why he was talking to me—he wants me to stay on the job."

Jeremy added, "Our country, even the pledge of allegiance to the flag, is based on religious principles: 'One nation, under God, indivisible, with liberty and justice for all.' That's the kind of principle I'd like to see in the workplace!"

We talked over the pros and cons at length, and Jeremy decided to heed his boss's advice because he really did like his job. However, at the close of the session, he remarked, "I'm going to be keeping my eyes and ears open for other opportunities because I still don't like this watchdog bit when I'm on a lunch hour!"

This situation had a humorous conclusion. After our discussion, Jeremy made it a point not to discuss religion on the job. Then came the day when, to Jeremy's delight, a major client told Jeremy's boss that the reason the firm got his business was that he respected Jeremy as a solid church-goer. The client added, "There are too few firms who uphold religious values!"

## *The Psychological Impact of Energy*

The great adepts and teachers who have walked the earth have demonstrated how to live by their actions, words and deeds. And their teachings have been simple yet profound. They have taught us to honor one another, which is not only a spiritual ideal but also practical if we are trying to be true to higher principles. When we respect one another, lead from the heart and give other people the benefit of the doubt, we usually come to a meeting of the minds.

All of us identify with our own consciousness, and we are sensitive to circumstances that we interpret as an affront. Yet, if we put ourselves in the place of the other person, we can usually figure out why that person is reacting in a certain way. If we are sensitive to the needs and goals of the other person, we can usually maintain our poise while fostering a meeting of the minds.

We may be having a difficult time because of the psychological impact of negative energy in a situation. Most people feel uncomfortable with negative energy and uplifted by positive energy. Simply recall how you feel when you turn on the TV and find only murder and mayhem. This is likely in stark contrast to how you feel when you discover a program that is humorous, positive or uplifting. That is when most of us breathe a sigh of relief and say, "Yessss!"

The ascended master Kuthumi has given spiritual instruction about our energy levels and how they relate to the self and to the soul.

He gave the following teaching:

> In order to create a more crystal-clear picture of the self, we wish to discuss the self in terms of energy levels. The parable of the talents reveals that individuals vary according to the gifts given unto them. This is also true of energy levels. Health, karma, and aspiration are among the various factors that govern the abundance of energy one has at his disposal. Energy levels also vary within the framework of a norm—a high and a low.
>
> Most individuals do not realize that the potential of the self is related to the quantity and quality of the energy which they use. Very little progress in the study of

the self has been made by mankind, for they have not
known just how to proceed. For instance, the idea of the
soul has been preserved as a sacred cow. Men have not
considered the soul as energy bestowed. They suppose
that the soul is a unique but undefined quality of reality.

### The Energetic Nature of the Soul

If you will think of the nature of the soul as the
nature of God and consider the facts (1) that God is
boundless energy, (2) that man has been given a limited
quantity of God's energy, and (3) that the energy which
he has been given does comprise the content of the soul,
you will be on the right track in your investigations of
the self.

Jesus warned that men could lose their souls,[73] and
of course there are many trials and taxing situations
which may deplete the amount of energy available to the
individual. I do not say that all energy used by man comes
from the soul, for as you know man's supply of every
good and perfect gift is from above.[74] But I do relate
soul energy to the temporal manifestation of identity.

### Karma: The Governor of Energy Flow

This soul energy, or solar energy, is limited in quantity—some having a great deal more of it than others.
"As a man soweth, so shall he reap."[75] Therefore, karma
acts as the governor, in part, of the flow of man's energy
from his Presence just as it regulates the amount of soul
energy given to the lifestream at the beginning of each
embodiment....

The more energy a person has, the more he is apt to
attract; and the less he has, the less he is apt to attract.
The need to purify one's energies becomes more and more
apparent as the individual sees that his life potential is

dependent upon the quality of his energy. Actually a great deal of energy which was once his to use is now imprisoned in the imperfect patterns of his own human miscreations. Like money in the bank which has been pledged as collateral, this energy cannot be withdrawn until one's spiritual obligation has been met. . . .

### Releasing Tensions—Redeeming Energy

Those who treat the mind or emotional nature of man know full well that where there is a drop in energy levels, where fatigue occurs, there is a much greater tendency to mental disorders.

What man must do, then, is learn how to release himself from tensions—physically, mentally, and emotionally. He must learn to use all of the energy which God has given him, some of which is in a state of rest and some of which is in a state of movement. He must learn to undo the misqualifications of energy for which he bears responsibility; he must learn to requalify that which has been misqualified. This will give him a greater quotient of energy that can be used in the development of true soul consciousness, for the purposes of life are that man might master the universe through first mastering himself.

### Attracting a Greater Portion of Divinity

In a very real sense the spiritual energies of the divine image are reflected in the mirror of mortal consciousness. These energies bring about the advent of soul force within the lifestream, but they must be continuously augmented in order that the expanding soul may attract a greater portion of divinity to the life of the individual.

All undesirable karmic manifestations return to their point of origin—which is the individual being of man—

when the attractive force within him, whether qualified with good or ill, has reached a certain intensity. Therefore, it is well that individuals recognize the fact that when they draw to themselves the higher nature of being, they are also drawing a definitive quantity as well as a definitive quality of energy that will serve to fortify the being of man against the day of karmic reckoning when all negatives and positives must be adjusted.

### The Supreme Art of Transmutation

In our considerations of man's energy potential we are concerned with both quality and quantity. Although it is true that the Absolute is all and, therefore, possesses all (in a sense being possessed by all), the universal desire for the manifestation of purity by the self—whether it be the desire of the macrocosmic Lord of the Universe or the desire of the individual monad—should be a progressive reaching out for more and more of the reality of right qualification.

As you think of the soul as the repository of the energies of the fiery world,[76] you will feel a greater sense of responsibility to maintain the soul and its contents upon the altar of purity. And perhaps you will consider more often how vastly beneficial it will be—not only to you as an individual but also to the universe as a whole—if you will learn how to summon the will to requalify negative thoughts, feelings, and creations with the pristine beauty of the first creation of God. Think of the worlds of misqualified substance that are waiting to be conquered when you practice this supreme art of transmutation!

### "Except Ye Become as a Little Child"

Following the master in the regeneration, cradling the infant Messiah of reality in the crèche of the heart, men will begin the process of expanding their understanding of the self through becoming all that which is real and discarding, through requalification, all that which is not.

This task may seem interminable, the process involved. It is not. Except that ye become as a little child ye cannot enter in.[77] To manifest the little child consciousness is to develop the masterful Christ consciousness that will successfully take dominion over the earth.[78]

Wait, watch, and work. For the Father works with you and within you.[79]

## *Strengthening Our Heart Ties*

When we practice the art of self-transformation, we realize that every day is a renewal of opportunity to redeem our energy and strengthen our heart ties with friends and loved ones. How do we do this? By choosing to say a kind word, to do a good deed or to give a friend a pat on the back. In every act of kindness, we generate positive energy and uplift our soul and spirit.

We accelerate our spiritual awareness through prayer and meditation and in the process of our communion with God we identify more and more with our Higher Self. When we open our heart to the flow of light and love from the heart of God, we cultivate kindness and compassion and bring ourselves into alignment with our higher values and sense of purpose.

We experience a sense of exhilaration in the presence of a saint or ascended master when we pray or decree, or when we have done a good deed or fulfilled a higher purpose. When we pursue our own higher aspirations and heed the wisdom of the heart, we experience peace of mind and joy in our heart.

I correlate these states of bliss with the superconscious, that realm of higher motives and ideals that vibrates at a higher frequency than our normal conscious awareness. When we identify with our superconscious, we make wiser and more compassionate decisions. We find it natural to love our neighbors and forgive others their misdeeds.

## A Dream of Ancient Times

I would like to conclude this chapter with a dream that I had of ancient times. In the dream, I am a storyteller and I gather the stories of ancient people. I am looking down from above, observing a beautiful island. There is beauty in the greenery and the shining waters and the island seems to be broken off from the mainland. I realize this is ancient Lemuria.

My teacher, Mrs. Prophet, and another woman are telling a story as if they had lived it. This is the story of a people displaced from their homeland. And the storytellers are seeking to raise the spirits of these people.

As I listen to the story, I become aware of other women with their heads covered. They are wearing long dresses like Middle-Eastern women, or nuns' habits. A third woman is present, an older Wise Woman with a kindly face. And she tells me as I awaken, "All of this is worthy of being recorded."

I meditated upon this dream glyph upon awakening and again as I prepared to include it in this chapter. I realized that I was embodied in this ancient time. The beauty of the greenery and the shining waters were Lemurian, and the sadness of the people represented a certain sadness of my soul. And I realized that I am meant to transmute the records of my ancient Lemurian lifetimes.

As a storyteller in the dream, I am seeking to raise the spirits of the people as are Mrs. Prophet and the other woman, both of whom represent the role of spiritual teacher. One I am very familiar with, the other is a mystery to me. And the woman who is a mystery needs to be explored by bringing her to conscious awareness. As I meditated upon her, I realized that she represents a feminine aspect of me that was hidden but is now ready to be revealed.

The Wise Woman symbolizes who I am in a state of oneness with my Higher Self. Her kindly face is the face of my Divine Feminine, who is kindness personified. She prompted me to record all of this and to meditate upon it because all of the dream elements are dimensions of the daughter of God that I really am.

The women in nuns' habits represent my lifetimes as a nun. And the women in Middle-Eastern type clothing symbolize my embodiments in the Middle East. I relate the sadness of my soul to my grief concerning the Middle East of today, so filled with turbulence and turmoil and the antics of those who have been influenced by the fallen angels.

In contemplating the dream, I realized that I needed to pray for the lightbearers who are trapped in the struggle. And I also needed to pray for the return of my soul parts that have been stolen by the fallen ones in ancient encounters.

What is the dream message? I understand it as a message from my Real Self, my Higher Self:

"I am meant to claim my wisdom and my oneness with my Real Self, to make the calls for my soul parts to return home, to leave the debris of centuries behind and to complete my mission of teaching others what God has taught me. I am walking the upward path—and by God's grace I am coming Home!"

Every lightbearer is called to the upward journey according to God's timing. We have been on earth many lifetimes, and we are meant to complete our mission and return to our loving Father-Mother God. So be it in accordance with God's grace and the continued striving of our soul and spirit.

# 11

# Interweaving Science and Religion

*The more I study physics
the more I am drawn to metaphysics.*

—ALBERT EINSTEIN

*I*n this age of acceleration in scientific discovery, we realize that science and religion are not alien to one another but rather augment the understanding of each other and contribute to the healing of body, mind and soul.

Through science, we advance technology and explore the universe and in so doing, as Einstein indicated, we come closer to God as the Creator and progenitor of life. In religion, we give glory to God for scientific advances that bring us ever closer to the full realization that God is science, God is religion, God is the Creator of all life.

Both science and religion are credited with healing the body, mind and soul. Clergy may attribute the healing of the physical body to divine intervention while doctors are likely to give full credit to the medical intervention. I believe both are correct because God works miracles in many ways, including through the skills of excellent doctors. Indeed, faith and trust in God are valuable healing aspects.

The ideal clinical situation is for scientists, physicians and clergy to work hand in hand for the healing and comfort of the sick and dying. In a number of healing centers, such as Cancer Treatment Centers of America and the Mayo Clinic, this is happening. And many doctors and pastors serve together in hospice facilities to care compassionately for those nearing the end of life.

## *Mysteries of the Universe*

Relatively few studies have been published on how religion and faith influence the healing process. Thus, scientists often cannot explain a healing that is not attributable to medical intervention.

I believe the more we study the mysteries of the universe, the more we have difficulty attributing the orbiting of planets and the rise and fall of continents—or miraculous healings—to anything less than the hand of the Divine.

Kabbalah, the record of the Jewish mystical tradition, sheds light on this subject. This body of wisdom recorded in the Aramaic text indicates how the ancient peoples understood the origin of the universe and of mankind. Hidden in its mysteries are explanations that may very well lead to a decoding of the secrets of the universe—if that is in accordance with God's will.

In the introduction to her book *Kabbalah: Keys to Your Inner Power*,[80] Mrs. Prophet writes:

> If there is common ground among the world's religions, it is to be found in mysticism. Adventurers of the spirit, the mystics have dared to push beyond the

boundaries of orthodox tradition to pursue a common goal: the direct experience of God—not in the hereafter, but in the here and now. And they teach that while you may seek him in temple or mosque or church, you must ultimately find him in your own heart. . . .

Through the inspiration of mystics who have gone before, I would remind you of your birthright as a son or daughter of God. That birthright, which is your unique portion of God himself, is right inside of you. Only you can unlock it.

What is Kabbalah? It is a subject so mysterious that for centuries only married men over the age of forty were allowed to study it.[81] That view is no longer universally held, and today both men and women of any age study the basic principles of Kabbalah. As one Kabbalist wrote, "From 1540 onward, the most important commandment will be for all to study [Kabbalah] in public, both old and young."[82]

The term *Kabbalah* refers to the mystical tradition of Judaism. No one knows exactly when Kabbalah first began. As a body of knowledge it sprang from mysticism but was not a continuation of any known mystical tradition. Jewish mystical practices can be traced back to around the first century B.C., and the movement known as Kabbalah first emerged around 1200 in Provence, France. But some Kabbalists say the first Kabbalistic revelations dated back to the time of Adam.

Although the teachings of Kabbalah are highly mystical, they are also highly practical. Jewish mystics received revelations about the creation of the universe that are strikingly similar to modern science's big bang theory. They came up with a language and a symbology to describe the qualities of God, our relationship to God, our spiritual purpose in life and the origins of evil.

Most importantly, Kabbalists developed an understanding of the mysteries of God that can help us unlock our spiritual power—the power that God endowed us with from the beginning. The power that launched the big bang.

How can we use the keys of Kabbalah to access that power? By becoming mystics ourselves. Yes, we have the right to become mystics in our own time, using the map that Kabbalists have left us.[83]

## *The Big Bang Theory and Jewish Mysticism*

In her book on Kabbalah, Mrs. Prophet includes scientific theories and mystical explanations about the origin of our physical universe.[84]

The first chapter is titled "The Big Bang and Jewish Mysticism" and the following epigraph is taken from the Zohar:

*The "Beginning" extended itself and made a palace for itself, for glory and praise. There it sowed the holy seed....*

*As soon as [the seed] entered, the palace filled up with light. From that light are poured forth other lights, sparks flying through the gates and giving life to all.*

Mrs. Prophet gives an excellent summary of the big bang theory along with related teachings from the Jewish mystical tradition.

She writes:

In the beginning, there was a seed of energy infinitely smaller than a proton, surrounded by nothingness. In a fraction of a second, that seed exploded into a blazing inferno of matter and energy that cooled and eventually formed galaxies, stars and planets.

That is the big bang theory—the creation myth of today's cosmologists. Scientists first proposed the theory in the 1920s. It fell from favor for a time, but in 1965 scientists discovered microwave radiation that appeared to be from the big bang. With that discovery, they were close to proving the theory, but they needed more evidence of ripples in the seemingly uniform microwaves that surround everything in space.

Then in 1989, NASA launched the Cosmic Background Explorer satellite (COBE) to look at the microwaves. The satellite enabled scientists to see how the universe was evolving when it was only 300,000 years old. What they saw were the imprints of tiny ripples in space that were caused by the big bang.

When the findings were announced on April 23, 1991, excitement in the scientific community could hardly have been higher. George Smoot, head of the research team that made the discovery, said that looking at radiation patterns just after the big bang was "like looking at God."[85] Celebrated physicist Stephen Hawking called it "the discovery of the century—if not of all time."[86]

These findings are a great breakthrough, not only for science but also for religion. For if the big bang theory is accurate, scientists may be confirming the creation myths of Jewish and Hindu mystics.

### In the Beginning, There was "Nothing"

Like modern scientists, Jewish mystics of the thirteenth century said that in the beginning there was nothing—nothing, that is, except the "divine nothingness," the hidden, transcendent God. The God of Genesis who "created the heaven and the earth" was not even manifest. The term the mystics used to describe God before creation was *Ein Sof. Ein Sof* means "without end," or "the Infinite." *Ein Sof* is the First Cause. It is ultimate reality—unmanifest incomprehensible and indescribable.

The major text of the Jewish mystical tradition, the *Sefer ha-Zohar* (Book of Splendor), or Zohar, reveals a process of creation that started deep within the hidden recesses of the formless *Ein Sof* and unfolded as a series of emanations. Central to this drama was a single point that gave forth light and sowed "the holy seed," creating a cosmic conception that is depicted as an explosion of light....

The sixteenth-century Kabbalist Rabbi Issac Luria came up with a different theory of the Creation. While other Kabbalists said the Creation began with an act of expansion, Luria started with the concept of contraction, or *tzimtzum*. According to Luria, *Ein Sof,* the Infinite, contracted itself to its centermost point and then withdrew to the sides of the circle surrounding that point in order to create a vacuum. The reason for *Ein Sof's* contraction was this: For the creation of the finite world to occur, the Infinite needed to define an empty space where its finite creation could exist separately from itself.

From the edge of the vacuum, *Ein Sof* issued a ray of light that launched all of creation. The sequence of events is complicated but, in essence, *Ein Sof's* light manifested ten divine emanations. Each emanation was to be preserved in a special vessel. Some of these vessels, however, were unable to hold that light and consequently shattered. As a result sparks of divine light, along with shards of the vessels, scattered, giving birth to the material world. You could say that what happened was Luria's own version of the big bang.

Like the cosmologies of scientists and Jewish mystics, one ancient Hindu creation myth begins with "nothing." The Creation Hymn of the Rig-Veda says:

> The non-existent was not,
>> the existent was not:
>> there was no realm of air,
>> no sky beyond it....
> Death was not then,
>> nor was there aught immortal:
>> no sign was there,
>> the day's and night's divider.
> That One Thing, breathless,
>> breathed by its own nature:
>> apart from it was nothing whatsoever.
> Darkness there was:
>> at first concealed in darkness
>> this All was indiscriminated chaos.
> All that existed then was void and formless:
>> by the great power of Warmth was born
>> that Unit.
> Thereafter rose Desire in the beginning—
> Desire, the primal seed and germ of Spirit.
> Sages who searched with their heart's thought
>> discovered the existent's kinship
>> in the non-existent.[87]

The hymn sounds similar to the opening words of Genesis, the first book of the Old Testament. The Zohar, in fact, teaches that these verses symbolically describe the mystery of emanation from *Ein Sof*.

> In the beginning God created the heaven and the earth. And the earth was without form, and void; and darkness was upon the face of the deep. And the Spirit of God moved upon the face of the waters.

> And God said, "Let there be light": and
> there was light.
> And God saw the light, that it was good:
> and God divided the light from the darkness.
> And God called the light Day, and the dark-
> ness he called Night. And the evening and the
> morning were the first day.[88]

The dividing of the light from the darkness could
also be compared to Luria's idea of contraction. At first,
there was only darkness, nothingness. Then came the
light, which launched the process of creation.

Just as science has confirmed the idea behind Jewish
and Hindu creation myths, so it has lent credibility to
other statements Jewish mystics have made about the
universe. Although scientists are still refining their cal-
culations, they believe that the universe is somewhere
between nine billion and sixteen billion years old. About
seven hundred years ago, the mystic Rabbi Isaac of Acco
reached the same conclusion. He said the universe was
over fifteen billion years old, but he didn't base his conclusion on precise scientific measurement. In his book
*The Treasury of Life*, he said he based it on the hidden
oral tradition.[89]

If this mystical tradition can tell us something about
the age of the universe, then perhaps it can solve other
mysteries of the universe that scientists have not yet
cracked.

### How Does This Apply to Me?

You may be wondering, "How does this mystical tradition apply to me?" I believe that the study of Kabbalah can
teach us more about who we are and what we are intended
to do during our sojourn on planet Earth. I also believe that

we can fulfill a higher purpose when we tap the fullness of our spiritual potential.

As described above, according to Kabbalah, in the beginning of worlds there was only *Ein Sof,* the nature of the Infinite yet unmanifest. Kabbalah describes the original creation coming from the unfolding of the vastness of *Ein Sof* into ten energy emanations called *sefirot,* which we can think of as dimensions of the personality of God, as facets of the jewel of Infinite Being.

This action of the Divine provided the model for all creation, including the androgynous archetype of man and woman, known as *Adam Kadmon,* the beginning of human evolution. This may very well be the ancients' understanding of the biblical story of Adam and Eve.[90]

Thus each of us, according to the mystical teaching, is patterned after the archetypal *sefirot:*

> *Keter,* our divine essence, represents our free will and awareness of God as the Divine Presence.
>
> *Hokmah* and *Binah* correspond to the right and left hemispheres of the brain, *Hokmah* manifests as genius, inspiration and originality; *Binah* represents our ability to reason and discriminate.
>
> *Hesed* manifests as love, mercy, tolerance and unconditional giving; *Gevurah/Din* as discipline, discrimination, justice and true judgment.
>
> *Tiferet* is our essential awareness of beauty, harmony, balance and serenity; *Da'at,* sometimes thought of as the quasi *sefirah* of knowledge, gives us the ability to express our thoughts and is also the omniscience and universal consciousness of God.
>
> *Netzah* and *Hod* govern our involuntary and voluntary processes. *Yesod* provides the foundation of

spiritual birth, physical procreation and the ego; it is the seat of physical and spiritual pleasure.

*Malkhut/Shekhinah* is the connector of the Infinite with the earth plane, the focal point for the meeting of our spiritual and physical forces; these sefirot also represent our physical body and our receptivity to divine emanations.[91]

### *Spirituality and Practicality*

I believe that the *sefirot* are the etheric pattern of our higher consciousness, the inner foundation of our faith and trust in God, which is a given for people on the spiritual path. Many of my clients pray on a regular basis and receive answers in tangible ways.

I am reminded of a friend of mine who had a special gift of knowing the perfect way to reach out to people in distress. I believe she outpictured the essence of *Hesed*—love, mercy, tolerance and unconditional giving—in her interactions with other people and with animals.

Becky was a humble soul who tended to stay in the background in large gatherings but spent much of her life helping others. She made it a point to be kind and generous to anyone who came her way. She also had a great love for animals and was always the one who would bring home the stray cat or lost dog. Becky was a soft touch for any animal that needed a temporary home.

She told me, "I feel I have a gift for helping people but I'm not really trained to do that. So I just try to be kind and generous when I see someone in need. I actually think my strongest connection is with animal life. Every time I have an opportunity to help a lost pet, I do my best to find its owner. Do you think that's strange?"

I responded, "I don't think so. Animal life is often neglected and your love for animals reminds me of Saint Francis. He had such a love for animals and birds and all elemental life. And now he is known as the ascended master Kuthumi. Maybe helping animals is your way of serving life. Why don't you ask Kuthumi to help you with your mission?"

Becky thought that was a great idea. She said, "I have always loved the stories about Saint Francis so this is a real key for me." She immediately began a novena* to Kuthumi to guide her in her service to animal life. She also told him she would love to help people if he would just show her the way to do it.

I lost track of Becky for several years after she moved to another state, until one day she called to give me an update. "You won't believe this!" she said excitedly. "My prayers to Kuthumi really worked! I am running an animal rescue service and I'm married to a veterinarian who helps me take care of them when they are sick. And the best part is that Tim and I really love each other. It's a perfect match!"

I responded, "That's great!" And I couldn't help being amused at the way God had answered Becky's fervent prayers. He gave her not only a perfect way to help animals but also a loving veterinarian husband as her helpmate. What a blessing!

## Faith Healing

I believe that prayer and faith connect us with the healing power of God. Evangelist Aimee Semple McPherson was a marvelous example:

The evangelist was born Aimee Kennedy in 1890

---

* See Glossary.

near Ingersoll, Ontario, Canada. The daughter of devout Methodists, she loved Sunday school and grew up reciting Bible stories instead of nursery rhymes.

At age 17, Aimee attended a prayer meeting conducted by Robert Semple, an Irish evangelist. She described that life-changing event, "Suddenly, in the midst of his sermon the evangelist closed his eyes and with radiant face began to speak in a language that was not his own. To me this Spirit-prompted utterance was like the voice of God thundering into my soul."[92]

Aimee prayed earnestly to be infused with God's "Spirit of power." For seven days, Aimee's prayers besieged heaven and then "ripples, waves, billows, oceans, cloudbursts of blessing" flooded her being.

Aimee married the evangelist Semple in 1908. Within two years, he was called to minister in China. And Aimee preached her first sermon en route in London, England.

The China mission was cut short when Semple died from dysentery shortly after arriving. Aimee returned to the United States and married Harold McPherson under the condition that, if called, she would obey God and return to active ministry.

To supplement the family income, she worked for the Salvation Army in New York. During this time, Aimee remembers "a voice kept hammering at the doorway of my heart" to "preach the word!"

Following the birth of her son and a serious operation, Aimee was strongly prompted to resume preaching the gospel. She had been so ill that she felt either she would die or Jesus would heal her for further service. She prayed for healing and the strength to preach—and Jesus answered her prayer.

Leaving home and husband, Aimee began her mission in tents and churches in Canada and the eastern United States. Her first healing came during a revival meeting in 1916 when Aimee prayed for a young woman severely crippled by rheumatoid arthritis.

In 1918, Jesus answered Aimee's prayer to heal her seriously ill daughter and instructed her to move her headquarters to California. Settling in Los Angeles, Aimee continued ministering and glorifying Jesus throughout the country. Jesus continually guided her ministry, "When you lay your hands on them, I will lay my hands on yours. And all the time you are standing there, I will be standing right back of you. And when you speak the Word, I will send the power of the Holy Ghost. You are simply the mouthpiece of the telephone. You are the key on the typewriter. You are only a mouth through which the Holy Ghost can speak."

On January 1, 1923, Aimee opened the Angelus Temple in Los Angeles where she preached Jesus' message of "the Foursquare Gospel" to thousands.

Three years later, Aimee disappeared from a Pacific Coast beach, presumed drowned. A month later, she reappeared in a Mexican border town, describing her escape from two kidnappers.

An investigation was launched into charges of conspiracy and misappropriation of church funds by staging a phony kidnapping. Publishing tycoon William Randolph Hearst intervened on Aimee's behalf; charges were dropped, and Aimee resumed her ministry.

Her ministry and life ended in 1944. Aimee lived in anticipation that Jesus would come and receive her as his waiting bride. The theme of her preaching was always "Jesus Christ, the same yesterday, and today and forever."[93]

## A Message to the American Woman
## "The Work Is Not Yet Finished"

Aimee's work goes on as the ascended lady master Magda. On June 13, 1982, she spoke to the American woman in a dictation, saying:

> My beloved, this era of my life that has passed, its very manifestation, was greatly opposed. People remember me as Aimee Semple McPherson. But, precious ones, those who saw me or believed in the works of God in my presence truly saw the One who sent me.[94]
>
> I knew myself then and now as his bride,[95] as the soul merging with the inner light. And so, this victory of the feminine ray is a sign that God has ordained this nation as the place of the victory of the soul. And the one out of whom he cast seven devils[96] is the first to see him.

### A Precious Treasure

> This, beloved, becomes a precious treasure for those who sense themselves as sinners, though God himself has not decreed it. For they have so idolized the person of Jesus that no taint or mar could touch him. Having made him "the God," they allowed me to remain the human, and, therefore, identifiable is their consciousness with my own.
>
> People today consider that they may have walked the path I walked and still have an opportunity to attain the resurrection. Thus, you see, the open door of my heart becomes a more plausible, understandable way! And yet by contrast, whether the figure of Magda or the figure of Aimee—by comparison to him, in their sight, they consider the doctrine laughable that I should have attained the resurrection from this very city and have been received by my LORD in the ritual of the ascension....

## The Gift of the Violet Flame

In those very days, some in America had the gift of the violet flame. Jesus gave me that gift by direct transfusion, you might say, so that it was in and assimilated by me without the prior understanding or knowledge of its use or affirmation.

It was indeed the violet light, as the akashic records will prove, that flowed from his heart through mine for the healing miracles that took place. Yet I was in the tradition of the Church, for these were the sheep that must be reached. And Jesus desired to use me, in the fullest sense of the word, before the hour of my own ascension, that he might bear witness of the truth of God's life in me and of the opportunity of all souls to ascend—especially from the level of imperfection, the level of mutability, shall we say, which orthodoxy does not permit to be ascribed to him.

## A Message to the Soul

Precious hearts, the message of Jesus this day is a message to the American woman and to the man who understands himself to be the manifestation of light. It is a message to the soul of all nations, and it does indeed concern itself with the very present possibility of transmutation and forgiveness of sin when there is repentance.

It is a message of the Holy Spirit! It is a message of believability in the power of the Spirit to transcend the frail, the imperfect, the incomplete—and that to occur right where you are.

Let us not allow the false measuring rod of that mortal consciousness to enter this congregation whereby you take measure of yourself, in the outer sense, and of everyone else and you consider that because you are so many inches high on the Path, it will take you so many miles and so many years to arrive at the point where you could be the instrument of the Holy Spirit! It is almost the sense, "Well, we are growing up now. We are children. And when we are all grown up, then we will be able to be like Jesus, then we will be able to be like Mary."

### Believe in the Holy Spirit

Dear hearts, believe in the Holy Spirit! Believe in the power of the Son of God to come down from the cross in this hour and to stand where you stand and to deliver the full fire of the body and the blood of his Presence for the healing of the whole world!

Understand, when you place a limitation on your capacity to deliver light, you are limiting God and his ability to use your temple. In reality you are saying, "I do not want to be God's instrument in this moment, and so I will hold the concept of myself as *not able.*"

Well, if you are not "able," then you must be Cain! And, you see, Cain killed Abel.[97] It is the Cain consciousness that kills the sense of ability within you! And to be carnally minded is death. You cannot be both. You must choose. . . .

### Be Your Transcendent Self

Thus, when the worst of the human self is overcome by the best of the human self, when your Abel overcomes your Cain, you must not rest there. For the best of your human self is still not the instrument of the LORD—but the transcendent Self that you really are, the one who is the Doer. . . .

Jesus has called me to walk with him with you, at your side. As you teach and preach and lecture and deliver this most stupendous light and message, I will be a witness at your side that the sinner can be saved—that the Saviour can come, cast out seven devils in that one, in one generation, and two thousand years later raise up that same one in the fullness of his power of healing and miracles!

### You Will Be Able to Teach

Thus, you will be able to teach: If he did it unto Magda,[98] he can do it unto you. And you yourself can become the transparency for the Bridegroom—you, the one who becomes the instrument of the Teacher [on behalf of] the one to whom you speak, self-conceived as a sinner. None can deny the reality. None must deny it!

And I charge you to preach of my own reincarnation, as well as that of the messengers! Allow people to face the great dazzling reality of my Presence. Allow them to realize that a so-called modern woman, having passed through the decades of this century in Canada and in the United States, could actually be received in heaven and take the initiation of the ascension—that one who made mistakes, even in the final incarnation, can be forgiven and move on.[99]

## The Power of Forgiveness

As I contemplate Magda's words, I am reminded of a mother and daughter who learned about the power of forgiveness. Martha was praying earnestly for her 86-year-old mother, Irene, to make peace with God before she passed on. Irene had been a stalwart churchgoer, but she had seemingly lost faith due to reversals in her health and finances.

Martha explained, "Mother was upset when she had to stop working and live on a much smaller pension income. And then her health deteriorated, which cost her more money, and she gave up on God. That's what is really upsetting me. I'm worried about what's going to happen when she passes on because she's mad at God. I have been praying for her every day, but my prayers aren't changing her mind."

"What do you think she is most angry about?" I asked.

"I think it's because she has always been a stalwart churchgoer and she expects God to keep her in good health," Martha responded. "I used to tell her that everyone's body gets older and she isn't an exception to the rule. I don't say things like that to her anymore because she got really mad at me. What I said seems to be engraved in her mind, and she's not about to forgive me. I hope I haven't ruined her relationship with God."

"I don't see how what you said could ruin her relationship with God. There must be something else troubling her," I replied. "Do you suppose she would be willing to talk it over with me?"

"I could ask her," Martha replied. "She's always respected you and considers you to be her minister."

Martha was somewhat relieved and decided to talk to her mother the next day. When she called me back, she was feeling better and said her mother would like to talk with me.

When I visited Irene a few days later she was upbeat compared to the way her daughter had described her. She invited me in and we sat down over a cup of tea.

"I'm worried about Martha," Irene confided. "I think she's mad at me because I told her I gave up on God. I didn't really but I was mad at her so I told her that, and then I didn't want to take it back. And now it's engraved in stone in her mind, and that annoys me no end!"

"I think Martha is more worried than mad," I responded.

"She took you seriously when you told her you gave up on God."

"She deserved it," Irene retorted. "I don't like people telling me what to do, especially my daughter!"

I couldn't help but smile. "Does she make it a habit to tell you what to do? I know that wouldn't work because you are just as strong-minded as she is."

Irene laughed, "You're right about that. Maybe she comes by it honestly. Do you think she's learned her lesson by now?"

"Well, I think it will be a long time before she tries to tell you what to do again, but I also think you are underestimating her love for you. She said what she did because she was worried about you," I responded.

There was a long pause. Irene looked chagrined and finally said, "I know she loves me, but I do like to make my own decisions. Maybe I wouldn't have reacted the way I did if I hadn't felt that she was trying to control me."

"Actually, Irene," I responded, "I don't think Martha really wants to control you, and I believe that the two of you could talk that out. What really got to her was that you convinced her you were mad at God. And that scared her."

I saw a twinkle in her eyes. "Okay, I get it. I overdid the damage control thing," Irene said. "But you've known me a long time; do you think I would do something that stupid?"

"I'll have to admit I was surprised, but you did a good job of convincing Martha," I responded. "What do you want to do about it now?"

"I suppose I should apologize for scaring her, but then I expect an apology from her for telling me what to do!" was Irene's quick response.

"Okay," I responded. "But there's one piece of advice that I'd like to give you because I've heard you give it to other people. Remember, 'You can catch more flies with honey than vinegar.'"

Irene had a good laugh and asked Martha to join us. They talked over the situation and I intervened when I could be helpful. At the end of their talk, they put their arms around each other and apologized to one another.

"I am so relieved, Mom," Martha said. "I really thought you meant it when you told me you had given up on God. And I knew that part of it was my fault. I was actually trying to help but I wasn't very gracious about it. I'm sorry that I overreacted."

"That's okay," Irene responded. "I wasn't particularly gracious myself. I'm sorry I made you feel bad."

"I'm glad you are feeling better," I said. "You are both lovely people, and I trust you both realize how much you love each other. Right?"

"Right!" they responded.

Martha called a few weeks later to tell me that sharing their faith in God, forgiving each other and being more diplomatic was working. She added, "Our relationship is better than it has been in years. I believe we both learned a big lesson."

# 12

# Transcending the Human Drama

*Ah, but a man's reach should exceed his grasp,*
*Or what's a heaven for?*

—ROBERT BROWNING

*M*any people today are seeking a higher vision, a more integrated relationship with their soul and spirit and more enlightened ways to handle life's challenges. My clients tell me that their greatest desire is to make right decisions, to balance their karma, to transcend the human drama and to make it home to God.

In order to do this, we need to make the goal of the ascension our first priority. And one way to move toward that goal is to walk the path of loving-kindness and selfless giving, which has been the upward path since ancient times.

The action of giving to God as a prelude and postlude to receiving a healing or a blessing is a custom that is as old as time itself—people have brought offerings to places of worship for thousands of years. And when a healing occurred they offered gifts of thanksgiving. The ancients knew the connection between giving their offering to God and receiving a blessing.

Our forefathers in America offered their love and devotion to God when they established this nation "under God, with liberty and justice for all" and expressed gratitude for the blessings of life, opportunity and the pursuit of happiness. They had a vision and fulfilled it—it is up to us to see that their wisdom and compassion continues to be preserved for future generations.

In his "Proclamation of Thanksgiving" in 1863, President Abraham Lincoln offered the American people another magnificent vision:

> The year that is drawing toward its close has been filled with the blessings of fruitful years and healthful skies....
>
> No human counsel hath devised nor hath any mortal hand worked out these great things. They are the gracious gifts of the Most High God who, while dealing with us in anger for our sins, hath nevertheless remembered mercy.
>
> It has seemed to me fit and proper that they should be solemnly, reverently, and gratefully acknowledged, as with one heart and one voice, by the whole American people. I do therefore invite my fellow-citizens in every part of the United States, and also those who are at sea and those who are sojourning in foreign lands, to set apart and observe the last Thursday of November next, as a day of Thanksgiving and Praise to our beneficent Father who dwelleth in the Heavens.[100]

Thanking our Father-Mother God brings a return current of God's love and grace, which is essential for those who are striving on the path to the ascension. When we give of ourselves to others and to God, we are called to give lovingly.

The vibration of our giving indicates whether it is a gift from the heart or simply an act of arbitration.

We can ask ourselves, are we giving because we love to give or are we giving with the underlying thought, "I am giving something to you and I expect you to give something back." If the latter is our motivation, we will likely not feel good about our giving unless we get something back. And we will have sacrificed the joy that comes from simply giving because of a love to give.

All of the saints have walked the path of selfless giving and we are meant to follow in their footsteps. So, we give freely with no strings attached. We give a gift to our church, synagogue or mosque or a gift to a friend or loved one or a stranger we meet along the road of life just because we want to give. This was the spirit of Mother Teresa who always gave whatever she had to whomever she met.

Gratitude and kindness are also beautiful ways of giving. We can be mindful and appreciative of those who are thoughtful and helpful to us, and we can honor those who have helped us get to where we are today. We can make it a point to show our appreciation, to write a thank-you note, to send a card or flowers or whatever will spark a smile and a feeling of warmth in another person's heart. We can choose to do these simple acts of kindness because we love people and want to brighten their day.

When we appreciate the goodness in other people and open our heart to those we meet along the road of life, we begin to emanate the energy of loving-kindness that blesses the giver, the receiver and the entire world. In so doing we raise our energy to a higher frequency, which accelerates our higher consciousness and brings us ever closer to a state of oneness with God.

## *Preparing for the Upward Journey*

As a therapist and minister, I offer a seven-point program for those who pursue the journey upward:

- Pray for inspiration, guidance and courage
- Be a loving companion to your soul
- Be patient, kind and generous to others
- Be thoughtful, practical and decisive
- Be a lifelong learner
- Take the high road at every choice point
- Thank God for the opportunity!

Thus, we walk in faith, heed the guidance of our Higher Self and leave the outcome to God as we set ourselves to win our victories on earth and to return Home in the victory of the ascension.

When we praise God for our blessings, we are uplifted and strengthened by the return current of divine love. When we surrender our will to God's will and become his instrument, the rhythm of our life becomes a flow of light and grace. And when we listen with our heart and soul, we may inwardly hear the music of the angels.

The shepherd boy David composed a beautiful psalm of praise that is as inspiring to us today as it must have been for the Israel of yesterday:

PSALM 100
A PSALM OF PRAISE.

Make a joyful noise unto the LORD, all ye lands.

Serve the LORD with gladness: come before his presence with singing.

Know ye that the LORD he is God: it is he that hath made us, and not we ourselves; we are his people, and the sheep of his pasture.

Enter into his gates with thanksgiving, and into his
courts with praise: be thankful unto him, and bless his
name.

For the LORD is good; his mercy is everlasting; and
his truth endureth to all generations.[101]

## To Those Who Desire to Achieve the Ascension

When we synchronize our aspirations, thoughts, emotions
and actions with the currents of divine energy flowing from
our I AM Presence and Christ Self, we walk the path of life
in a state of continuous transcendence which accelerates
enlightenment and prepares us for the ascension in accordance with God's timing.

Each of us has the opportunity to achieve the victory of
the ascension, our soul's permanent reunion with God. The
ascended masters teach that, at the conclusion of life, we will
meet with spiritual overseers to review our progress. This
meeting includes a life review so that we understand what we
have accomplished and the lessons we still need to learn.

If we have balanced 51 percent or more of our karma, we
will be given the choice to ascend to the heaven-world or to
return to earth to balance 100 percent of our karma. Some
may choose the path of the bodhisattva and reembody to continue serving earth's evolutions. However, due to the turbulent
conditions on earth today the ascended masters have encouraged people on the spiritual path to take their ascension when
it is offered. We may very well be of more help to our loved
ones once we have ascended to the heaven-world.

## The Ascension Temple over Luxor

Through their teachings, the ascended masters have
given us a vision of the Ascension Temple in the higher

realms above Luxor, Egypt. It is here that the ritual of the ascension is held under the direction of the ascended master Serapis Bey, chohan of the fourth ray. This temple is a part of the spiritual retreat at Luxor, which is presided over by Serapis, who was a high priest in the ascension temple during the ancient civilization of Atlantis. After establishing etheric retreats and mystery schools adjacent to the temples to the Divine Mother, Serapis and his band departed from Atlantis before the final cataclysm to transfer the ascension flame to Luxor.

Serapis embodied on earth as the famous Spartan king Leonidas, whose name means "Son of the Lion." His heroism and selfless devotion to a greater cause and glory more precious than life secured him a singular place in history. He later embodied as the Egyptian pharaoh Amenhotep III and constructed the temple at Luxor on the Nile River.

The temple was constructed to correspond to the outline of the human skeletal framework, and its courtyards and rooms correspond closely to the human body.

In their book *Lords of the Seven Rays,* the Prophets quote R. A. Schwaller de Lubicz, who studied the temple's architecture for fifteen years and came to a similar conclusion: "The Temple of Luxor is indisputably devoted to the Human Microcosm. This consecration is not merely a simple attribution: the entire temple becomes a book explaining the secret functions of the organs and nerve centers."[102]

The Prophets explain how the temple relates to the mystery of rebirth and transformation:

> In truth this temple displays the idea of the rebirth of
> the divine man based on his transformation through the
> universal Mother Principle. And to those who have eyes

to see and ears to hear, the mysteries are unveiled. The Principle and Presence of the Mother in the matter body is taught by the Lord of the Fourth Ray as in metaphor he raises our consciousness to the plane of causation:

[Serapis Bey says] "Out of the Word is Mother and the Word is Mother and in this Word was the soundless sound that passing through her lips became the AUM of the creation. Thus the science of sound and the science of the Word are known in the white-fire core of the fourth ray. And Alpha stepped forth and Omega was the One and through her the beginning became the ending.

"For the sake of her children's restoration to the House of Spirit," he explains, "Omega entered the Matter universes. And our Dear Mother became one with the Matter cycles below even as She is in—for her Blessed Being constitutes—the Matter cycles Above. And now in the last days the Mother, even the Great Kali, strips from her own all violations of Her Matter Body by the dark ones.

"Therefore I give you this prayer to sustain you through the rigorous initiations of the fourth ray: 'Even so, come quickly, Dearest Mother, to liberate our souls forever from the bondage of the senses, the illusion of time and space and the violators of thy Word incarnate in our souls! Come, Blessed Mother, Come.' "[103]

## Initiations Precede the Ascension

In order to be eligible for the ascension, each initiate must balance at least 51 percent of his or her karma and balance the threefold flame of power, wisdom and love. The action of the violet transmuting flame invoked through prayers and decrees purifies the aura and chakras, transmuting the records of karma and facilitating the balancing of the threefold flame.

The initiate is also called to raise the Kundalini fire, the sacred energy of the Mother light, from the base-of-the-spine chakra to the crown chakra. The raising of the Kundalini is accomplished through prayers, mantras and meditation. This process is not completed in a few days or weeks but comes about as a steady, gentle raising of consciousness over time.

Another important element is service to God and to those we meet along life's way. The initiate welcomes the challenges of life as a testing of soul and spirit, and greets problematic individuals or situations with a spirit of joy and appreciation. This process gradually raises our consciousness and readies the soul for the advanced initiation of the ascension.

We have been told that we can pray to be taken to the violet flame room at Luxor for transmutation and acceleration of the homeward path. And we can help ourselves by invoking the violet flame to transmute the records of karma and misqualified energy that may block our vision or interfere with our ability to make wise decisions.

Invoking the violet flame on a daily basis will accelerate our consciousness and propel us toward the fulfillment of the goal of the ascension. Serapis gives instruction that can help us make progress in identifying with our Real Self:

> "The real miracle and first lesson of alchemy at Luxor is the separating out of the Real from the unreal in the psyche (soul) of the individual," explains Serapis. "What is real in you, what is unreal? I charge you this day, students of the Most High God, to give answer; for you are not students of Serapis Bey or Morya or Saint Germain, but you are students of the Almighty, of the Christ, and we stand as mentors and fellow servants of the Most High God.

### Separate the Real from the Unreal

"I charge you, then, this day to take a page in your book of Christhood,* to make two columns. The first column—Myself, What Is Real; the second column—Myself, What Is Unreal. You will head the first column with the word *God, the I AM THAT I AM; Christ, the only begotten Son.* This is that which is real within you. You will head the second column with: *the human ego, the human will, the human intellect, the human pride.*

"And then you will list the virtues of the light, the virtues of the Christ and of God in the first column, which you know to be real and to be outpictured within you. And in the second, you will list those faults, those sins which are not real. Then you will return to the first column and list those attributes that you desire to have as real, that you know exist, that you honor and adore, but which you have not yet mastered. These you must also claim as yourself, as reality; for unless and until you claim them, you cannot be them. And thus, you will clearly mark the truth and the falsehood of identity.

### Invoke God's Grace—Remove Unreality

"This is the starting place of the ascension. That which is in the first column must rise, that which is in the second must be transmuted before the energy thereof can rise.

"Then step by step each day, with rejoicing in your heart, you take the power, the dominion of the God qualities you have listed in the first column and all energies that you have listed there and you use them as your authority, your substance, your collateral to invoke the

---

*A special notebook or diary in which the student records spiritual experiences, reflections, devotions and prayers, lessons learned and those still to be mastered.

grace of God, his will, and his healing to remove the stain of sin and all unreality which you have listed as the misqualified energies and momentums in the second column. This, then, becomes an objective and practical exercise in the demonstration of the science of the laws of God."[104]

## *Training Candidates for the Ascension*

Superimposed over the physical temple at Luxor is Serapis' etheric retreat. Here initiates pursue the ascension disciplines under the tutelage of Serapis and the 144 instructors who work with him in preparing candidates for the alchemical process of the ascension.

The Prophets describe this process of preparation:

> Serapis Bey's methods of discipline are tailor-made for each candidate for the ascension. After an initial interview by himself or one of Twelve Adepts presiding in his mystery school, devotees who come to his retreat are assigned in groups of five or more to carry out projects with other initiates whose karmic patterns (graphically illustrated in their astrology) forecast the maximum friction between their lifestreams. This test must be given in order that they may choose to be or not to be centered in God. Soon it is clear that *all* idols of the tyrant self or karmic past must be surrendered if one is to merge with the confluent stream of the Law of the One.
>
> Each group must serve together until they become harmonious—individually and as a cohesive unit of hierarchy—learning all the while that those traits of character that are most offensive in others are the polar opposite of their own worst faults and that what one criticizes in another is apt to be the root of his own misery.
>
> Aside from this type of group dynamics, individuals

are placed in situations (both in the retreat and in their day-to-day activities) that provide them with the greatest challenges, according to their changing karmic patterns. In this course of Serapis one cannot simply up and leave a crisis, a circumstance, or an individual that is not to his liking. He must stand, face and conquer his own carnal mind and misqualified energy by disciplining his consciousness in the art of nonreaction to the human creation of others, even as he learns how not to be dominated or influenced by his own human creation.[105]

## The Ritual of the Ascension

At the close of their final embodiment of service to earth's evolutions, candidates who have been accepted for the ascension rite come to the Ascension Temple at Luxor to receive the initiation that will reunite them with their God Presence. Accompanied by ascended and unascended masters, the initiate is bidden to the flame room by the Lord of the Fourth Ray where he must stand on a dais in the center of a large circle with masters, adepts, seraphim and brethren in attendance on the periphery.

At a certain moment when all is in readiness the individual's cosmic tone is sounded, and the current from Alpha is released from the circle on the ceiling and the current from Omega rises from the base. The moment the individual's tone is sounded, and simultaneous with the bursting forth of the flame formed by the caduceus action of both currents, the seraphim in the outer court trumpet the victory of the ascending soul with a magnificent rendition of the "Triumphal March" from *Aïda*. The discipline that is the keynote of this retreat is felt in their precise, golden-tone rendition of the piece.... [106]

### The Glorified Physical Body

Serapis says, "Although the form of an individual may show signs of age prior to his ascension, all of this will change and the physical appearance of the individual will be transformed into the glorified body. The individual ascends, then, not in an earthly body but in a glorified spiritual body into which the physical form is changed on the instant by total immersion in the great God flame.

"Thus man's consciousness of the physical body ceases and he achieves a state of weightlessness. This resurrection takes place as the great God flame envelops the shell of human creation that remains and transmutes, in a pattern of cosmic grids, all of the cell patterns of the individual—the bony structure, the blood vessels, and all bodily processes which go through a great metamorphosis.

"The blood in the veins changes to liquid golden light; the throat chakra glows with an intense blue-white light; the spiritual eye in the center of the forehead becomes an elongated God flame rising upward; the garments of the individual are completely consumed, and he takes on the appearance of being clothed in a white robe—the seamless garment of the Christ. Sometimes the long hair of the Higher Mental Body appears as pure gold on the ascending one; then again, eyes of any color may become a beautiful electric blue or a pale violet....

"Lighter and lighter grows the physical form, and with the weightlessness of helium the body begins to rise into the atmosphere, the gravitational pull being loosened and the form enveloped by the light of the externalized glory which man knew with the Father 'in the beginning' before the world was.

"This is the glory of the ascension currents. It is the glory of attainment which Jesus demonstrated on Bethany's hill. . . .

### Serving the Earth after the Ascension

"These changes are permanent, and the ascended one is able to take his light body with him wherever he wishes or he may travel without the glorified spiritual body. Ascended beings can and occasionally do appear upon earth as ordinary mortals, putting on physical garments resembling the people of earth and moving among them for cosmic purposes. This Saint Germain did after his ascension when he was known as the Wonderman of Europe. Such an activity is a matter of dispensation received from the Karmic Board." Generally, however, ascended beings do not return to the physical plane unless there is some specific service requiring this change in vibratory rate.

Some who have earned their ascension volunteer to surrender this blessing temporarily and continue to reembody in order to assist those who are still in the process of overcoming. This is called the bodhisattva ideal. There are many in both the unascended and ascended octaves who have volunteered to remain with the evolutions of earth until every last man, woman and child is free in the ascension.[107]

Serapis Bey tells us, "You ascend daily." Our thoughts, our feelings, our daily deeds are all weighed in the balance. We do not ascend all at once but by increments as we pass our tests and win our individual victories. The entire record of all our past lives and momentums of both good and evil must be counted; and then, when we have brought at least 51 percent of all the energy that has ever been allotted to us into balance with the purity and harmony of the Great God Self, we may be offered the gift of the ascension, which is indeed by the grace of God. The remaining 49 percent must be transmuted, or purified, from the ascended octaves through service to earth and her evolutions performed by the soul after the ascension.[108]

As a loving father prodding the soul onward and upward, Serapis Bey says:

> "You need not expect, precious ones, that as the swoop of a great bird of paradise, heaven will come down to you and raise you instantly up into the light. Each day you weave a strand of light substance back to the heart of your Presence by the shuttle of your attention; each strand strengthens the anchor beyond the veil and thus draws you into a state of consciousness wherein God can use you more as an effective instrument for good."[109]

## *The Infinite Grace of Heaven*

Lord Maitreya, the Great Initiator, has given us a glimpse of immortality and the infinite grace of heaven that uplifts our consciousness and ignites hope and joy in our soul. This loving ascended master delivered a memorable dictation to Mark Prophet, "A Study in Christhood by the Great Initiator: Immortality and the Cosmic Sense."[110] His words are as apt today as they were when he gave this dictation in Boston, Massachusetts, in 1961.

Lord Maitreya speaks to our heart and soul:

> I AM come today to charge into your midst the radiance that is familiar to your souls, the radiance that is our natural habitat, the light that will exalt you and

raise you and comfort you, the light that will be a solace unto you when you seem to be separate one from another and from all forms of comfort.

For the light of God will penetrate your consciousness as you lie upon your beds and cannot sleep, when the cares and oppressions of the world seem to press in upon you and you find difficulty in finding peace. If you will turn your hearts toward the Christ and make a call unto him, he will respond and with blazing light come into your forcefield to bring you that same peace and love which he brought to mankind long ago.

You are dealing now, beloved ones, with immortality. You are dealing with the realm of the ascended masters. You are dealing with the compassion of heaven. It is no ordinary or mortal concept that comes to your mind, but it is the concept of Life, the concept of eternal Life, the concept of the grace of heaven.

The grace of heaven, beloved ones, transcends history. It transcends the known world. It transcends your human thoughts. The grace of God is sufficient for you[111] or every occasion which you may ever face. And with the waning of all human sensibilities, mankind will find the dawning of the cosmic sense wherein they are able to cognize the nearness of the heavenly octaves and the spheres of light to their own consciousness.

## Become as a Little Child

The tiny babe lifts its eyes toward its own God Presence, and it smiles. And those individuals in the presence of that babe are pleased to see the smile upon the face of the child, but they do not know of the vision of the angels which appears to the tiny one. Much later in life, when familiarity with the world scene has closed the door and the curtain that separate the consciousness of the child from the wonders of heavenly spheres, those visions come, then, no more. And the child becomes a part of the mass consciousness—guided by parents, guided by teachers, guided by companions, many of whom are fit and many of whom are unfit to guide.

The pressure, then, of mass consciousness builds up a synthetic man—not a manifestation of the eternal light, but a manifestation of carnality destined to be confused, destined to confuse, and destined eventually to perish as an individual entity and pass from the screen of life.

But this is not the plan of immortality, and God is immortal. God is immortal! And in his immortality there is peace and joy forever without end.

The harshness of the world, the clanging furor of the tides of mortality do not comfort mankind; and therefore, they run to and fro, seeking peace. And no peace is given to them, and yet they continue to seek. For it is the Great God Self within, that manifested in the cosmic sense in the tiny babe, that must awaken. This cosmic sense, like a rosebud, must unfold. Like a lotus it must breathe its perfume into space.

When the consciousness of man begins to unfold, it becomes as a little child. And as it becomes as a little child, the entire glory of heaven is revealed to that individual. And man realizes that outer life has been a chimera, and that all that the eyes have seen and that the ears have heard is nothing to be compared to the wonders of the eternal spheres!

### God Is as Close as Our Heart and Breath

I, Maitreya, come to you as a father would to his children. And I come to you today to breathe upon you concerning the cosmic sense, that you may awaken within yourselves to the glory of God, which is present in space wherever you are. Individuals have the idea that God is far removed from them. But this God that I declare unto you today, beloved ones, is as near as your hands and feet, or as close as your heart and breath.

The inflowing of the cosmic light within the body of man is a gift of the Presence of God, which is perpetuated momentarily by the intelligence of heaven in action. The Christ mind—the divine power that beats your heart while you sleep, that gives to your physical consciousness, your body elemental,[112] and your mind the understanding to govern all of the senses that control the body movements, both voluntary and involuntary—is a gift of God.

Be grateful, then, for this gift, but above all be grateful for the gift that is the eyes of your soul, the hearing of your soul, the understanding of your heart. For you are not your garments that you wear. You are not these physical bodies. You are a living soul! At inner levels you wear garments of immortality, and these are real and tangible; but because you have diverted your attention from the inner realm to the outer, you are not aware of the inner garments that you wear—and it is as though you were bereft of your attire.

## Be Clothed upon with Immortality

Pause now and think, beloved ones, what it means to be clothed upon with immortality. Beloved Hilarion, when embodied as Saint Paul, warned mankind of the fact that they must first put off mortality if they would put on immortality.[113]

I, today, admonish you, beloved ones of the light, that you likewise recognize the need to put off the mortal senses during those moments when you desire to awaken the senses of immortality. In the name of

Almighty God, precious students of the light, if you are thinking of entertainment, if you are thinking of food, if you are thinking of some accomplishment that you wish to do in order to expand your own personality, during a time when you are trying to make attunement with your God Self, how can you possibly make that attunement?

You must, then, put off the consciousness of the outer man, of the human self. You must come in full faith to the fount of Almighty God, believing that he is "and that he is a rewarder of them that diligently seek him."[114]

This is a truth pursued of old by Enoch,[115] pursued of old by every ascended master who ever made the ascension. This Christ-seeking must become the goal of man if he would awaken to all of the potency and power of the sacred fire.

### Put On the Mind of Christ!

Beloved ones, some of you have idly dreamed of moments when you would be able to say to a man with a withered hand, "Be thou made whole!"[116] Some of you have idly dreamed of a moment when you could at a glance pass an individual on the street who was suffering from habitual drunkenness and be able to speak to that one at inner or outer levels and say, "Be thou free! Be thou whole!"[117] Some of you have been more ambitious, and you have dreamed of how you could reach out your hand as the Christ did and raise men from the dead.[118]

Well, beloved ones, this power is within you. But it is most important that you recognize that you as individuals must first put off the old man and his deeds[119]—you must put off the consciousness of the world sense and put on the new mind of the Christ if you are to accomplish these specific feats and enjoy these cosmic graces, these cosmic gifts.

These gifts are given to you. They are free—they are without money, they are without price.[120] They are held for you now by your own Mighty I AM Presence and they will manifest in your world, and no power in heaven or earth can possibly prevent their manifestation at that moment when you are ready to receive them.

## Accept the Radiance of Angelic Hosts

But, beloved ones, you cannot be made ready to receive them until you yourself have elected to open up the senses of heaven—to recognize the angelic hosts, to recognize the ascended masters, to recognize your own Mighty I AM Presence as the only power in your world. There is no other power but God. There is no other power that can act in your world but the power of God!

I ask, therefore, that you pause as I make contact with the beloved angelic hosts and ask them to pour their radiance into the chalices of your hearts. I ask that they saturate you with the pure light rays from their hearts, charged with the essence of roses and the fragrance of pine. I ask that you be made aware, then, of the sweetness of the soul of God that is within you and of the eternal Presence of God within you.

The eternal Presence of God within you is forever and forever and forever. It is without end. Therefore accept this gift from the angelic hosts that are part of my band of light. I ask you now to be at peace.

## Fulfill the Hopes of Heaven

Children of the Light, I want to remind you that each one of you was conceived by God. I want to remind you that you came not through the gate of birth by accident, but you came by conscious, divine intent. I want to remind you that your life was as divinely intended a manifestation as was the birth of beloved Jesus and other great avatars.

I want to remind you that the hopes of heaven for you were and are great, that simply because individuals have permitted their own self-hope to become dim does not prevent the immortal concept of God from being held steadfast for every lifestream. And it is this anchor—it is this anchor, beloved ones of the light—that causes each man to feel the pull of immortality, leading him onward to seek, to understand the great cosmic laws and the great cosmic light.

### The Word of God Is the Progenitor

I am known as the Great Initiator, and it is my responsibility to take interest concerning the unfoldment of the individual chelas in coming through the stages of initiation of the Great White Brotherhood. Today, as I gaze not only upon those lifestreams who are assembled within this room but upon the lifestreams of all humanity, I behold among mankind many who are ready for various stages of initiation. Some are ready for cosmic stages of initiation. Some are ready for less advanced stages of initiation. But many are making themselves ready by application to their own divinity.

The bonds of divinity are so far greater than mortal concepts that it is sometimes difficult to bridge the gap between human words and divine ideas so that mankind will understand the wonder of which I speak. Mankind today are plagued because of the fact that, through the semantics of words, they do not always understand or conceive of the true power of the Word of God. But the Word of God is the progenitor of every individual within this place, upon this planet, and everywhere in the universe.

This Word of God, beloved ones, is ever blessed. It is tangible and real, it is intelligent, it is light! And in it there is no shadow, nor is there a shadow of turning.... [121]

### The Light of Heaven Will Lift You Up

Beloved ones, when an individual comes into manifestation as a tiny babe, that individual in time comes to recognize its own father and mother and members of its household. So it is of the Spirit of Light. When an individual becomes as a babe in Christ—aware of the ascended masters, although dimly—there is a gradual expansion of consciousness until at last that individual is able to walk and talk with the ascended masters and cosmic beings as freely as you have your social familiarity here among mankind. And this is as it should be.

For the patriarchs of old communed with the angels, communed with the cosmic beings. And this will happen to you, and eventually, precious ones, you will find that heaven is all around you, and the roses of heaven will blossom at your feet. The fragrance of heaven will penetrate your body and your mind. The light of heaven will lift you up in consciousness until you will feel at home beneath the stars! For you will know that there are points of light—chakras within your body, and centers of light—and that in time all of these points of light will blend into one beautiful star, the star of initiation whereby you are able to pass through the star doorway and commune with nature, with the elementals, with the angelic hosts.

You will no longer be possessed with a mere sense of a physical body and the limitations of that body. You will be able to leave the body at will, and you will be able to move anywhere upon this planet or upon many planets at will. And you will find a freedom from fear, from bondage, from the need to partake of food, from the need to be subject to natural and man-made laws in an ordinary sense. For you will become subject to the great cosmic laws, and these transcend all other laws.

### The Goal Is Mighty: Make the Call!

Precious ones of the light, the goal is mighty. The race needs the help of the ascended masters. This we are willing to give. We ask that you make the call within yourself; we do not ask that you necessarily make the statement before mankind concerning your inner intention.

Those of you who may be timid today and may not quite recognize the voice of the Good Shepherd,[122] I ask tonight, before you close your eyes in sleep, that you make a call to God, to your own Mighty I AM Presence, and that you ask him to guide your footsteps that you may understand the power of light, the power of the ascended masters, the power of the Christ in action— and that you consciously elect to further your progress in the things of the Spirit, that this which passeth away, these "former things,"[123] be no longer cleaved to, but that you anchor within the veil that permanent God consciousness that no man can take from you.

And then you will be a part of our band and you will have begun in newness of life,[124] in renewing the consciousness of the atoms and electrons of your body, in charging yourself with the sacred fire. You will be eventually victors, not vanquished.

I thank you, and bid you good evening.

# Questions and Answers
## with Dr. Marilyn Barrick

Q: I know it is not good to criticize, condemn or judge other people, but I get frustrated when someone is being inconsiderate or hurtful. In spite of my best intentions, out pops a critical comment. Then I get upset and criticize myself. It is as if criticism, condemnation and judgment have a life of their own. How do I stop it?

A: Most people feel upset when another person is inconsiderate or hurtful, particularly if the hurtful drama involves someone we love or respect. Yet, a critical comeback on our part can be equally hurtful. We add fuel to the fire when we then get upset with ourselves, typically followed by a surge of resentment toward the person who ignited the fire in the first place. It's no wonder that criticism, condemnation and judgment (ccj) take on a life of their own.

We can outwit our tendency to be critical or to react with a critical comeback if we remind ourselves that ccj is instigated and propelled by the forces of darkness, who take great delight in getting us to criticize, condemn and judge one another. Why do they go to so much trouble? One major reason. They want to steal our energy and entice us into making karma, which ties us to the earth plane—until at least 51 percent of the karma is balanced.

God is calling his sons and daughters to come Home and the fallen angels and their tools are angry. They know that they have defied God and will no longer exist once they have no light to keep them going. That is the reason they devil the lightbearers, to steal the light.

Why do they have to steal it? Because they have cut themselves off from God's light by misusing it. Tricking the lightbearers into misqualifying the light and then stealing that energy is the way the fallen ones continue to exist.

When we fall for the tricks of the fallen angels, we lose some of our light, we have less energy and we feel vulnerable, inadequate and distant from God—and this is how we feel when we criticize and condemn others.

So, if all of this is a "trick of the force" as Mark Prophet put it, how can we outwit it? First, we remind ourselves that if someone else is inconsiderate or hurtful, it is natural to feel vulnerable, hurt or frustrated. Secondly, we ask ourselves, "What do I want to do about these feelings?" And it is at that strategic moment that Mr. CCJ will likely come riding in from the unconscious or subconscious to do the right job in a wrong way.

The right way is to stand up for the soul—our soul or anyone else's. The wrong way is to tear someone down in the process of trying to stand up for the soul. And that is exactly what ccj does. It rips the fabric of the soul, eats away at the criticizer's self-worth and erodes our sense of honor and compassion.

When we get our hackles up, Mr. CCJ becomes convinced that he is being properly protective. Using our voice, he will explain that this is a natural reaction—like a porcupine that shoots its quills when someone comes too close to the soft underbelly. And, after all, Mr. CCJ is doing an even more important job, protecting our vulnerable self and our soul.

In order to counter this move, we remind ourselves that when we are critical, condemning and judgmental, we give light to the forces of darkness. These forces continue to exist only by the light we release when we are in a discordant vibration. We affirm that we will no longer be "a tool of the force," as Mark Prophet used to describe it.

So, with God's help we begin the redemption of Mr. CCJ. We take a leap of faith! We toss the bristly cloak of ccj into the sacred fire (through fiery ruby ray or violet flame decrees), and we put on the full armor of inner strength, allegiance to truth and obedience to harmony. And we teach the recalcitrant Mr. CCJ, step by step, to stop reacting and to adopt the demeanor of a knight in shining armor who serves God and protects the soul.

We claim the motto, "I will be true to myself and to my God." We choose forbearance in the face of turmoil. And we practice forgiveness and self-correction whenever we make a mistake. We also ask the angels in the outfield to remind us to keep our mouths shut when we don't feel harmonious.

Each time we feel tempted to criticize someone we remind ourselves that Father-Mother God made us of the *love stuff.* We determine to behave lovingly and to stop returning evil for evil. We decide to view hurtful happenings as a lesson about the importance of harmony. And we practice harmony over and over again in order to form a habit of harmonious behavior.

Step by step, we build a momentum of harmony, grace and Christly aplomb. And we send our gratitude to Father-Mother God for the opportunity to correct our flaws, to strengthen our virtues and ultimately to return Home in the victory of the ascension.

**Q:** My friend and I were having dinner, and my friend's escort was critical and rude to her. I debated whether I should say something like "what you're saying is really unkind!" but I decided it was not my business. Do you think I should have told him he was being rude?

**A:** That is a difficult one, but I think you were wise to refrain from saying what you were thinking! This reminds me of the saying, "Don't step in where angels fear to tread."

If you had corrected your friend's escort, you might have ignited a scene your friend would not appreciate. Unless you were able to be in perfect balance and as diplomatic as Saint Germain and as loving as Jesus, you likely would have stirred a pot that was already brewing and made it boil over.

Since the man was your friend's escort and they obviously have a relationship, I would be inclined to offer a silent prayer, let it go and talk with your friend privately if she opens the door to a conversation about it. I would also suggest that you keep your friend in your prayers and pray for the highest resolution possible for her.

**Q:** I am an Aquarian and I know I am called to be loving but my parents are very good at pushing my buttons. I love them and I do my best not to react, but they continually find fault with me. I am of age and not even living with them. Do you have any suggestions to help me stay loving instead of reacting?

**A:** None of us can keep people from finding fault with us, especially our parents, who are used to telling us what to do because they raised us. I suggest that you give yourself a big hug and tell yourself:

"Okay, this is the way they are and I'm not going to change them, but what I can control is my reaction. I choose not to let my parents' adverse reactions ruin my day. I choose to remain centered. I choose to remain unattached. I choose to sit under my Bodhi tree as a Buddha. I choose to be loving and kind—and I choose to walk out the door if it gets to be too much!"

According to spiritual astrology, Aquarians are intended to express divine love. You might ask yourself, "What would the masters of great love, like Jesus, Mother Mary or the ascended lady master Nada do in a situation like this?"

Write down what comes to mind when you contemplate these exemplars of divine love. Then open the floodgates of your heart's love and send love to your parents. You can send your love silently when they are upset, and you will feel much better doing that than reacting to their comments.

I suggest that you pray for the love of God to sustain you, keep your heart open, let the love flow—and trust God's love to heal the relationship between you and your parents.

**Q:** I would like to know what to do with people I love who are closed up and have built barriers around them?

**A:** Pray for them and be kind in your interactions with them. Kindness lets your loved ones know it is safe to come

244 Everything Is Energy

out from behind the barriers, at least when they are with you. And remember it is their decision as to whether they do that or not. Maybe they need their barriers at the moment. Most people who erect barriers do so because they have been hurt and are trying to protect themselves. If we continue to behave lovingly, eventually they tend to lower the barriers. So be a safe haven when they are with you, pray for their well-being and ask God to help them through whatever is troubling them.

Q: What do you think about self-hypnosis?

A: The only difference between self-hypnosis and hypnosis is that in self-hypnosis you are putting yourself into the trance state. The ascended masters teach that it is not a good idea because you are in a completely receptive state and not in conscious control of your environment.

Hypnosis is not the same as meditation, in which you connect with your Higher Self and the etheric plane. Whether it is self-hypnosis or hypnotism by someone else, the chances are the person who is hypnotized is a sitting duck for any astral forces that happen to be around.

Some people have also asked me whether it is wise to use a tape made by a hypnotist. And my response is that using someone's tape connects you with that person's consciousness, as well as with your own unconscious. Bad dreams, even nightmares, can result from probing the depths of the unconscious without the assistance of a qualified therapist—the depths of the unconscious realm can overwhelm any of us.

This is why we pray before we go to sleep. We invoke our tube of light and ask to be overshadowed by the ascended masters. Yet, all of us have occasional bad dreams, which are typically triggered by difficulties in our lives and lessons we need to learn. When you wake up from a bad dream, I suggest writing it down to gain a conscious understanding of what you and your soul are trying to resolve in the dream state.

The state of being awake, whether in the light of day or the darkness of night, is mindful of the words of Gautama Buddha when he won his victory under the Bo tree. He said, "I am awake!" And that is what we are called to be—awake to who we are as sons and daughters of God.

Q: What is the difference between opening ourselves to pain and letting down our guard?

A: It could be at times one and the same. I think the difference is the way it is usually spoken of, the connotation of it, the underlying meaning of it.

When you open your heart, the connotation is opening oneself, allowing the flow of light, of love, wisdom and power and the tenderness of your being to flow out. Letting down your guard has the connotation of being off guard, opened up without conscious intent—and therefore, without conscious protection.

Our protection is the flow of God's light, having that flow of light moving through us like a waterfall that will not allow any negativity to flow in. In contrast, when we have not invoked the light, energy can penetrate our aura and become a part of us without our consent. So letting down our guard is risky—it's like playing football without a helmet!

**Q:** I have heard that Carl Jung's theory is outdated and many therapists are using transactional analysis in its place. What are your thoughts on different kinds of therapy?

**A:** Jung's theory, known as analytical psychology, is not at all outdated. It is a beautiful way of working and connects with what the ascended masters teach. I would add that any therapy is as good as the consciousness of the practitioner.

Transactional analysis, developed by Eric Burn, has roots in Jungian thinking. This is the therapy where one works with the parent, child and adult parts of one's self—it was one of the precursors of inner child work.

Psychosynthesis, developed by Roberto Assagioli, is another therapy that derives from Jungian psychology. In psychosynthesis, the therapist includes the sub-personalities, which are similar to working with the inner child. Assagioli also introduced the concept of the superconscious, the inner arena of our hopes, dreams and aspirations. In psychosynthesis, the client partners with the Higher Self.

I use elements of all of these theories that connect with the healing of the soul and spirit, which is my major focus. In my practice I focus on the issues the client wishes to resolve. And I firmly believe that a positive rapport between therapist and client is essential to healing.

**Q:** When I am invoking the light, I become choked up and my eyes water. If I am alone at home, I just let it flow and sometimes it's sorrow and sometimes it's joy. Should I be concerned that sorrow might keep me from making my ascension?

**A:** Tears of joy and bliss are very different from tears of sadness and grief. When we have tears of joy and bliss we are raised to higher consciousness. And when we have tears of sadness and grief we are focused on some aspect of our humanness that needs to be redeemed.

When you have this experience, you have a marvelous opportunity to praise God in the bliss and to pray for God's guidance to correct the human condition that is creating the sorrow. I suggest that on a daily basis you give violet flame decrees to transmute the sorrow, and make it a point to thank God for the blessing of life and opportunity.

**Q:** Can you tell me whether a situation I remembered during a therapy session was really a past life or a figment of my imagination?

**A:** Only the soul and God know the reality of whether or not a memory is actually a past-life remembrance or a figment of our imagination. We also need to be mindful that memories are subject to our mental interpretation. Thus, a recall may or may not be completely accurate in the details of what actually occurred.

I do believe there is a lesson to be learned from whatever comes to mind because it is an aspect of our consciousness. In my therapeutic work I simply accept the remembrance of the client. And we work together to understand the lesson and how the individual might apply it in his or her life today.

With respect to the situation being a figment of your imagination, it would still reflect your thoughts and feelings. So it might be useful to ask yourself, "What might be my purpose in imagining this? What am I trying to heal within myself? What lesson am I trying to learn? How might I apply it in my life today?"

**Q:** Many people today do not seem to respect the values I was brought up with. What do you think is happening to our culture?

**A:** I too believe we are experiencing a decline in traditional morality and values throughout the world. It has been precipitated by a number of factors: worldwide violence, terrorist activities, hate-mongering, the addictive use of drugs and alcohol, sexual promiscuity and the ignoring of traditional values in the service of expediency.

Add to the mix the influence of atheism, the trappings of Satanism and the degrading and blasphemous lyrics in pop culture and we begin to understand the roots of cultural decline. In addition, we have the negative influence of good people tending to turn a blind eye toward cultural degradation because they do not know what to do about it.

What is the solution? I believe it is to open our eyes and do our part to change our small portion of the world. Archangel Jophiel gave a simple key to students of the ascended masters. He told them in a dictation delivered through Mrs. Prophet, "Good people must do better."[125] If all the good people in the world united to do better, we would see swift and major change because the vibration of the world would be raised up.

In other words, we can choose to be the loving, compassionate people we really are and dedicate ourselves to fulfilling the mission of our Higher Self. We can pay attention to the prick of conscience and join with good people everywhere to confront personal and planetary problems from an enlightened and practical point of view. When we do this, we shift the energy in our small corner of the world. And when enough of us do it worldwide, the world will become a better place.

# Alchemical Energy Formulas

Strengthening the aura and purifying the chakras is an important key in helping us balance our energy and achieve higher consciousness. And invoking the violet flame to transmute the debris of centuries of embodiments is essential if we would make the fastest progress possible in the journey to enlightenment.

In order to outwit the forces of darkness and protect the soul and spirit during the earthly journey, we also need to invoke the fires of illumination and seal our chakras and aura in the blue-fire protection of Archangel Michael and the blue-flame angels.

We begin by invoking the tube of light, which envelops us in the radiant light of God, uplifting our energies and establishing a protective forcefield that prevents negative energies from invading our consciousness. Coupled with the violet fire of transmutation, the tube of light seals our connection with our Higher Self, Christ Self, or Buddha Self and enables us to walk through the veils of maya and fulfill our higher purpose without succumbing to the forces of darkness.

The inner opponent we encounter is the dweller-on-the-threshold, the conglomerate of negative energy that we have accumulated over many lifetimes on planet Earth and beyond. The sacred power that dethrones the dweller-on-the-threshold is the blue-fire power of God. Archangel Michael and the blue-fire angels release that fire when we call to them for protection and for the will of God to manifest in our life.

We prepare ourselves for the action of the blue fire by invoking the light of God to cleanse and uplift our consciousness. First, we take several deep breaths, exhaling slowly, as we focus our attention on our heart. Then we envision a shower of brilliant white light enfolding us, descending from the I AM Presence into our aura, consciousness, being and world as we give the following decree* as a spoken prayer:

---

*See *Prayers, Meditations, Dynamic Decrees for the Coming Revolution in Higher Consciousness* published by The Summit Lighthouse, Corwin Springs, Montana, 1984.

## VIOLET FIRE AND TUBE OF LIGHT DECREE

O my constant, loving I AM Presence, thou light of God above me whose radiance forms a circle of fire before me to light my way: I AM faithfully calling to thee to place a great pillar of light from my own Mighty I AM God Presence all around me right now today!

Keep it intact through every passing moment, manifesting as a shimmering shower of God's beautiful light through which nothing human can ever pass. Into this beautiful electric circle of divinely charged energy direct a swift upsurge of the violet fire of freedom's forgiving transmuting flame!

Cause the ever expanding energy of this flame projected downward into the forcefield of my human energies to completely change every negative condition into the positive polarity of my own Great God Self!

Let the magic of its mercy so purify my world with light that all whom I contact shall always be blessed with the fragrance of violets from God's own heart in memory of the blessed dawning day when all discord—cause, effect, record and memory—is forever changed into the victory of light and the peace of the ascended Jesus Christ.

I AM now constantly accepting the full power and manifestation of this fiat of light and calling it into instantaneous action by my own God-given free will and the power to accelerate without limit this sacred release of assistance from God's own heart until all men are ascended and God-free in the light that never, never, never fails!

Next, we invoke Archangel Michael's blue-fire power and protection as we give the following decree aloud, repeating the refrain after each verse:

## LORD MICHAEL

1. Lord Michael, Lord Michael,
   I call unto thee—
   Wield thy sword of blue flame
   And now cut me free!

Refrain: Blaze God-power, protection
   Now into my world,
   Thy banner of faith
   Above me unfurl!
   Transcendent blue lightning
   Now flash through my soul,
   I AM by God's mercy
   Made radiant and whole!

2. Lord Michael, Lord Michael,
   I love thee, I do—
   With all thy great Faith
   My being imbue!

3. Lord Michael, Lord Michael
   And legions of blue—
   Come seal me, now keep me
   Faithful and true!

Coda: I AM with thy blue flame
   Now full-charged and blest,
   I AM now in Michael's
   Blue-flame armor dressed! (3x)*

---

* Repeat the coda three times in recitation of the decree. Give this decree 3x or as many times as you like to reinforce Archangel Michael's protection.

Now we are ready to invoke the circle and sword of Mighty Astrea, "The Starry Mother," who wields a circle and sword of fiery blue-white energy to cut us loose and set us free from energies and projections that are a burden to the body, mind and spirit. We can also give the Astrea decree for our loved ones and people in the vanguard of service to the Light:

### DECREE TO BELOVED MIGHTY ASTREA—
### "THE STARRY MOTHER"

In the name of the beloved Mighty Victorious Presence of God I AM in me, Mighty I AM Presence and Holy Christ Selves of Keepers of the Flame, Lightbearers of the world and all who are to ascend in this life, by and through the magnetic power of the sacred fire vested in the Threefold Flame burning within my heart, I call to beloved Mighty Astrea and Purity, Archangel Gabriel and Hope, beloved Serapis Bey and the seraphim and cherubim of God, beloved Lanello, the entire Spirit of the Great White Brotherhood and the World Mother, elemental life—fire, air, water and earth! to lock your cosmic circles and swords of blue flame in, through, and around:

[my four lower bodies, my electronic belt, my heart chakra and all of my chakras, my entire consciousness, being and world.]

Cut me loose and set me free (3x) from all that is less than God's perfection and my own divine plan fulfilled.

1. O beloved Astrea, may God Purity
   Manifest here for all to see,
   God's divine Will shining through
   Circle and sword of brightest blue.

First chorus:*   Come now answer this my call,
Lock thy circle round us all.
Circle and sword of brightest blue,
Blaze now, raise now, shine right through!

2. Cutting life free from patterns unwise,
Burdens fall off while souls arise
Into thine arms of infinite Love,
Merciful shining from heaven above.

3. Circle and sword of Astrea now shine,
Blazing blue-white my being refine,
Stripping away all doubt and fear,
Faith and goodwill patterns appear.

Second chorus:   Come now answer this my call,
Lock thy circle round us all.
Circle and sword of brightest blue,
Raise our youth now, blaze right through!

Third chorus:   Come now answer this my call,
Lock thy circle round us all.
Circle and sword of brightest blue,
Raise mankind now, shine right through!

Once we have invoked the tube of light, Archangel Michael's protection and Astrea's circle and sword of blue flame, we are ready to give the fiery decree for the angels to bind the dweller-on-the-threshold. This is an alchemical formula for casting out the conglomerate of the carnal mind.

---

*Give the decree once, using the first chorus after each verse. Give it a second time, using the second chorus after each verse. Give it a third time, using the third chorus after each verse. These three sets of three verses followed by each of the three choruses comprise one giving of the Astrea decree.

The dweller decree is a dynamic prayer that liberates us from layers of unreality—the scar tissue of bygone traumas that needs to be cleared for our soul's resurrection. When we give this decree, we are championing our soul and defending our right to be who we are as our Real Self.

We center in our heart and envision the angels binding and casting out the dweller-on-the-threshold and freeing our soul as we give this decree with the full power of our throat chakra:

I CAST OUT
THE DWELLER-ON-THE-THRESHOLD!

In the name of my beloved mighty I AM Presence and Holy Christ Self, Archangel Michael and the hosts of the LORD, in the name Jesus Christ, I challenge the personal and planetary dweller-on-the-threshold, and I say:

*You* have no power over me! *You* may not threaten or mar the face of my God within my soul. *You* may not taunt or tempt me with past or present or future, for I AM hid with Christ in God. I AM his bride. I AM accepted by the LORD.

*You* have no power to destroy me!

Therefore, be *bound!* by the LORD himself.

Your day is *done!* You may no longer inhabit this temple.

In the name I AM THAT I AM, be *bound!* you tempter of my soul. Be *bound!* you point of pride of the original fall of the fallen ones! You have no power, no reality, no worth. You occupy no time or space of my being.

You have no power in my temple. You may no longer steal the light of my chakras. You may not steal the light of my heart flame or my I AM Presence.

Be *bound!* then, O Serpent and his seed and all implants of the sinister force, for *I AM THAT I AM!*

I AM the Son of God this day, and I occupy this temple fully and wholly until the coming of the LORD, until the New Day, until all be fulfilled, and until this generation of the seed of Serpent pass away.

*Burn* through, O living Word of God!

By the power of Brahma, Vishnu and Shiva, in the name Brahman: I AM THAT I AM and I stand and I cast out the dweller.

Let him be bound by the power of the LORD's host! Let him be consigned to the flame of the sacred fire of Alpha and Omega, that that one may not go out to tempt the innocent and the babes in Christ.

*Blaze* the power of Elohim!

Elohim of God—Elohim of God—Elohim of God

Descend now in answer to my call. As the mandate of the LORD—as Above, so below—occupy now.

*Bind* the fallen self! *Bind* the synthetic self! Be *out* then!

*Bind* the fallen one! For there is no more remnant or residue in my life of any, or any part of that one.

Lo, I AM, in Jesus' name, the victor over death and hell! (repeat sentence two times)

Lo, *I AM THAT I AM* in me—in the name of Jesus Christ—is *here and now* the victor over death and hell!

Lo! it is done.


To complete the alchemy, we invoke the violet flame to transmute any residual debris or sense of burden:

## VIOLET FLAME FROM THE HEART OF GOD

Violet flame from the heart of God,  (3x)*
    Expand thy mercy through me today!  (3x)
Violet flame from the heart of God,  (3x)
    Transmute all wrong by forgiveness ray!  (3x)
Violet flame from the heart of God,  (3x)
    Blaze into action through all to stay!  (3x)
Violet flame from the heart of God,  (3x)
    O mercy's flame, fore'er hold sway!  (3x)
Violet flame from the heart of God,  (3x)
    Sweep all the earth by Christ-command!  (3x)
Violet flame from the heart of God,  (3x)
    Thy freeing power I now demand!  (3x)

> Take dominion now,
> To thy light I bow;
> I AM thy radiant light,
> Violet flame so bright.
> Grateful for thy ray
> Sent to me today,
> Fill me through and through
> Until there's only you!

I live, move, and have my being within a gigantic fiery focus of the victorious violet flame of cosmic freedom from the heart of God in the Great Central Sun and our dearly beloved Saint Germain, which forgives, transmutes, and frees me forever by the power of the three-times-three from all errors I have ever made.

Now we affirm our union with our Higher Self as we give the Introit to the Holy Christ Self:

_____

*Repeat each line three times when the notation "(3x)" appears.

## INTROIT TO THE HOLY CHRIST SELF

1. Holy Christ Self above me,
   Thou balance of my soul,
   Let thy blessed radiance
   Descend and make me whole.

Refrain: Thy flame within me ever blazes,
   Thy peace about me ever raises,
   Thy love protects and holds me,
   Thy dazzling light enfolds me.
   I AM thy threefold radiance,
   I AM thy living presence
   Expanding, expanding, expanding now.

2. Holy Christ Flame within me,
   Come, expand thy triune light;
   Flood my being with the essence
   Of the pink, blue, gold, and white.

3. Holy lifeline to my Presence,
   Friend and brother ever dear,
   Let me keep thy holy vigil,
   Be thyself in action here.

We seal the action of these mantras and decrees by accepting and amplifying the light we have called forth:

And in full faith I consciously accept this manifest, manifest, manifest! (3x)* right here and now with full power, eternally sustained, all-powerfully active, ever expanding, and world enfolding until all are wholly ascended in the light and free! Beloved I AM! Beloved I AM! Beloved I AM!

_____

* Repeat the preceding words three times beginning with "And in full faith ... "

We conclude the transformational process by affirming the I AM, our higher qualities and the victory of our soul's mission:

## I AM AFFIRMATIONS

I AM a soul of light.
I AM walking the path home to God.
I AM the will of God manifesting in my life.
I AM the wisdom of the Christ and the Buddha.
I AM the compassion of the Divine Mother.
I AM the purity of my Higher Self.
I AM one with the flame of Truth.
I AM the servant of the Christ in all.
I AM joyfully balancing my karma.
I AM lovingly obedient to my Real Self.
I AM passing my soul initiations.
I AM winning my ascension.

We may also offer personal prayers for our families and God's people everywhere. Upon completion of our supplication and communion with God, we give the following benediction.

## SEALING BENEDICTION

May the words of my mouth and the meditations of my heart be acceptable in thy sight, O LORD, my strength and my redeemer.

THE CHART OF YOUR DIVINE SELF

# The Chart of Your Divine Self

We are able to pray to God and he will answer because we are connected to him. We are his sons and daughters. We have a direct relationship to God and he has placed a portion of himself in us. In order to understand this relationship better, the ascended masters have designed the Chart of Your Divine Self.

The Chart of Your Divine Self is a portrait of you and of the God within you. It is a diagram of yourself and your potential to become the being of light that you really are. It is an outline of your spiritual anatomy.

The upper figure is the "I AM Presence," the Presence of God that is individualized in each one of us. It is your personalized "I AM THAT I AM." Your I AM Presence is surrounded by seven concentric spheres of spiritual energy that make up what is called your "causal body." The spheres of pulsating energy contain the record of the good works you have performed since your very first incarnation on earth.

They are like your cosmic bank account.

The middle figure in the Chart represents the "Holy Christ Self," who is also called the Higher Self. You can think of your Holy Christ Self as your chief guardian angel and dearest friend, your inner teacher and voice of conscience. Just as the I AM Presence is the presence of God that is individualized for each of us, so the Holy Christ Self is the presence of the universal Christ that is individualized for each of us.

"The Christ" is actually a title given to those who have attained oneness with their Higher Self, the Christ Self. That is why Jesus was called "Jesus, the Christ." Christ comes from the Greek word *christos* meaning "anointed"—anointed with the light of God.

The Chart shows that each of us has a Higher Self, or "inner Christ," and that each of us is destined to become one with that Higher Self—whether we call it the Christ, the Buddha, the Tao or the Atman. This "inner Christ" is what the Christian mystics sometimes refer to as the "inner man of the heart," and what the Upanishads mysteriously describe as a being the "size of a thumb" who "dwells deep within the heart."

We all have moments when we feel that connection with our Higher Self—when we are creative, loving, joyful. But there are other moments when we feel out of sync with our Higher Self—moments when we become angry, depressed, lost. The spiritual path is all about learning to sustain the connection to the higher part of ourselves so that we can make our greatest contribution to humanity.

The ribbon of white light pictured descending from the I AM Presence through the Holy Christ Self to the lower figure in the Chart is the crystal cord (sometimes called the silver cord). It is the "umbilical cord," the lifeline that ties you to Spirit.

Your crystal cord also nourishes that special, radiant flame of God that is ensconced in the secret chamber of your heart. It is the threefold flame, or divine spark, literally a spark of sacred fire that God has transmitted from his heart to yours. This flame is called "threefold" because it engenders the primary attributes of Spirit—power, wisdom and love.

The mystics of the world's religions have contacted the divine spark, describing it as the seed of divinity within. Buddhists, for instance, speak of the "germ of Buddhahood" that exists in every living being. In the Hindu tradition, the Katha Upanishad speaks of the "light of the Spirit" that is concealed in the "secret high place of the heart" of all beings.

Likewise, the fourteenth-century Christian theologian and mystic Meister Eckhart taught of the divine spark when he said, "God's seed is within us." There is a part of us, said Eckhart, that "remains eternally in the Spirit and is divine. . . . Here God glows and flames without ceasing."

When we decree, we meditate on the flame in the secret chamber of our heart. This secret chamber is your own private meditation room, your interior castle, as Teresa of Avila called it. In Hindu tradition, the devotee visualizes a jeweled island in his heart. There he sees himself before a beautiful altar, where he worships his teacher in deep meditation.

Jesus spoke of entering the secret chamber of the heart when he said: "When thou prayest, enter into thy closet, and when thou hast shut thy door, pray to thy Father which is in secret; and thy Father which seeth in secret shall reward thee openly."

The lower figure in the Chart of Your Divine Self represents you as a soul on the spiritual path, surrounded by the violet flame and the protective white light of God known as the tube of light. Your soul is the living potential of God— the part of you that is mortal but can become immortal. The high-frequency energy of the violet flame can help you reach that goal more quickly.

The purpose of your soul's evolution on earth is to grow in self-mastery, balance your karma and fulfill your mission on earth so that you can return to the spiritual dimensions that are your real home. When your soul at last takes flight and ascends back to God and the heaven-world, you will become an "ascended" master, free from the rounds of karma and rebirth.

# Notes

1. An ascended master is one who, through Christ and the putting on of the mind which was in Christ Jesus (Phil. 2:5), has mastered time and space and in the process gained the mastery of the self in the four lower bodies and the four quadrants of Matter, in the chakras, and the balanced threefold flame. An ascended master has also transmuted at least 51 percent of his karma, fulfilled his divine plan and taken the initiations of the ruby ray unto the ritual of the ascension—acceleration by the sacred fire into the Presence of the I AM THAT I AM (the I AM Presence). Ascended masters inhabit the planes of spirit—the kingdom of God (God's consciousness)—and they may teach unascended souls in an etheric temple or in the cities on the etheric plane (the kingdom of heaven).

2. The superconscious is a concept of psychosynthesis, a psychological theory developed by Roberto Assagioli, based on unifying the personality with a higher source of purpose and direction. He called this higher source the transpersonal self. Others refer to it as the Higher Self or the Christ Self.

3. See *One on One*, explorefaith.org, "Interview with Lauren Artress" with moderator Kathy Carmean, April 7, 2003, regarding the Reverend Dr. Lauren Artress' book, *Walking a Sacred Path: Rediscovering the Labyrinth as a Spiritual Tool*, published in 1995. Rev. Artress is an Episcopal priest, a psychotherapist and author of *Walking a Sacred Path*,

which reintroduced the labyrinth as a form of walking meditation and prayer. Since 1986, she has served as canon for special ministries at Grace Cathedral in San Francisco and is founder of Veriditas, a worldwide labyrinth project.

4. See Charles W. Leadbeater, *Ancient Mystic Rites* (Wheaton, Ill., Theosophical Publishing House, 1986).

5. See *Isis Unveiled: A Master Key To The Mysteries of Ancient and Modern Science and Theology,* Vol. 1. – Science, by H. P. Blavatsky (Pasadena, Calif., Theosophical University Press, 1877; reprinted in soft cover, 1998), pp. 522–23.

6. Manly P. Hall, in his renowned compilation: *An Encyclopedic Outline of Masonic, Hermetic, Kabbalistic and Rosicrucian Symbolical Philosophy* (Los Angeles: Philosophical Research Society, 1972).

7. Rev. 7:17; 21:4.

8. This instruction was given to Elizabeth Clare Prophet in a dictation from the ascended master Lanello, October 6, 1995. See *Pearls of Wisdom,* vol. 38, no. 37.

9. For a thorough understanding of how to analyze your dreams, including Tibetan dream yoga, I suggest my book *Dreams: Exploring the Secrets of your Soul* (Corwin Springs, Mont., Summit University Press, 2001).

10. Elizabeth Clare Prophet's lecture, "Karma, Reincarnation and Christianity," was given at the *Class of the Golden Cycle,* New Orleans Airport Hilton, October 11, 1991.

11. W. R. Alger, *A Critical History of the Doctrine of a Future Life* (Boston: Roberts Brothers, 1886), p. 475, quoted in Joseph Head and S. L. Cranston, comps. and eds., *Reincarnation: The Phoenix Fire Mystery* (New York: Julian Press/Crown Publishers, 1977), p. 8.

12. David Christie-Murray, *Reincarnation: Ancient Beliefs and Modern Evidence* (1981; reprint, Bridport, Dorset: Prism

Press, 1988), p. 17.

13. Ignatius Donnelly, *Atlantis: The Antediluvian World,* rev. ed., ed. Egerton Sykes (New York: Gramercy Publishing Company, 1949), pp. 251, 254–55.

14. Pythagoras, quoted in *Continuum: The Immortality Principle* (San Bernardino, Calif.: Franklin Press, 1978), p. 19.

15. Diogenes Laertius, *Lives of the Eminent Philosophers* 8.8.4.

16. Plato, *the Republic,* 10.617, trans. Josiah Wright, quoted in Head and Cranston, *Reincarnation: The Phoenix Fire Mystery,* p. 216.

17. Josephus, *The Wars of the Jews* 2.8.14, in *The Works of Josephus,* new updated., trans. William Whiston (Peabody, Mass.: Hendrickson Publishers, 1987).

18. Josephus, *The Antiquities of the Jews,* 18.1.3, in *The Works of Josephus,* trans. Whiston.

19. Xenophanes, quoted in Diogenes Laertius, *Lives* 8.8.20.

20. Matt. 5:18.

21. Deut. 32:35; Rom. 12:19; Heb. 10:30.

22. Paramahansa Yogananda, *Man's Eternal Quest* (Los Angeles: Self-Realization Fellowship, 1975), p. 474.

23. Phylos the Thibetan, *A Dweller on Two Planets or The Dividing of the Way* (New York: Harper & Row, 1974).

24. Matt. 25:21.

25. This lecture of the ascended master Ernon, Rai of Suern, was delivered by the messenger Elizabeth Clare Prophet on November 27, 1991. Published in *Pearls of Wisdom,* vol. 34, no. 61.

26. The sacred fire (also known as the Kundalini fire) is the precipitation of the Holy Ghost for the baptism of souls, for purification, for alchemy and transmutation, and for the realization of the ascension, the sacred ritual whereby the soul returns to the One. When the sacred fire is spent

through inordinate or perverted sexual activity, it remains in the lower chakras; thus, the ascended masters recommend conservation of the sacred fire for the soul's victory of the ascension.

27. Lost sheep of the House of Israel: When Jesus left his golden-age civilization on Atlantis 34,500 years ago, two million souls followed him. They went to Suern, present-day India. One million of these souls ascended from Suern. The other million continued to reincarnate, some among the Suernis and some on Atlantis in the realm of the Poseid. Thirteen thousand years ago, the Suernis rebelled against their ruler, Rai Ernon. Those of the one million who were incarnated in Suern did not rebel. However, they too were subject to the doom the Rai pronounced upon the Suernis: to dwindle and wait for ninety centuries and suffer until the time of Moses. He told the Suernis that at that time they would be called "the seed of Abraham," the twelve tribes of Israel. The one million who had been with Jesus on Atlantis reincarnated in the tribe of Joseph through his sons, Ephraim and Manasseh, whom Jacob blessed as his own. The tribe of Joseph was one of the ten tribes of the Northern Kingdom of Israel. Today, these one million are reincarnated principally among the peoples of the British Isles, the United States and Canada. The Suernis reincarnated in the remaining nine of the ten tribes of the Northern Kingdom of Israel and in the two tribes of the Southern Kingdom of Judah. Today those nine tribes of the Northern Kingdom are generally reincarnated among the European nations as Christians, whereas the two tribes of the Southern Kingdom (Judah and Benjamin) and some Levites are generally reincarnated among the modern-day Jews. For reasons of karma, the seed of Abraham have also reincarnated in every nation. See "A Profile of Ernon, Rai of Suern," delivered by the messenger Elizabeth Clare Prophet

on Sunday, October 13, 1991, during the four-day *Class of the Golden Cycle* held at the New Orleans Airport Hilton. Published in *Pearls of Wisdom,* vol. 34, no. 60.

28. Misqualification of energy and misuse of the sacred fire refer to the negative qualification of God's consciousness and life-force to multiply darkness, doubt, disease, degeneracy, and death instead of light, love, divine wholeness, peace, and freedom; also referred to as maya or illusion.

29. See *A Dweller on Two Planets* by Phylos the Thibetan (New York: Harper & Row, 1974).

30. Sanat Kumara in dictation to Elizabeth Clare Prophet, "The Buddha and the Mother" conference, San Diego, California, May 25, 1975. See *Pearls of Wisdom,* vol. 42, no. 25.

31. After a period of obscurity lasting 1500 years, the Scottish explorer James Bruce discovered *The Book of Enoch the Prophet,* translated from an Ethiopic MS. in the Bodleian Library by the late Richard Laurence, LL.D., Archbishop of Cashel. Laurence's first translation appeared in 1821.

32. This dictation of Lady Master Venus was given to Elizabeth Clare Prophet on March 30, 1975, at the *Class of the Resurrection Flame,* in Los Angeles, California. See *Pearls of Wisdom,* vol. 42, no. 27.

33. Elizabeth Clare Prophet developed a spiritual matrix for retrieving the lost elements of the soul, which she named "Soul Retrieval." She led a service in which she invoked the assistance of the ascended masters and she and the congregation gave prayers and decrees for the recovery of soul parts. This dynamic service continues to be given by students of the ascended masters during the quarterly conferences of Church Universal and Triumphant.

34. Shapiro discovered the energy method serendipitously in 1987. As she was walking in a park in Los Gatos, California, she found herself preoccupied with a disturbing

thought, which then disappeared. At the same time she noticed that her eyes were spontaneously moving back and forth. When she focused on another situation that aroused mild anxiety and intentionally moved her eyes back and forth, that upsetting thought disappeared as well. Shapiro realized she was onto something vital for the relief of anxiety. She completed her master's and doctorate degrees in clinical psychology and focused her research efforts over the next decade upon developing EMDR (eye movement, desensitization and reprocessing), a therapy increasingly acclaimed by clinicians, crisis intervention organizations and academicians for the healing of PTSD, post-traumatic stress disorder. Shapiro is the author of a textbook as well as the popular book, *EMDR: The Breakthrough Therapy for Overcoming Anxiety, Stress, and Trauma,* co-authored with Margot Silk Forrest. Shapiro was awarded the 1994 Distinguished Scientific Achievement in Psychology Award by the California Psychological Association and has trained over 20,000 clinicians in the United States.

35. See Shapiro's book, *EMDR: The Breakthrough Therapy for Overcoming Anxiety, Stress, and Trauma* (New York: HarperCollins Publishers, 1997), Chapters 5 & 6.

36. For further information see *Dreams: Exploring the Secrets of Your Soul* by Marilyn C. Barrick, Ph.D. (Corwin Springs, Mont.: Summit University Press, 2001), Chapter 3. Also see *Working with Dreams in Psychotherapy* by Clara Hill (New York: Guilford Press, 1996); *The Mystical, Magical, Marvelous World of Dreams* by Wilda B. Tanner (Tahlequah, Okla.: Sparrow Hawk Press, 1988); *Some Must Watch While Some Must Sleep* by William Dement, M.D. (San Francisco: San Francisco Book Co., 1976).

37. *EMDR: The Breakthrough Therapy for Overcoming Anxiety, Stress, and Trauma* by Francine Shapiro, Ph.D. & Margot Silk Forrest (New York: HarperCollins Publishers,

1997), pp. 1–4 and "Update: EMDR and Life After The Blast, Controversial Therapy Praised in Oklahoma City" by Don Oldenburg, Washington Post staff writer, *The Washington Post,* July 21, 1995.

38. See Elizabeth Clare Prophet, *Forbidden Mysteries of Enoch: Fallen Angels and the Origins of Evil* (Corwin Springs, Mont.: Summit University Press, 1992).

39. See *Saint Germain's Prophecy for the New Millennium* by Elizabeth Clare Prophet with Patricia R. Spadaro and Murray L. Steinman (Corwin Springs, Mont.: Summit University Press, 1999), pp. 6–9.

40. This meditation is an adaptation of the HeartMath exercise developed by Doc Lew Childre and The Institute of HeartMath, Boulder Creek, California.

41. Elizabeth Clare Prophet, "Christ and the Dweller: A Perpetual Path of Victory," *Pearls of Wisdom,* vol. 26, no. 38a.

42. See 2-audiocassette album, *The Fourteenth Rosary: The Mystery of Surrender,* published by The Summit Lighthouse, Corwin Springs, Mont., 1991.

43. Elizabeth Clare Prophet, "The Labyrinth of Human Creation," Summit University, March 10, 1981.

44. Elizabeth Clare Prophet, "Buddhism: Religions of the World," November 27, 1974.

45. Ascended Master Kuthumi, "Remember the Ancient Encounter," *Pearls of Wisdom,* vol. 28, no. 9.

46. Lord Maitreya is an ascended being, known as the Cosmic Christ and the Planetary Buddha. His name means "loving-kindness" and he focuses the radiance of the Cosmic Christ to the evolutions of earth. Maitreya is worshiped in Tibet, Mongolia, China and Japan and throughout Asia, where he is revered by Buddhists as "the Compassionate One" and as the coming Buddha. For further information, see *The Masters and Their Retreats* by Mark L. Prophet and Elizabeth

Clare Prophet, complied and edited by Annice Booth.

47. Mrs. Prophet charted the cycles of psychological and spiritual development on what she named the "cosmic clock." This is a way of mapping our spiritual initiations from birth to our present age and into future years. For a complete description of these cycles including color charts, see *A Spiritual Approach to Parenting: Secrets of Raising the 21st Century Child* (Corwin Springs, Mont.: Summit University Press, 2004), Chapters 3 and 4. Also see *Predict Your Future: Understand the Cycles of the Cosmic Clock* by Elizabeth Clare Prophet (Corwin Springs, Mont.: Summit University Press, 2004).

48. The messenger Elizabeth Clare Prophet's response to the ascended master El Morya's dictation: "Free El Morya!" given to Mrs. Prophet during a Sunday service, August 14, 1988.

49. Ascended Master Serapis Bey, "The Path of the Ascension Is the Path of Love," published in *Mirror of Consciousness: Lords of the Seven Rays*, Book Two, Chapter the Fourth, by Mark L. Prophet and Elizabeth Clare Prophet (Corwin Springs, Mont., Summit University Press, 1986), pp. 138–41.

50. Elizabeth Clare Prophet, "Studies of the Human Aura," Summit University, April 17, 1975.

51. *Alchemy of the Heart: How to Give and Receive More Love*, Elizabeth Clare Prophet and Patricia R. Spadaro (Corwin Springs, Mont., Summit University Press, 2000), p. 5.

52. Elizabeth Clare Prophet, given in the Palm Sunday Service, March 31, 1985.

53. This dictation by Helios was given to the messenger Elizabeth Clare Prophet, July 4, 1991.

54. This instruction from the ascended master Jesus was

delivered in dictation to Elizabeth Clare Prophet on March 30, 1997. See *Pearls of Wisdom,* vol. 40, no. 35.

55. Elizabeth Clare Prophet, given during a prayer vigil at the Royal Teton Ranch, Corwin Springs, Montana, April 19, 1990.

56. This dictation from Jesus, "The Christmas Rose: I Call You to the Heart of God," was given to the messenger Elizabeth Clare Prophet on December 25, 1991. Published in *Pearls of Wisdom,* vol. 34, no. 67; also in *Walking with the Master: Answering the Call of Jesus* by Elizabeth Clare Prophet and Staff of Summit University (Corwin Springs, Mont., The Summit Lighthouse Library, 2002).

57. Ecclesiastes 1:9.

58. Luke 6:31, "And as ye would that men should do to you, do ye also to them likewise."

59. "Blessed are the meek: for they shall inherit the earth." Matt. 5:5.

60. Lord Lanto, "Human Moods," published in *Understanding Yourself: Opening the Door to the Superconscious Mind—A Study in the Psychology of the Soul by the Masters of the Far East* by Mark L. Prophet (Corwin Springs, Mont., Summit University Press, 1985), pp. 90–93. Also published in *Pearls of Wisdom,* vol. 12, no 35.

61. Shakespeare, *Henry IV, Part II,* III, i, 56.

62. Serapis Bey, "Love That Has the Courage to Be," published in *Mirror of Consciousness: Lords of the Seven Rays,* Book Two, Chapter the Fourth, by Mark L. Prophet and Elizabeth Clare Prophet (Corwin Springs, Mont., Summit University Press, 1986), pp. 166–68.

63. Frank Purcell quoting from *Rufus Jones Speaks To Our Time: An Anthology,* edited by Harry Emerson Fosdick (New York: Macmillan, 1951), p. 47 as quoted in *Parabola:*

*The Search for Meaning,* vol. 29, no. 4, November 2004, pp. 36–37.

64. Frank Purcell quoting from *Rufus Jones: Essential Writings,* edited by Kerry Walters (Maryknoll, N.Y.: Orbis, 2001), p. 74 as quoted in *Parabola: The Search for Meaning,* vol. 29, no. 4, November 2004, p. 37.

65. See *The Science of the Spoken Word* by Mark L. Prophet and Elizabeth Clare Prophet (Corwin Springs, Mont.: Summit University Press, 1983), p. 72.

66. Luke 11:33–36.

67. This dictation by the ascended master Djwal Kul was delivered through the messenger Mark L. Prophet on February 6, 1959, and is published in *Pearls of Wisdom,* vol. 2, no. 5.

68. Mark Prophet in *The Soulless One: Cloning a Counterfeit Creation* (Corwin Springs, Mont., Summit University Press, 1981), pp. 45–46, 48–49.

69. Matt. 5:1–12.

70. Luke 6:20–23.

71. *Alchemy of the Heart: How to Give and Receive More Love,* Elizabeth Clare Prophet and Patricia R. Spadaro (Corwin Springs, Mont., Summit University Press, 2000), pp. 168–71.

72. Ibid., pp. 8–10.

73. Matt. 10:28.

74. James 1:17.

75. Gal. 6:7.

76. The place where God is—"Our God is a consuming fire" (Heb. 12:29).

77. Matt. 18:3.

78. Gen. 1:26, 28.

79. This teaching by the ascended master Kuthumi is published

in *Understanding Yourself: Opening the Door to the Super-conscious Mind—A Study in the Psychology of the Soul by the Masters of the Far East* by Mark L. Prophet (Corwin Springs, Mont.: Summit University Press, 1985), pp. 45–50.

80. See *Kabbalah: Key to Your Inner Power* by Elizabeth Clare Prophet with Patricia R. Spadaro and Murray L. Steinman (Corwin Springs, Mont.: Summit University Press, 1997), Introduction, pp. xiii–xiv.

81. Endnote from *Kabbalah: Key to Your Inner Power:* "According to Professor Daniel Matt, the restriction that only married men over the age of 40 were allowed to study Kabbalah originated in Islamic tradition, which warned scholars not to study philosophy until they were ready. The injunction spread to Jewish philosophy and made its way to Kabbalah. Matt says the restriction is a warning that students of Kabbalah should be grounded in an occupation and the practical life, perhaps to be married or to have a trade, before exploring inner truths. (Telephone interview with Daniel Matt, professor at the Center for Judaic Studies, Graduate Theological Union, Berkeley, California, 22 October 1993)."

82. Endnote from *Kabbalah: Key to Your Inner Power:* "Quoted in Abraham Azulai, *Or ha-Hammah*. See Gershom Scholem, *Kabbalah* (1974; reprint, New York: New American Library, Meridian, 1978), p. 68; David Biale, 'Jewish Mysticism in the Sixteenth Century,' in Paul E. Szarmach, ed., *An Introduction to the Medieval Mystics of Europe* (Albany, N.Y.: State University of New York Press, 1984), p. 315."

83. *Kabbalah: Key to Your Inner Power* by Elizabeth Clare Prophet with Patricia R. Spadaro and Murray L. Steinman (Corwin Springs, Mont.: Summit University Press, 1997), p. xiv.

84. The following information on "The Big Bang and Jewish Mysticism" is taken from *Kabbalah: Key to Your Inner Power* by Elizabeth Clare Prophet with Patricia R. Spadaro and Murray L. Steinman (Corwin Springs, Mont.: Summit University Press, 1997), Chapter 1, pp. 1–5.

85. Rae Corelli, Marci McDonald, and Hilary Mackenzie, "Looking at God," *Maclean's*, 4 May 1992, p. 38.

86. Ibid, p. 39.

87. Creation Hymn, Rig-Veda, 10.129.1–4. Translation from Ralph T. H. Griffith, *Hymns of the Rgveda*, rev. ed., 2 vols. (New Delhi: Munshiram Manoharlal Publishers, 1987), 2:621–22; and Jai Guru Dev, *Rig Veda: Tenth Mandala*, p. 236.

88. Gen. 1:1–5. King James Version of the Bible.

89. David Sheinkin, *Path of the Kabbalah*, ed. Edward Hoffman (New York: Paragon House, 1986), pp. 25–27.

90. For further information see *Kabbalah: Key to your Inner Power* by Elizabeth Clare Prophet with Patricia R. Spadaro and Murray L. Steinman, and *Emotions: Transforming Anger, Fear and Pain* by Dr. Marilyn C. Barrick, pp. 189–94.

91. For further understanding of the Kabbalah, see *Kabbalah: Key to Your Inner Power* by Elizabeth Clare Prophet with Patricia R. Spadaro and Murray L. Steinman, Chapters 3 and 4. Also see *Anatomy of the Spirit: The Seven Stages of Power and Healing* by Caroline Myss, Ph.D. (New York: Harmony Books, 1996).

92. See *Pearls of Wisdom*, vol. 25, no. 24; published by The Summit Lighthouse.

93. Ibid.

94. John 12:44, 45.

95. Rev. 19:7; 21:9.

96. Mark 16:9; Luke 8:2.
97. See the biblical story of Cain and Abel in Gen. 4:1–8.
98. Magda is referencing her embodiment as Mary Magdalene. The ascended masters have told their students that Mary Magdalene, now the ascended lady master Magda, is Jesus' twin flame. See *Mary Magdalene and the Divine Feminine: Jesus' Lost Teachings on Woman* by Elizabeth Clare Prophet with Annice Booth (Corwin Springs, Mont.: Summit University Press, 2005).
99. This dictation of the ascended lady master Magda was delivered through the messenger Elizabeth Clare Prophet on April 9, 1982, during the Easter conclave at Camelot in Los Angeles, California, and published in *Pearls of Wisdom,* vol. 25, no. 24.
100. Abraham Lincoln, "Proclamation of Thanksgiving," October 3, 1863.
101. Psalm 100.
102. R. A. Schwaller de Lubicz, *The Temple in Man: Sacred Architecture and the Perfect Man,* trans. Robert and Deborah Lawlor (New York: Inner Traditions International, 1977), p. 24. As quoted by Mark L. Prophet and Elizabeth Clare Prophet in *Mirror of Consciousness: Lords of the Seven Rays,* Book One, Chapter 4 (Corwin Springs, Mont.: Summit University Press, 1986), pp. 152, 158.
103. See Mark L. Prophet and Elizabeth Clare Prophet, *Mirror of Consciousness: Lords of the Seven Rays,* Book One, Chapter 4 (Corwin Springs, Mont.: Summit University Press, 1986), pp. 158–59.
104. Ibid, pp. 163–64.
105. Ibid, pp. 165–66.
106. Ibid, pp. 171–72.
107. Ibid, pp. 172–74.

108. Ibid, pp. 169–70.
109. Ibid, p. 170.
110. This dictation by Lord Maitreya was delivered through the messenger Mark L. Prophet on October 21, 1961, in Boston, Massachusetts. It is published in *Pearls of Wisdom,* vol. 27, no. 8.
111. II Cor. 12:9.
112. "Almost everyone (with the exception of those who suffer severe psychological detachment from self and body) forms an emotional attachment to the body. After all, this is the body we have worn and worked through, the body that has provided the temple for our soul and the means by which we experience pleasure and pain on this plane, balance our karma and do good deeds. . . . Emotions connected with our attachment to the body are natural, and you should be aware that your body elemental has a consciousness and its consciousness permeates the physical body. But you are the master of your body elemental. And, of course, body elementals cannot do the best job, even though they would like to, when you don't give them the best food and exercise, spiritual teaching and practices. Don't mistake your body elemental's fears for your own. Your body elemental is also attached to the body, because that's his job. He takes care of the body. No more body, no more job! So he's wondering where he's going and what he's going to do when you lay that body aside in your final embodiment. You have to comfort your body elemental as you would a little child and promise him that you are taking him with you to the next octave because he has been a very faithful servant. Tell him he can still be your aide-de-camp after you've ascended and he'll have plenty of assignments." Instruction given by Elizabeth Clare Prophet, published in *Pearls of Wisdom,* vol. 35, no. 30, July 26, 1992.

113. I Cor. 15:53.

114. Heb. 11:6.

115. Also see Elizabeth Clare Prophet, *Fallen Angels and the Origins of Evil: Why Church Fathers Suppressed the Book of Enoch and Its Startling Revelations* (Corwin Springs, Mont.: Summit University Press, 2000).

116. Matt. 12:9–14; Mark 3:1–6; Luke 6:6–11.

117. Mark 5:34; Luke 17:19; John 5:6, 8–9, 14–15.

118. Matt. 9:18–26; Mark 5:22–43; Luke 7:11–15; 8:41–56; John 11:1–44.

119. Eph. 4:22–24; Col. 3:9–10.

120. Isa. 55:1.

121. James 1:17.

122. John 10:1–16.

123. Rev. 21:4.

124. Rom. 6:4; 7:6.

125. This dictation by Archangel Jophiel, "An Age of Crisis at the Crossroads of Life: Good People Must Do Better," was delivered through the messenger Elizabeth Clare Prophet, May 24, 1986, in Vancouver, B.C., Canada. Published in *Pearls of Wisdom*, vol. 29, no. 53.

# Glossary

**Alpha-Omega.** The divine wholeness of the Father-Mother God affirmed as "the beginning and the ending" by the Lord Christ in Revelation (Rev. 1:8, 11; 21:6; 22:13.)

**Ascended masters.** Enlightened spiritual beings who once lived on earth, fulfilled their reason for being and have reunited with God.

**Ascension.** A spiritual acceleration of consciousness that takes place at the natural conclusion of one's final lifetime on earth whereby the soul reunites with God and is free from the rounds of karma and rebirth.

**Astral plane.** The lowest vibrating frequency of time and space; the repository of mankind's thoughts and feelings, conscious and unconscious.

**Bilateral brain stimulation.** The stimulation of the left and right brain by one of three methods: 1) a back-and-forth movement of the eyes—left, right, left, right; 2) listening via a headset to an alternating sound—left, right, left, right; 3) a gentle tapping of the hands—left, right, left, right.

**Bodhisattva.** (Sanskrit, 'a being of *bodhi* or enlightenment.') A being destined for enlightenment, or one whose energy and power is directed toward enlightenment. A bodhisattva is destined to become a Buddha but has forgone the bliss of nirvana with a vow to save all children of God on earth. An ascended master or an unascended master may be a bodhisattva.

**Body elemental.** A being of nature (ordinarily invisible and functioning unnoticed in the physical octave) that serves the soul from the moment of its first incarnation in the planes of Matter to tend the physical body. About three feet high and resembling the individual whom he serves, the body elemental, working with the guardian angel under the generative Christ Self, is the unseen friend and helper of man.

**Carnal mind.** The lower aspects of the human ego, human intellect and human will; the animal nature of man.

**Causal body.** Interpenetrating spheres of light surrounding each one's I AM Presence at spiritual levels. The spheres of the causal body contain the records of the virtuous acts we have performed to the glory of God and the blessing of mankind.

**Chart of Your Divine Self.** See pp. 260–64.

**Christ Self.** See Holy Christ Self.

**Conscious mind.** The arena of the mind of which an individual is consciously aware; the aspect of mental life that one accesses in daily conversation and decision-making.

**Cosmic Clock.** A way of charting the cycles of psychological and spiritual development from birth to the conclusion of life (created by Elizabeth Clare Prophet). For further information, see the bibliography for *A Spiritual Approach to Parenting: Secrets of Raising the 21st Century Child* and *Predict Your Future: Understand the Cycles of the Cosmic Clock.*

**Crystal Cord.** The stream of God's light, life and consciousness that nourishes and sustains the soul and her four lower bodies. Also called the silver cord (Eccles. 12:6).

**Decree.** A dynamic form of spoken prayer used by students of the ascended masters to direct God's light into individual and world conditions. The decree may be short or long and is usually marked by a formal preamble and a closing or acceptance. It is the authoritative Word of God spoken by man in the name of the I AM Presence and the living Christ to bring about constructive change on earth through the will of God. The decree is the birthright of the sons and daughters of God, the "Command ye me" of Isaiah 45:11, the original fiat of the Creator: "Let there be light and there was light" (Gen. 1:3). It is written in the Book of Job, "Thou shalt decree a thing, and it shall be established unto thee: and the light shall shine upon thy ways" (Job 22:28).

**Demon.** A devil; an evil spirit.

**Dictation.** The messages of the ascended masters, archangels and other advanced spiritual beings delivered through the agency of the Holy Spirit by a messenger of the Great White Brotherhood.

**Divine Mother.** "Divine Mother," "Universal Mother" and "Cosmic Virgin" are alternate terms for the feminine polarity of the Godhead, the manifestation of God as Mother.

**Elementals.** The nature spirits of earth, air, fire and water.

**El Morya.** The ascended master who is the teacher and sponsor of the messengers Mark L. Prophet and Elizabeth Clare Prophet and the founder of The Summit Lighthouse.

**EMDR.** Acronym for "Eye Movement Desensitization and Reprocessing," an innovative method of psychotherapy originated and developed by Dr. Francine Shapiro. Acclaimed by practitioners and crisis intervention organizations, EMDR has proven to be effective in helping people resolve depression, phobias, recurrent nightmares, post-traumatic stress disorder and long-standing grief. As one of the most extensively researched and supported methods for treating trauma, the effectiveness of EMDR is well documented; the method is practiced around the world.

**Entities.** Conglomerates of misqualified energy or disembodied individuals who have chosen to embody evil. Entities that are focuses of sinister forces may attack disembodied as well as embodied individuals.

**Fallen angels.** Also called the *dark ones,* those angels who followed Lucifer in the Great Rebellion, whose consciousness "fell" to lower levels of vibration. They were "cast out into the earth" by Archangel Michael (Rev. 12:7–12)—constrained by the karma of their disobedience to God and his Christ to take on and evolve through dense physical bodies. Here they walk around, sowing seeds of unrest and rebellion among men and nations.

**Four lower bodies.** The four sheaths surrounding the soul; the vehicles the soul uses in her journey on earth: the etheric, or memory, body; the mental body; the desire, or emotional, body; the physical body. The etheric body houses the blueprint of the soul's identity and contains the memory of all that has ever transpired in the soul and all impulses she has ever sent out. The mental body is the vessel of the cognitive faculties; when purified, it can become the vessel of the mind of God. The desire body houses the higher and lower desires and records the emotions. The physical body is the miracle of flesh and blood that enables the soul to progress in the material universe.

**Great White Brotherhood.** A spiritual order of Western saints and Eastern adepts who have reunited with the Spirit of the living God; the heavenly hosts. They have transcended the cycles of karma and rebirth and ascended (accelerated) into that higher reality which is the eternal abode of the soul. The word "white" refers not to race but to the aura (halo) of white light surrounding their forms.

**Holy Christ Self.** The Higher Self; our inner teacher, guardian, friend and advocate before God; the universal Christ individualized for each of us.

**I AM Presence.** The Presence of God, the I AM THAT I AM, individualized for each soul.

**Karma.** Sanskrit, meaning 'act,' 'action,' 'work' or 'deed.' The consequences of one's thoughts, words and deeds of this life and previous lives; the law of cause and effect, which decrees that whatever we do comes full circle to our doorstep for resolution. The law of karma necessitates the soul's reincarnation so that she can balance her misuses of God's light, energy and consciousness.

**Karmic Board.** The Karmic Board, also known as the Lords of Karma, dispense justice to this system of worlds, adjudicating karma, mercy and judgment on behalf of every lifestream. All souls must pass before the Karmic Board before and after each incarnation on earth, receiving their assignment and karmic allotment for each lifetime beforehand and the review of their performance at its conclusion.

**Light.** The universal radiance and energy of God.

**Lightbearer.** A soul of light on earth for a heavenly purpose.

**Messenger.** One trained by an ascended master to receive and deliver the teachings, messages and prophecies of the Great White Brotherhood.

**Nirvana.** The goal of life according to Hindu and Buddhist philosophy; the state of liberation from the wheel of rebirth through the extinction of desire.

**Novena.** The recitation of prayers and the practicing of devotions for nine successive days for a special religious purpose.

**REM sleep.** A state of sleep characterized by the rapid back-and-forth movement of the eyes. Pioneering research discovered that if people were awakened during REM sleep, 80 percent of the subjects reported vivid dreaming. EEG readings indicate that brain waves during REM sleep are much like those of the normal waking state. REM sleep is also called "paradoxical sleep" because although the brain appears activated and alert, the muscles of the dreamer are flaccid and relaxed. Depriving people of REM sleep can cause a variety of reactions including irritability, increased anxiety, and disorientation. Research findings also indicate that REM sleep enables emotional processing and a vast amount of learning can occur in a short period of time.

**Retreat.** A focus of the Great White Brotherhood, usually on the etheric plane where the ascended masters preside. Retreats anchor one or more flames of the Godhead as well as the momentum of the masters' service and attainment for the balance of light in the four lower bodies of the planet and its evolutions.

**Secret Chamber of the Heart.** The sanctuary of meditation behind the heart *chakra,* the place to which the souls of lightbearers withdraw. It is the nucleus of life where the individual stands face to face with the inner Guru, the beloved Holy Christ Self, and receives the soul testings that precede the alchemical union with the Holy Christ Self—the marriage of the soul to the Lamb.

**Sons of the Solitude.** The Sons of the Solitude are an ancient brotherhood of advanced adepts. In the book *A Dweller on Two Planets* by Phylos the Thibetan, we learn that they were the highest initiates on Atlantis. The Sons of the Solitude were celibate, lived without families and often apart from civilization. They attained their mastery through years of training in many lifetimes. Examples in scripture of the Sons of the Solitude include Melchizedek, Jesus Christ and John the Baptist.

**Subconscious.** The subconscious refers to the level of consciousness and mental activity just below conscious awareness. It is the arena of consciousness that we reference when we say, "It's just on the tip of my tongue."

**Superconscious.** The inner region of the mind from which we access our higher intuitions and inspirations, artistic, philosophical or scientific, ethical imperatives and urges to humanitarian and heroic action. It is the realm of genius and of what people refer to as "high dreams," as well as altruistic love and the states of contemplation, illumination and ecstasy.

**Threefold flame.** The divine spark, the flame of God ensconced within the secret chamber of the heart; the soul's point of contact with the I AM Presence and Holy Christ Self.

**Transmutation.** A change of one element, form, species, condition, nature or substance into another. (In chemistry, the conversion of atoms of a given element into atoms of a different isotope or of a different element, as in radioactive disintegration or by nuclear bombardment.)

**Twin Flame.** The soul's masculine or feminine counterpart conceived out of the same white fire body, the fiery ovoid of the I AM Presence.

**Unconscious mind.** The unconscious mind is the arena of the psyche that is the repository of instinctual drives, primitive urges and repressed desires; these aspects of human nature are sometimes referred to as the "dark side."

**Violet flame.** The sacred fire that transmutes the cause, effect, record and memory of sin or negative karma. Also called the flame of transmutation, of freedom and of forgiveness.

# Bibliography

Barrick, Marilyn C., Ph.D. *A Spiritual Approach to Parenting: Secrets of Raising the 21st Century Child.* Corwin Springs, Mont.: Summit University Press, 2004.

Barrick, Marilyn C., Ph.D. *Soul Reflections: Many Lives, Many Journeys.* Corwin Springs, Mont.: Summit University Press, 2003.

Barrick, Marilyn C., Ph.D. *Emotions: Transforming Anger, Fear and Pain.* Corwin Springs, Mont.: Summit University Press, 2002.

Barrick, Marilyn C., Ph.D. *Dreams: Exploring the Secrets of Your Soul.* Corwin Springs, Mont.: Summit University Press, 2001.

Barrick, Marilyn C., Ph.D. *Sacred Psychology of Change: Life as a Voyage of Transformation.* Corwin Springs, Mont.: Summit University Press, 2000.

Barrick, Marilyn C., Ph.D. *Sacred Psychology of Love: The Quest for Relationships That Unite Heart and Soul.* Corwin Springs, Mont.: Summit University Press, 1999.

Bennett-Goleman, Tara. *Emotional Alchemy: How the Mind Can Heal the Heart.* New York: Harmony Books, 2001.

Booth, Annice. *Memories of Mark: My Life with Mark Prophet.* Corwin Springs, Mont.: Summit University Press, 1999.

Booth, Annice. *The Path to Your Ascension: Rediscovering Life's Ultimate Purpose.* Corwin Springs, Mont.: Summit University Press, 1999.

Chödrön, Pema. *Awakening Loving-Kindness.* Boston: Shambhala Publications, 1996.

Diamond, John, M.D. *Your Body Doesn't Lie.* New York: Harper & Row, 1979.

Epstein, Mark, M.D. *Going to Pieces without Falling Apart: A Buddhist Perspective on Wholeness.* New York: Broadway Books, 1998.

Gilbert, Rob, Ph.D., ed. *Bits and Pieces.* Fairfield, New Jersey: Economics Press, April 19, 2001.

Goldstein, Joseph, and Jack Kornfield. *Seeking the Heart of Wisdom: The Path of Insight Meditation.* Boston: Shambhala Publications, 1987.

Hall, Manly P. *The Secret Teachings of All Ages.* Los Angeles: The Philosophical Research Society, 1972.

Hill, Clara E. *Working with Dreams in Psychotherapy.* New York: Guilford Press, 1996.

Inayat Khan, Pir Vilayat. *Introducing Spirituality in Counseling and Therapy.* New York: Omega Press, 1982.

John of the Cross, Saint. *Dark Night of the Soul.* Translated and edited by E. Allison Peers. Garden City, N.Y.: Doubleday and Company, 1959.

Kornfield, Jack. *A Path with Heart: A Guide through the Perils and Promises of Spiritual Life.* New York: Bantam Books, 1993.

Laurence, Richard, trans. *The Book of Enoch the Prophet.* San Diego: Wizards Bookshelf, 1976.

Leadbeater, C. W. *Ancient Mystic Rites.* New York: Theosophical Publishing House, 1986.

McPherson, Aimee. *Life Story of Aimee Semple McPherson.* Los Angeles: Foursquare Publications, 1979.

McPherson, Aimee. *This Is That.* Los Angeles: Echo Park Evangelistic Assoc., 1923.

Myss, Caroline, Ph.D. *Anatomy of the Spirit: The Seven Stages of Power and Healing.* New York: Harmony Books, 1996.

Phylos the Thibetan. *A Dweller on Two Planets.* New York: Harper & Row, 1974.

Prabhupada, Swami A. C. Bhaktivedanta. *Bhagavad-Gita As It Is.* Abr. ed. New York: Bhaktivedanta Book Trust, 1972.

Prophet, Elizabeth Clare. *Fallen Angels and the Origins of Evil: Why Church Fathers Suppressed the Book of Enoch and Its Startling Revelations.* Corwin Springs, Mont.: Summit University Press, 2000.

Prophet, Elizabeth Clare. *The Great White Brotherhood in the Culture, History and Religion of America.* Corwin Springs, Mont.: Summit University Press, 1987.

Prophet, Elizabeth Clare. *The Opening of the Seventh Seal: Sanat Kumara on the Path of the Ruby Ray.* Corwin Springs, Mont.: Summit University Press, The Summit Lighthouse Library, 2001.

Prophet, Elizabeth Clare. *Predict Your Future: Understand the Cycles of the Cosmic Clock.* Corwin Springs, Mont.: Summit University Press, 2004.

Prophet, Elizabeth Clare. *Saint Germain's Prophecy for the New Millennium.* Corwin Springs, Mont.: Summit University Press, 1999.

Prophet, Elizabeth Clare. *Violet Flame to Heal Body, Mind and Soul.* Corwin Springs, Mont.: Summit University Press, 1997.

Prophet, Elizabeth Clare, with Annice Booth. *Mary Magdalene and the Divine Feminine: Jesus' Lost Teachings on Woman.* Corwin Springs, Mont.: Summit University Press, 2005.

Prophet, Elizabeth Clare, with Erin L. Prophet. *Reincarnation: The Missing Link in Christianity.* Corwin Springs, Mont.: Summit University Press, 1997.

Prophet, Elizabeth Clare, and Patricia R. Spadaro. *Alchemy of the Heart: How to Give and Receive More Love.* Corwin Springs, Mont.: Summit University Press, 2000.

Prophet, Elizabeth Clare, with Patricia R. Spadaro and Murray L. Steinman. *Kabbalah: Key to Your Inner Power.* Corwin Springs, Mont.: Summit University Press, 1997.

Prophet, Elizabeth Clare, and Staff of Summit University. *Walking with the Master: Answering the Call of Jesus.* Corwin Springs, Mont.: The Summit Lighthouse Library, 2002.

Prophet, Mark L. *The Soulless One: Cloning a Counterfeit Creation.* Corwin Springs, Mont.: Summit University Press, 1981.

Prophet, Mark L. *Understanding Yourself: Opening the Door to the Superconscious Mind—A Study in the Psychology of the Soul by the Masters of the Far East.* Corwin Springs, Mont.: Summit University Press, 1985.

Prophet, Mark L., and Elizabeth Clare Prophet. *Climb the Highest Mountain: The Path of the Higher Self.* 2d ed. Corwin Springs, Mont.: Summit University Press, 1986.

Prophet, Mark L., and Elizabeth Clare Prophet. *The Masters and the Spiritual Path.* Corwin Springs, Mont.: Summit University Press, 2001.

Prophet, Mark L., and Elizabeth Clare Prophet. *Mirror of Consciousness: Lords of the Seven Rays.* Corwin Springs, Mont.: Summit University Press, 1986.

Prophet, Mark L., and Elizabeth Clare Prophet. *Saint Germain On Alchemy: Formulas for Self-Transformation.* Corwin Springs, Mont.: Summit University Press, 1993.

Prophet, Mark L., and Elizabeth Clare Prophet. *The Science of the Spoken Word.* Corwin Springs, Mont.: Summit University Press, 1991.

Rossman, Martin L., M.D. *Guided Imagery for Self-Healing.* Tiburon, Calif.: An H. J. Kramer Book, published in a joint venture with New World Library, 2000.

Salzberg, Sharon. *Lovingkindness: The Revolutionary Art of Happiness.* Boston: Shambhala Publications, 1995.

Schwaller de Lubicz, R. A., *The Temple in Man: Sacred Architecture and the Perfect Man.* New York: Inner Traditions International, 1977.

Serapis Bey. *Dossier on the Ascension: The Story of the Soul's Acceleration into Higher Consciousness on the Path of Initiation.* Corwin Springs, Mont.: Summit University Press, 1979.

Shapiro, Francine, Ph.D., and Margot Silk Forrest. *EMDR: The Breakthrough Therapy for Overcoming Anxiety, Stress, and Trauma.* New York: BasicBooks, 1997.

The Summit Lighthouse. *Prayers, Meditations, Dynamic Decrees for the Coming Revolution in Higher Consciousness.* Corwin Springs, Mont.: Summit University Press, 1984.

Tishby, Isaiah, and Fischel Lachower, comps. *The Wisdom of the Zohar: An Anthology of Texts.* 3 vols. Translated by David Goldstein. 1989. Reprint. New York: Oxford University Press for the Littman Library of Jewish Civilization, 1991.

Tolle, Eckhart. *The Power of Now: A Guide to Spiritual Enlightenment.* Novato, Calif.: New World Library, 1999.

Wheatley, Margaret. *Leadership and the New Science: Learning about Organization from an Orderly Universe.* San Francisco, Calif.: Berrett-Koehler Publishers, 1994.

Yogananda, Paramahansa. *Autobiography of a Yogi.* Los Angeles: Self-Realization Fellowship, 1974.

Zweig, Connie, Ph.D., and Steve Wolf, Ph.D. *Romancing the Shadow: Illuminating the Dark Side of the Soul.* New York: Ballantine Books, 1997.

# A Spiritual Approach to Parenting
## Secrets of Raising the 21st Century Child

As we face the complexities of the Aquarian age, spiritually advanced souls are being born to usher in a prophesied time of peace and enlightenment. In this perceptive guidebook, Dr. Marilyn Barrick discusses the Indigo, Crystal and Spirited children, their mission to help earth fulfill her divine destiny and the special challenges to the parents raising these extraordinary children.

Dr. Barrick also reveals the "cycles of life" we all pass through and shows how we can deal with their corresponding life lessons. She gives valuable insights into how karma and past-life records influence our marriages and families—and teaches us ways to master these important relationships.

ISBN: 0-922729-96-4
Trade Paperback  $15.95

"As we welcome the Indigo and Crystal children who are our future leaders, Dr. Barrick has written a valuable and timely book. Drawing on ancient wisdom and personal experience, she offers sound advice to help parents support the growth and creativity of these wonderful young people."

—CHRISTINE PAGE, M.D., author of
Spiritual Alchemy: How to Transform Your Life

"Filled with remarkable insights into the psychology of the child's soul, this book goes way beyond current parenting approaches. By exploring children's deep spiritual needs through their developmental stages and ways to raise up the inner genius, A Spiritual Approach to Parenting offers real healing and hope to the many sensitive, bright children that have been mislabeled as 'learning disabled' or 'problem' children."

—DR. JOYE B. BENNETT, child psychologist and co-editor of
Nurturing Your Baby's Soul: A Spiritual Guide for Expectant Parents

# Soul Reflections
## Many Lives, Many Journeys

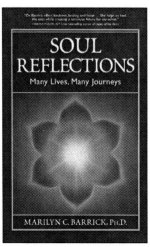

ISBN: 0-922729-83-2
Trade Paperback $14.95

The journey of our soul has lasted many lifetimes...

As we move into the 21st century, many of us feel a yearning for spiritual awakening and divine guidance. We look to therapists, coaches and ministers for answers, but ultimately the healing of soul and spirit is an inner quest.

In *Soul Reflections: Many Lives, Many Journeys*, through intriguing studies of factual and legendary heroes, inspiring meditations and practical exercises, Dr. Barrick shows how love and compassion initiate a healing process for the soul. And she reveals alchemical formulas to enrich our quest for soul liberation.

*"Marilyn Barrick fervently believes in the power of compassion as a potent tool for healing human sorrow and suffering. She offers us the possibility—nay, the promise—of spiritual companionship and support the moment we honor our brief time on earth as a gift to be opened, rather than as a problem to be solved."*

—WAYNE MULLER, N.Y. *Times* best-selling author of *Legacy of the Heart*

*"Dr. Barrick has outlined a clear path for your soul's homeward journey, illumined by her many years of experience in guiding souls through life's difficult moments."*

—DR. NEROLI DUFFY, author, lecturer and medical doctor

*"This book is a must-read for any serious seeker who hungers for knowledge of the path that can lead to enlightenment and the ascension in the light."*

—REV. E. GENE VOSSELER, public speaker, writer and spiritual counselor

# Emotions
## *Transforming Anger, Fear and Pain*

Scientists have demonstrated the link between emotional balance and physical and mental well-being. When we learn how to handle our emotions, we can achieve balance in body, mind and soul. In *Emotions: Transforming Anger, Fear and Pain,* Dr. Marilyn Barrick, a transformational psychologist, takes the study of our emotions—and how to deal with them—to the next level.

In *Emotions,* you will discover how to release anger, guilt and grief in a healthy way to experience inner joy. The author shares techniques such as trauma-release therapy, peaceful self-observation and using nature as healer to help us realize loving-kindness, mindfulness and tolerance. She also shares

ISBN: 0-922729-77-8
Trade Paperback   $14.95

successful spiritual techniques she has developed in her practice. In these uncertain times, *Emotions: Transforming Anger, Fear and Pain* is an invaluable guide to creating heart-centeredness in a turbulent world.

*"Marilyn Barrick is on the mark. While we search for the understanding of our physical, mental and spiritual selves, we often forget the source of the balance between all of them—our emotional self. This book addresses the issue magnificently. Read it and grow."*

—DANNION BRINKLEY, N.Y. *Times* best-selling author of
*Saved by the Light* and *At Peace in the Light*

*"Emotions is a wise, heartfelt and deeply spiritual path that can lead you from fear to courage, anger to joy, and helplessness to effectiveness—whatever challenges you may be facing. I have found it tremendously helpful."*

—MARTIN L. ROSSMAN, M.D., author of *Guided Imagery for Self-Healing*

*"Written in an easily understandable style,* Emotions: Transforming Anger, Fear and Pain *offers a wealth of information. Dr. Barrick provides excellent methods for freeing ourselves from some of our most destructive emotions—thus opening the door to improved health at all levels. This book is deserving of wide reading and rereading."*

—RANVILLE S. CLARK, M.D., psychiatrist, Washington, D.C.

# Dreams
## Exploring the Secrets of Your Soul

ISBN: 0-922729-63-8
Trade Paperback   $14.00

Everyone and everything in our dreams is part of us...We spend one-third of our lives asleep—and most of that time we are dreaming. Dr. Marilyn Barrick's fascinating work shows that our dreams are not only meaningful and connected with events in our lives, but they also hold valuable keys to our spiritual and emotional development. In fact, our souls are great dramatists and teachers, and the scripts of our dreams often contain profound and valuable guidance.

*Dreams: Exploring the Secrets of Your Soul* discusses Tibetan sleep and dream yoga, lucid dreaming and techniques to help you more clearly remember and understand your dreams. Learn how to interpret your dreams through the powerful insights in this book and the author's visionary analysis of actual dreams. And discover how to decode the metaphorical messages of your own soul.

*"This unique book on dreams integrates the soul's development on the spiritual path with personal dream work....*
*It invites us to consider a greater potential of the self beyond life's ordinary conflicts and helps us open up to a greater understanding of the purpose of life."*

—RALPH YANEY, M.D.,
psychiatrist/psychoanalyst and author of *10,001*

# Sacred Psychology of Change
## Life as a Voyage of Transformation

Catch the vision of your role in the 21st century. *Sacred Psychology of Change* shows how you can welcome cycles of change and even chaos as transformational opportunities. It is jam-packed with helpful information from cutting-edge change theories, psychology and spirituality.

Dr. Marilyn Barrick teaches us how to envision and explore the future while living productively in the present. Discover the importance of a creative mind-set, an open heart and the maturing of soul to successfully navigate the waves of change. Learn how to meet the challenges of endings and beginnings and emerge from the darkness of grief and loss into a bright new day.

ISBN: 0-922729-57-3
Trade Paperback  $14.95

The storytelling chapters and exercises bring your personal journey to life and suggest practical approaches to the challenging scenarios of our fast-moving world.

> *"This book asks us to 'focus our attention on the higher intelligence of our heart' and then describes in loving detail ways of doing just that. Those interested in the heart's ability to heal will find encouragement in these pages."*
>
> —RUTH BLY, licensed psychologist, Jungian analyst, author

> *"A profound treasure of spiritual truths and their practical application based on the author's many successful years of personal and professional experience. Written in the language of the heart and with remarkable clarity and sensitivity, this book will lead you, chapter by chapter and step by step, to a profoundly healing dialogue with yourself—and through an exciting spiritual and psychological journey of change."*
>
> —KENNETH FRAZIER, L.P.C., D.A.P.A., A.C.P.E.

# Sacred Psychology of Love
## The Quest for Relationships That Unite Heart and Soul

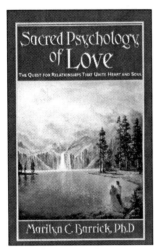

ISBN: 0-922729-49-2
Trade Paperback  $12.95

Searching for your perfect love? *Sacred Psychology of Love* unfolds the hidden spiritual and psychological dramas inherent in friendships, love relationships and marriage. It tells the story of each one's inner beloved and offers tender ways to spark divine love in your relationships.

After 39 years as a clinical psychologist and relationship counselor, Dr. Barrick is uniquely qualified to reveal the impact of childhood experiences upon adult relationships and to awaken us to the benefits of the reflecting mirror of the beloved. She shows the key role your inner "other half" plays in the eternal dance of love and gives practical self-help exercises to guide you on your quest for relationships that unite heart and soul.

*"A wonderful marriage of the mystical and practical, this soul-nourishing book is beautiful, healing and thought-provoking."*

–SUE PATTON THOELE,
author of *Heart-Centered Marriage*

*"In our search for the Beloved, whether inner or outer, we seek that mysterious blend of beauty and practicality which Dr. Marilyn Barrick masterfully conveys on every page. Synthesizing her knowledge of sacred text, her clinical expertise and her life's wisdom, she has written a book for anyone seeking to love or to be loved. With compassion and humor, she gives us an important tool for enriching relationships."*

–ANNE DEVORE, Jungian analyst

# *Wanting to Live*
## *Overcoming the Seduction of Suicide*
### by Dr. Neroli Duffy and Marilyn Barrick, Ph.D.

Practical tools and priceless insights that will save lives...

In this unique and inspiring book, a minister and former medical doctor along with a clinical psychologist part the veil for a startling look beyond the physical world into a realm we usually don't see: malignant spirits coaxing depressed but beautiful people into suicide; a bleak, painful existence in a dark, frightening level of consciousness; and lost souls

ISBN: 0-922729-92-1
5 1/2 x 6 1/2  **$8.95**

immediately coming back into a new lifetime to face the same test all over again.

Most important, *Wanting to Live: Overcoming the Seduction of Suicide*, by Dr. Neroli Duffy and Marilyn C. Barrick, Ph.D., tells us about powerful, life-changing partnerships with heavenly rescuers and offers priceless insights and practical tools for suicidal people and their loved ones. They shine the light of understanding to pierce the darkness and to bring hope to the despondent soul. This book is destined to save many lives.

The authors tell young people, "In reality there is no such thing as death. When we lay down the body, we do not die. Our soul and our spirit live on. The body is just a house, a temple for the spirit. If the near-death experience teaches us anything, it is the unreality of death and the reality of the continuity of the soul....

"In reality, your soul wants to live—not just in the finite sense of this earthly existence, but in the infinite sense of the great spiritual being that you are at inner levels."

SUMMIT UNIVERSITY ☙ PRESS
To order call 1-800-245-5445

## FOR MORE INFORMATION

Summit University Press books are available at fine bookstores worldwide and at your favorite online bookseller.

For a free catalog of our books and products or to learn more about the spiritual techniques featured in this book, please contact:

Summit University Press
PO Box 5000
Corwin Springs, MT 59030-5000 USA
Telephone: 1-800-245-5445 or 406-848-9500
Fax: 1-800-221-8307 or 406-848-9555
E-mail: info@summituniversitypress.com
www.summituniversitypress.com

MARILYN C. BARRICK, Ph.D., minister, psychologist and transformational therapist, is the author of a valuable seven-book self-help series on spiritual psychology. Her entire series of books is published and available in bookstores and on the Web:

*Everything Is Energy:*
*New Ways to Heal Your Body,*
*Mind and Spirit*

*A Spiritual Approach to Parenting:*
*Secrets of Raising the 21st*
*Century Child*

*Soul Reflections: Many Lives,*
*Many Journeys*

*Emotions: Transforming Anger,*
*Fear and Pain*

*Dreams: Exploring the Secrets*
*of Your Soul*

*Sacred Psychology of Change: Life as a Voyage of Transformation*

*Sacred Psychology of Love: The Quest for Relationships*
*That Unite Heart and Soul*

In *Everything Is Energy: New Ways to Heal Your Body, Mind and Spirit*—the seventh book in her spiritual psychology series—Dr. Barrick highlights the mysteries of the labyrinth of life and energy therapy as a jump-start to healing. She includes fascinating case histories and stories of past-life recall.

Dr. Barrick is also co-author with Dr. Neroli Duffy of *Wanting to Live: Overcoming the Seduction of Suicide*, a book written especially for today's teens and young adults.

In addition to her writing and private practice, Dr. Barrick conducts seminars and workshops in the U.S.A., Canada and Europe. Over her 39-year professional career, she has consulted as a psychological expert to schools, churches, government agencies, professional advisory boards and mental health facilities. She has also taught graduate psychology courses and served as a Peace Corps training development officer and field counselor.

Dr. Barrick's clinical practice includes individual, couple and family therapy, trauma release work, guided imagery, soul work and past-life analysis. For more information or to contact Dr. Barrick, visit her web site: www.spiritualpsychology.com.

Printed in the United States
211009BV00001B/8/A